American
Liberty & Justice

ALSO IN THE SERIES

Broke, Not Broken: Homer Maxey's Texas Bank War
Broadus Spivey and Jesse Sublett

A Clamor for Equality: Emergence and Exile of an Early Californio Activist
Paul Bryan Gray

A Conservative and Compassionate Approach to Immigration Reform: Perspectives from a Former US Attorney General
Alberto R. Gonzales and David N. Strange

Hers, His, and Theirs: Community Property Law in Spain and Early Texas
Jean A. Stuntz

Lone Star Law: A Legal History of Texas
Michael Ariens

Quite Contrary: The Litigious Life of Mary Bennett Love
David J. Langum, Sr.

The Reckoning: Law Comes to Texas's Edwards Plateau
Peter R. Rose

Sex, Murder, and the Unwritten Law: Courting Judicial Mayhem, Texas Style
Bill Neal

Showdown in the Big Quiet: Land, Myth, and Government in the American West
John P. Bieter, Jr.

Treasure State Justice: Judge George M. Bourquin, Defender of the Rule of Law
Arnon Gutfeld

SKULLDUGGERY, SECRETS, AND MURDERS

SKULLDUGGERY, SECRETS, AND MURDERS

THE 1894 WELLS FARGO SCAM THAT BACKFIRED

BILL NEAL

FOREWORD BY GORDON MORRIS BAKKEN

TEXAS TECH UNIVERSITY PRESS

This book is typeset in Minion Pro. The paper used in this book meets the minimum requirements of ANSI/NISO Z39.48-1992 (R1997). ♾

Text designed by Kasey McBeath
Cover design by Ryan Miller

Library of Congress Cataloging-in-Publication Data
Neal, Bill, 1936-
Skullduggery, secrets, and murders : the 1894 Wells Fargo scam that backfired / Bill Neal ; foreword by Gordon Morris Bakken.
pages cm. — (American liberty and justice)
Summary: “”Examines the 1894 Wells Fargo scam involving money packets falsely purported to contain $25,000. The plan goes awry and leads to the death of a sheriff and undercover agent; uncovers the identities of the masterminds”—Provided by publisher”— Provided by publisher.
Includes bibliographical references and index.
ISBN 978-0-89672-917-9 (hardback) — ISBN 978-0-89672-918-6 (e-book) 1. Swindlers and swindling—Oklahoma—History. 2. Trials (Murder)—Oklahoma—History. 3. Murder—Oklahoma—History. I. Title.
HV6698.O5N43 2015
364.152'3092—dc23 2014044544

15 16 17 18 19 20 21 22 23 / 9 8 7 6 5 4 3 2 1

Texas Tech University Press
Box 41037 | Lubbock, Texas 79409-1037 USA
800.832.4042 | ttup@ttu.edu | www.ttupress.org

For my friends in the "Free Thinkers Fellowship,"
Doctor Rosanna Herndon,
Doctor Dusty Blu Cooksey and General John Compere

CONTENTS

ILLUSTRATIONS

Maps

FOREWORD

Bill Neal's *Skullduggery, Secrets, and Murders* is another splendid analysis of a crime gone wrong. This book describes a unique conspiracy to commit insurance fraud, a crime that today continues to confound insurance companies and law enforcement. Bill Neal follows the conspiracy to its fatal conclusion and then explores the unindicted co-conspirators to their graves. The research is thorough, and the writing invites rapt attention to all of the culverts and gullies of the story.

Importantly, this book does what crime historians too often fail to do: follow the crime and the criminals to historical conclusions. Randolph Roth's *American Homicide* (2009) chronicles crime statistics and some criminals to statistical conclusions. Roth concentrates on regions and ethnicity. Bill Neal follows the criminal conspiracy to the murder of a law enforcement officer in the wrong place at the wrong time. He makes clear that the insurance fraud scheme was legally flawed and the criminal too uniformed to know the scheme could not work. Nonetheless, a man was dead, and law enforcement went to work. Unfortunately, only one of the guilty paid with incarceration. Yet a guilty verdict did not end the tale, and Neal follows each and every one of the parties to the grave regardless.

This book resonates with others that follow people and crime in detail. Robert Lansing's *Nimrod: Courts, Claims, and Killing on the Oregon Frontier* (2005) follows the travail of Nimrod O'Kelly through the Oregon criminal justice system in the 1850s as well as the problem of land claims of the time. Clare V. "Bud" McKanna brought his experience in crime scene investigation to his many books. His *The Trial of "Indian Joe"* (2007) and *White Justice in Arizona: Apache Murder Trials in the Nineteenth Century* (2005) in particular include his apt observations from a career in law enforcement. Kathleen A. Cairns follows

Nellie May Madison from Montana to California and a death sentence in *The Enigma Woman: The Death Sentence of Nellie May Madison* (2007). Her *Proof of Guilt: Barbara Graham and the Politics of Executing Women in America* (2013) tells of a botched robbery, the murder of an elderly widow, the trial of the three culprits, and their execution. Cairns places the trial and execution in the setting of anti–death penalty activism. John W. Davis, like Bill Neal, puts his years of law practice to use in *A Vast Amount of Trouble: A History of the Spring Creek Raid* (2005), *Goodbye, Judge Lynch: The End of the Lawless Era in the Big Hole Basin* (2006), and *Wyoming Range War: The Infamous Invasion of Johnson County* (2012). Carole Haber's *The Trials of Laura Fair: Sex, Murder, and Insanity in the Victorian West* (2013) tells of an 1870 California murder and two trials involving the insanity plea in the context of media frenzy, lawyerly theater, and popular attention to a woman condemned to death and, on retrial, set free to wander the lecture halls of America. Bill Neal's book goes beyond these excellent books to follow every detail to finality.

This is a deeply nuanced book, with the theme of order evolving out of unintended consequences and emerging as a rule of law for Texas. The details of the conspiracy make the book an important read. The author's insights make clear that justice is not always achieved in a courtroom.

GORDON MORRIS BAKKEN
Series Editor

PREFACE
CURIOUS REMARKS AN AUTHOR SOMETIMES HEARS

I didn't pay much attention to it at the time. I was about to give a book talk at the River Valley Pioneer Museum in Canadian, Texas, when the wife of a prominent local rancher pulled me aside and whispered, "I don't believe I'd get into that Isaacs mess if I were you."

The book I was to talk about was entitled *Getting Away with Murder on the Texas Frontier: Notorious Killings and Celebrated Trials*, and indeed one of the tales in the book had to do with the murder of the first sheriff of their county. It had happened in Canadian, and, yes, a dull-witted outlaw named George Isaacs, although not the triggerman, had been implicated in the crime. But George Isaacs had never been a resident of the Canadian community, and besides, most of the older generation in Canadian were familiar with the story. The murder happened more than a century earlier, after all—1894, to be specific. Now, why in the world would this Canadian native be apprehensive at this late date at the prospect of hearing the George Isaacs tale retold?

I was well aware, as is every Texas historian, of how tight-lipped and secretive folks are in those small, honor-sensitive communities about local scandals throughout the nineteenth century and well into the twentieth. The unwritten law of silence was the indelible—almost sacred—code adhered to not only within families but also within the entire community where the scandal occurred. Still, George Isaacs had never been a resident of Canadian. He did have three brothers who lived there at the time, but that too seemed an unlikely cause for concern. The brothers were all wealthy, prominent bankers and ranchers, and none of them to my knowledge had been parties to the Wells Fargo scam that backfired and triggered a tale of murders, secrets, and scandals. Moreover, the three respectable brothers had promptly denounced brother George as "the black sheep of the family" and then proceeded to ignore that unfortunate incident and never again had uttered the name George Isaacs. Besides all that, all the Isaacs brothers were long since dead and gone—half a century and more by 2009. And yet—still—it was taboo to whisper a word about "that Isaacs mess."

My book talk went off without incident, but afterward the lady's precautionary advice kept teasing my brain. I had done considerable primary research on the story of George Isaacs (and his rambunctious wife, Lizzie) when I wrote the original story and had uncovered a number of facts that had never seen the light of print. I had, I reckoned, gotten to the bottom of the George Isaacs story—put it to bed once and for all. But had I missed something? What could there have possibly been about "that Isaacs mess" that was so dark and disgraceful that it had prompted a local resident to make such a strange remark some 115 years after the fatal shot had been fired?

Perplexed, I decided to check the local Hemphill County history book. Surely, I figured, it would have a fairly detailed account of the most sensational crime that had happened in the century since the county was settled: the murder of their first sheriff by a gang of Oklahoma Territory hoodlums during an attempted robbery. It turned out that the book (written by a local author and published in 1977) did tell the story. And I quote: "Tom T. McGee died on the 24th day of November 1894 by murder."[1] End of story.

Somehow I just knew that there had to be more to the story than that. So I saddled up and started riding down that dim trail once again. I couldn't have imagined what a long and winding trail it would be—or how many fascinating and unlikely side trails would fork off the main branch. Nevertheless, no matter how many side trails it took or how many obstacles lay in the path, I was determined to solve that really, really cold case mystery.

When the jigsaw pieces of the puzzle finally fit together at the end of the trail, it turned out to be a true crime tale that no writer of fiction would have dared to concoct.

BILL NEAL
Canadian, Texas,
December 20, 2012

ACKNOWLEDGMENTS

Many acknowledgments are in order. First, and foremost, I thank my wife and companion, Gayla Neal, who is also my secretary, research assistant, and the doer of all manner of other unglamorous tasks. Next on the list has to be Mike Tower, of Elmore City, Oklahoma, author, western historian, and my expert go-to guy in helping me untangle the bewildering maze of facts, figures, events, laws, courts, lawyers, outlaws, lawmen, and other colorful characters in the Oklahoma Territory, the Indian Territory, and then the State of Oklahoma. Whew! Thanks again, Mike. I am also indebted to Dr. Rosanna Herndon, scholar and author, for her insightful suggestions on manuscript improvements.

Next in line are local historians: the late Robert E. King of Seiling, Oklahoma; Patsy Smart, also of Seiling; Carol Morse of Ardmore, Oklahoma; the late Jim Cloyd, lawman and former sheriff of Hemphill County, Texas; Mrs. Warren (Leta Jo) Haynie, director of the Firehouse Museum in Crowell, Texas; Marisue Burleson Potts, Motley County, Texas; Carol Ann Whitmire, editor of the *Quanah Tribune-Chief* newspaper; Jill Henderson, librarian at the Taylor County law library in Abilene, Texas; and the staff at the Hemphill County Museum at Canadian, Texas.

Valuable research resources included Tai Kreidler, Monte Monroe, Lynn Whitfield, and other staff at the Southwest Special Collections Library at Texas Tech University; Warren Stricker, research center director at the Panhandle-Plains Historical Museum; Donaly E. Brice and John Anderson at the Texas State Library and Archives Commission; Cathy Spitzenberger at the University of Texas at Arlington Library; and the staff at the Oklahoma State Archives library as well as district and county clerks at Crowell, Canadian, Vernon, Quanah, and Clarendon in Texas and Taloga in Oklahoma. Thanks also to western writers

Ellis Lindsey and Jerry Lobdill for research assistance, to H. Allen Anderson and the staff of *The New Handbook of Texas* at the Texas State Historical Association, and to the staff of the Haley Memorial Library and History Center at Midland, Texas.

Much appreciation also for the assistance and encouragement of Texas Tech University Press personnel, including Judith Keeling, former editor-in-chief now retired; Joanna Conrad, the present editor-in-chief; Amanda Werts, the managing editor; and staff including Kasey McBeath, Jada Rankin, and John Brock.

I must not conclude without expressing my appreciation to Dr. Garry L. Nall, retired editor of the *Panhandle-Plains Historical Review*, for his unfailing kind encouragement and support.

SKULLDUGGERY, SECRETS, AND MURDERS

PROLOGUE

THE APPROACH OF FOUR ARMED AND MOUNTED STRANGERS

The moment she spied those four mounted strangers riding into town, Mrs. John Miller knew they were up to no good. Canadian, Texas, was a small village in 1894, and she had never seen any of them before. All were well armed—she could see those Winchester rifles in their saddle scabbards—and when they got to the outskirts of town they reigned in, milled about, and held a powwow, seemingly uncertain about what to do next. When they noticed Mrs. Miller watching them, they wheeled their mounts around and rode out of sight over a hill. "They're here to rob the bank," she told her husband. "We ought to tell the sheriff."

Her husband, however, didn't think that was a good idea. "Best not busy yourself getting mixed up in something like that," he shrugged. So she kept quiet—until later, when she found out what those strangers really were up to.

CHAPTER ONE

MIDNIGHT AT WOODWARD

OKLAHOMA TERRITORY, MARCH 13, 1894

As the investigation into "that Isaacs mess" unfolded, it turned out that there was not only one cold case mystery to be solved. There were three.

First, who were the outlaws who executed the bizarre scheme to swindle Wells Fargo out of a large bundle of cash? Second, who were the triggermen who were responsible not only for the murder of the sheriff at Canadian, Texas, but also for the subsequent murder of an undercover Wells Fargo agent? Finally, and more perplexing yet, who were those behind-the-scene culprits—the ones who concocted that supposedly quick, easy, and nonviolent scam and then remained in the shadows while pulling the puppet strings on their cast of players? And just who the heck was that tall man who rode under the alias "Jim Stanley"?

This sleuth's investigation took him not only down the main trail, but also down several side trails—some productive, others leading only to dead ends, so typical of most criminal inquiries.

The investigation began with a focus on an earlier incident that happened around midnight, March 13, 1894, at the old Santa Fe Railroad depot in Woodward, Oklahoma Territory.

The cold winds of March swept across the lonely north plains of the Oklahoma Territory that night and swirled around the railroad hotel. Up in his second-story bedroom the Woodward Santa Fe Railroad agent, George W. Rourke, was warm, cozy, and fast asleep shortly after midnight when two outlaws emerged like ghosts from the pitch-black night and crept up the stairs. They knew exactly where Rourke's bedroom was, and they slowly opened the door and entered. The leader gently nudged Rourke awake with his pistol and calmly instructed the agent to get up, get dressed, and keep quiet. Rourke followed instructions.

Then the bandits marched Rourke downstairs and into the Santa Fe depot next door. As they passed through the baggage room en route to the Wells Fargo express office, they noticed a young man named Sam Peters asleep, apparently taking shelter from the frigid northern gale for a night's free lodging. They woke Peters. The leader told him to put up his hands and fall in. He did, without protest. The station agent unlocked the door to the express office, and all four entered. The outlaws forced Rourke to open the Santa Fe station safe that was in the office. They removed a large amount of cash and stuffed it into a large sack that the two intruders had thoughtfully brought along for that purpose. Then they turned their attention to a small Wells Fargo route safe. But Rourke, as a Santa Fe employee, didn't have the combination to the Wells Fargo safe, so they picked it up and took it with them—Rourke carrying the money sack and Peters carrying the route safe.

About a quarter of a mile east of the depot, they stopped and succeeded in breaking open the route safe, but it contained little of value. Then the odd, mismatched foursome continued their march to the Woodward stockyards, about half a mile east of the depot, where the horses were hitched. The leader directed Rourke to hang the money sack on the pommel of his saddle. The other robber handed young Peters $1.50 in silver for his services. After tying their victims securely, the outlaws mounted their horses and disappeared into the night.[1]

The victims were discovered at the stockyards shortly after daylight that morning, bound and shivering but unharmed. Rourke told officers that earlier the previous day, March 13, 1894, when the Santa Fe train chugged into the Woodward station, a Wells Fargo agent had delivered to him a large satchel filled with cash: government payroll money intended to be taken the next day to Fort Supply, the US Army base located some fifteen miles northwest of Woodward. Rourke took the money satchel and locked it in the Santa Fe railroad safe inside the Wells Fargo Express depot office.

Obviously the bandits had acquired inside information about the payroll shipment. The question was: Where did they get this information? That mystery was soon solved, however, when it was discovered that three days earlier the *Kansas City Times* had printed a detailed story about US Army payroll shipments. Ordinarily the army kept such information secret, but somebody at Fort Leavenworth, Kansas, had leaked the details to a correspondent for the *Times*. The resulting story described the intended movements of the army paymaster, the amount of money going to certain posts, and the means of transportation by which each would reach its destination. The news item went on to inform its readers that an estimated ten thousand dollars was to be sent by Wells Fargo via the Santa Fe Railroad to Woodward on March 13, 1894. The following day a horse-drawn wagon was scheduled to arrive from Fort Supply and pick up the payroll money.

It was also obvious that the uninvited visitors at the railroad station that night had read that story with a great deal of interest. Thus, the mystery was not how the outlaws found out about the army payroll stash of cash, but who leaked the story to the *Times*. Yet there was another, and much greater, unsolved mystery: Who were the bandits?

Although the bandits didn't wear masks, neither Rourke nor Peters recognized them. From their description of the pair and their modus operandi, officers suspected that the two culprits were the notorious Oklahoma Territory outlaws Bill Doolin and Bill Dalton. When officers followed the trail of their two horses, they noted that a short distance from the Woodward stockyards they were joined by six other riders, and all had fled in a southwesterly direction. Officers speculated that the other six riders were members of Doolin's infamous gang.[2]

Posses were soon formed, and the chase was on. US Marshal Evett Dumas Nix was notified, and he wired Deputy US Marshal Jack Love to "start in pursuit of the bold bandits and capture them dead or alive."[3] Colonel Dangerfield Parker, commanding officer at Fort Supply, detailed Lieutenant Kirby Walker and twenty cavalrymen for the hunt. Then he called on the army's famous civilian scout and tracker, Amos Chapman, and instructed him to "cut the flight of the outlaws toward the badlands along the Canadian River." Woodward itself was located practically on the banks of the North Canadian River, which flowed in a southeasterly direction from there, and the larger South Canadian River was only about thirty miles south of Woodward in D County, Oklahoma Territory. Until opened for settlement in 1892, D County had been a part of the Cheyenne-Arapaho Indian Reservation. It was a wild and sparsely settled area in rough terrain not accessible by roads or railroads, and it had no communication facilities—no telephones, no telegraph.

In short, it was outlaw heaven, and Colonel Parker hoped Amos Chapman could intercept the outlaws before the gang got there. Chapman gathered twenty Cheyennes and set off.

If ever there was a rough-hewed western frontiersman who fit Frederic Remington's description of that breed as being "men with the bark left on," it had to have been Amos Chapman. Some twenty years earlier in the Texas Panhandle, army scouts Chapman and Billy Dixon (hero of the previous Battle of Adobe Walls), together with four enlisted men, managed, without food or water for two days, to fight off a ferocious attack by a war party of 125 Comanche and Kiowa warriors by crawling into a slight depression in the prairie that had been made by wallowing buffaloes. During the Buffalo Wallow fight a bullet shattered Chapman's left knee, and later his leg had to be amputated. Chapman refused sedation while the operation was in progress but insisted on watching the procedure. For his role in the Buffalo Wallow fight he was awarded a US Medal of Honor for "gallantry in action." Now, more than two decades later, he refused to let his peg leg slow him down.[4]

In Woodward, as soon as it became known that a gang of desperadoes had robbed the Wells Fargo Express office, excitement escalated to a fever pitch. News of the heist was flashed to other towns in the area. Business was suspended. The posses rode hard but to no avail; the trail of the outlaws vanished in the canyons and gulches of the badlands south of Woodward. The outlaws were never captured, and the loot was never recovered.

Amos Chapman was a famous civilian Indian scout for the US Army. He was one of the five survivors of the 1874 Buffalo Wallow Fight in the Texas Panhandle. Courtesy of the Dewey County Historical Society.

Even though Amos Chapman had previously performed heroic deeds while serving as a civilian scout for the army, questions later arose as to just how diligent a pursuit he had conducted that day before losing the trail of the Woodward bandits. Several years earlier Chapman had married a Cheyenne woman, Mary Longneck, and had established a fairly sizable ranch on the Cheyenne-Arapaho Indian Reservation located along the North Canadian River only about thirty miles southeast of Woodward. It was no secret that on more than one occasion Chapman and his son-in-law and ranch manager, Lee Moore, had sheltered known outlaws on his remote ranch.[5]

Meanwhile, a clerk at the army's payroll office in Fort Leavenworth stated that the amount of US government payroll cash taken in the Woodward robbery was $6,540—quite a haul in 1894 (equivalent to approximately $175,000 in 2011 dollars). The government, however, did not lose that payroll cash. Since Wells Fargo still had official custody of the money and would have continued to retain custody of it until the day after the robbery, when the army wagons from Fort Supply were expected to arrive and receive the cash, Wells Fargo was the victim and suffered the loss.[6]

Before the year 1894 was out, Wells Fargo would be the target of another robbery at another Santa Fe depot in the same area: Canadian, Texas, to be exact.

Woodward, Oklahoma Territory, in the 1890s. Woodward was the site of a Wells Fargo heist on the night of March 13, 1894, when outlaws stole the US Army's payroll destined for Fort Supply. Woodward County 101, reprinted by permission of Western History Collections, University of Oklahoma.

CHAPTER TWO

THE $25,000 WELLS FARGO MONEY PACKETS

THE KANSAS CITY UNION DEPOT, NOVEMBER 21, 1894

November 21, 1894, was a day that A. A. Rinehart would recall vividly for the rest of his life. Rinehart, the station agent at the Wells Fargo Express office in the Kansas City Union Depot, thought he'd misunderstood what the customer said. This little fellow, whom he'd never seen before, never even heard of, calmly strolled up to the counter and announced that he had the enormous sum of $25,000 in cash that he wanted to ship via Wells Fargo Express to himself at Canadian, Texas. The man introduced himself as George Isaacs and explained that he had just sold some cattle at the Kansas City stockyards. Reinhart reckoned that his customer must have sold one mighty big herd of cattle: $25,000 in 1894 dollars amounted to more than $674,000 in 2011 money,[1] and that was by far the largest cash money shipment Rinehart had ever handled. November 21, 1894, would also be a day that George Isaacs would never forget. His life would never again be the same.

As requested, agent Rinehart gave George five Wells Fargo money packets, and George then left with the five empty packets. The next day he returned with all five packets bulging; each one, he claimed, contained five thousand dollars in cash. In truth, each packet contained only one hundred dollars in one- and two-dollar bills plus a lot of paper scraps. Printed on the face of each of the Wells Fargo packets were these two notations: "Said to Contain $5000.00" and "Contents NOT COUNTED BY AGENT, and Package Sealed in my presence." George signed his name on all five packets and handed them to Rinehart.

Rinehart, as clearly indicated on the face of each packet, did not verify the contents. Nevertheless, he sealed each packet with hot sealing wax. George paid the agent the $31.50 shipping fee and left. Agent Rinehart would later testify that another man—a fellow he didn't recognize—accompanied George Isaacs during this transaction, but that fellow stayed well in the background shadows and said nothing.

The money packets were to be shipped the following day by Wells Fargo via the Atchison, Topeka & Santa Fe Railroad. George told the agent that he would board the same train and receive his money packets at the Wells Fargo Express office in the Santa Fe depot in Canadian. The train was scheduled to arrive there at eight o'clock the following evening.

It is obvious that George plus his bashful confederate who discreetly kept in the background, as well as others in on the plot, were planning to scam Wells Fargo out of twenty-five thousand dollars. George's team of cutthroat pals intended to steal those five money packets either when they arrived at the Santa Fe station in Canadian or before they got there by robbing the train, thus enabling George to collect his "loss" from Wells Fargo. The problem with that plan was that George and his fellow thugs weren't as clever by half as they thought. The clever scheme they were so proud of was fatally flawed from the get-go.

Wells Fargo accepted shipments of cash in two quite different ways. If the shipper wanted to insure the cash shipment, he had to let the station agent count the cash and thus verify contents of the packet and then pay an insurance fee in addition to the ordinary shipping fee. At that point the Wells Fargo agent would seal it with hot wax and impress a "Wells Fargo" stamp on the wax. However, if the shipper did not let the agent count and verify the cash contents and did not pay an insurance charge, then a "For Public Use" seal was imprinted on the wax. According to the clear Wells Fargo rules, if the uninsured packets were lost or stolen, Wells Fargo would not be liable for any loss of the contents. Predictably, George Isaacs chose the latter method and paid only the nominal shipping fee, and his packets were clearly marked "For Public Use." Even had the heist gone down without a hitch, all genius George would have been entitled to recover from Wells Fargo was $31.50.[2]

In the end, however, those Wells Fargo rules didn't really matter. Some unanticipated events would intervene. And George Isaacs stood to lose a whole lot more than his $31.50 shipping fee.

George Isaacs had three prosperous brothers, who lived in Canadian, Texas: Will (aka Bill), Sam, and John. George, however, was not even close to being prosperous. At age thirty-six, George was a small man, standing only five feet, seven inches and weighing about 140 pounds. He could barely read (he had only a third-grade education), and he later listed his occupation as "laborer," although at the time of his encounter with the Kansas City Wells Fargo agent in November 1894, he was unemployed and lived in a shack along the Washita River near the town of Chickasha in the Chickasaw Nation in the Indian Territory.

Deputy US Marshal Walter Emerson "Jake" Hocker, who lived in the town of Purcell some thirty-five miles east of Chickasha, was well acquainted with George. He reported in 1894 that George Isaacs was "harboring the most notorious bands of desperadoes and thieves in the territory, and he was regarded as a member of them."[3]

Before that, sometime in 1892, Deputy Marshal Hocker had been assigned by his superior, US Marshal Sheb Williams, to conduct surveillance on several wealthy Texas cattlemen suspected of illegally running stock in the northwestern quadrant of the Chickasaw Nation. Hocker was also instructed to be particularly watchful of a fellow down there suspected of being a close associate of outlaws. His name was George Isaacs.

By that time, Bill Doolin, the most notorious desperado of all, was king of the Oklahoma and Indian Territory outlaws, a dubious crown that came with a handsome price—five thousand dollars to be exact—placed on the head of its bearer. Originally a member of the famous Bob Dalton gang, Doolin later formed his own gang after Bob Dalton was killed. Still later, as US marshals turned up the heat on his gang, Doolin took refuge in the Wichita Mountains in the southern part of Oklahoma Territory, not far from the shack where an outlaw-sanctuary host named George Isaacs resided.[4] George soon became well acquainted with Bill Doolin.

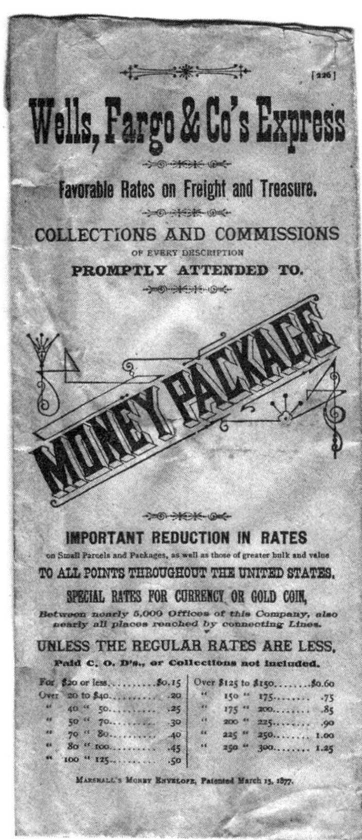

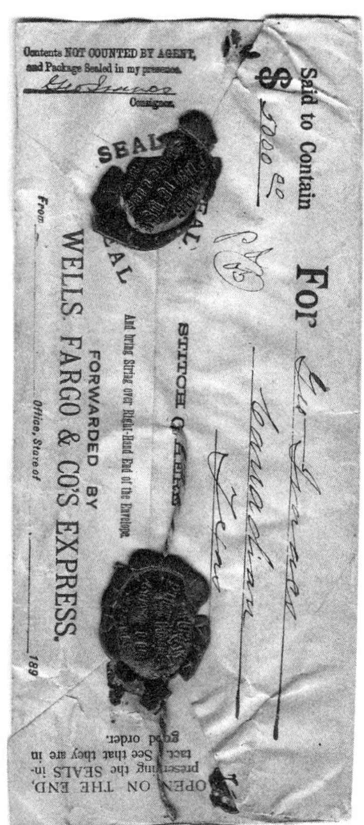

One of the five Wells Fargo money packets (front and back) that George Isaacs sent from Kansas City to himself in Canadian, Texas. The original money packets are in official court records, *State v. Jim Harbolt*, Cause No. 647, Donley County District Court, Clarendon, Texas.

Bill Doolin, king of the Oklahoma Territory outlaws in the early 1890s. Author's collection.

CHAPTER THREE

AN UNLIKELY AGGREGATION OF HEROES, VILLAINS, AND SPECTATORS

CANADIAN, TEXAS, NOVEMBER 23, 1894

They saddled up long before daylight—there were four of them—and they rode west along the South Canadian River, and by nine o'clock they were almost to the state line—out of the rough, brushy, outlaw-friendly haunts of the Oklahoma Territory and into the vast, rolling grasslands of the Texas Panhandle, treeless except for the towering cottonwoods that defined the banks of the river—headed for the frontier village of Canadian. By that time the Atchison, Topeka & Santa Fe train had already pulled out of the Kansas City station. It was also headed west, and Canadian, Texas, was also a distant stop on its route.

By ten o'clock that morning the four riders, their black overcoats buttoned tight against the bite of late autumn on the High Plains, had passed the Texas state line by about four miles and were some eighteen miles east of Canadian. J. W. Conaster spotted them there. Conaster was a settler in rural Hemphill County, and he was headed east en route from Canadian to his farm when he encountered the quartet. The strangers attracted his attention for several reasons: When he spoke to them, rather than returning a customary frontier greeting, they just glared at him; all four carried Winchester rifles in their saddle scabbards; they all had morrals (burlap bags filled with horse feed) dangling from their saddle horns—a sign they were long riders for sure; and each had a pair of overshoes lashed behind his saddle. Conaster would later testify that some other things also aroused his curiosity. It was unusual, he said, to see strangers not riding on any road or trail—they were riding along the south bank of the Canadian River—and it was also unusual to see that number of armed men riding together and astride some really good horses. That was why Conaster paid particularly close attention to the men. He noted that three of the riders had dark mustaches and that the fourth rider was a tall, light-complected man with small sideburns and a light mustache. Later, he would be able to identify two of the four riders. But he was never able to identify the tall, light-complected rider, the identity of whom would baffle lawmen for a long time.

By one o'clock in the afternoon the riders were about ten miles downriver from Canadian. That's where John N. Webb noticed them. Webb, a resident of Day County, Oklahoma, had been to Canadian, presumably for supplies, and was headed back home. Although the appearance of these four well-armed strangers aroused suspicion of other locals who crossed paths with them that day, Webb, curiously enough, seemed to have paid little attention to the riders. Instead, he focused his attention on the four horses they were riding—a fact that would later cause considerable speculation.

At three o'clock the riders were seen by Doc Walton some five or six miles east of Canadian, still heading west. Doc Walton had also been to Canadian and was on the way back to his home in Day County. (Day County, Oklahoma Territory, home to both Walton and Webb, was wedged between D County, Oklahoma Territory, on its east and Hemphill County, Texas, on its west.) Walton said that three of the riders were small men with dark mustaches, but he noted that the fourth rider was larger, appearing to weigh about 180 pounds, and that he was light-complected with small sideburns and a light-colored mustache. He couldn't identify the tall man, but by fortuitous chance he was able to positively identify one of the smaller men because Walton had previously become acquainted with him in Texas. His name was Will "Tulsa Jack" Blake, a known outlaw and member of the notorious Bill Doolin Oklahoma Territory gang. Walton spoke to Tulsa Jack as they passed, but Blake did not return his greeting and just kept riding. Later, when called to testify, Walton would also be able to positively identify one of the other men, but not the tall, light-complected man.

Meanwhile, the mighty iron horse from Kansas City was dragging a string of cars across the vast Kansas prairie, passing Topeka and heading southwest toward Woodward in the Oklahoma Territory. In that string of cars was the Wells Fargo Express car, and in that car were George Isaacs's five phony money packets. Also in that string of cars were some passenger cars, and in one of those cars was George Isaacs himself. His ticket would take him as far as the Santa Fe depot in Canadian, where the train was scheduled to arrive that night at eight o'clock. Another passenger on the train was a rancher named C. W. Jones. He had delivered a herd of cattle that day to a buyer in Gage, Oklahoma Territory, and was now en route to Amarillo. Although he had previously seen all four of the Isaacs brothers, he testified that he had not seen George Isaacs for eight or ten years, and he was unsure whether the Isaacs brother sitting across from him in the passenger car was George or George's brother, Will (or Bill) Isaacs. He initially identified him as Will.[1]

Now it was four o'clock in the afternoon. Mrs. John Miller saw those four riders about three hundred or four hundred yards from her home on the eastern edge of Canadian and near the south bank of the Canadian River. The moment she spied the strangers riding into town she knew they were up to no good. Canadian, Texas, was a small village in 1894, and Mrs. Miller had never before seen any of them. All were well armed, she noted, and when they got to the outskirts of town they reigned in, milled about, and held a powwow, seemingly uncertain about what to do next. She noted that one of the riders, the tall one, seemed especially cautious in his approach, keeping most of himself and his mount behind a low ridge. When the riders noticed her watching them, they wheeled their mounts around and rode out of sight over the hill.

Mrs. Miller immediately concluded that they were "up to some kind of devilment." She told her husband, "They're here to rob the bank. We ought to tell the sheriff." Her husband, however, didn't think that was a good idea. "Best not busy yourself getting mixed up in something like that," he shrugged.[2] So she kept quiet—until later, when she found out what those strangers really were up to.

Five o'clock, Friday, November 23, 1894: John Kirkham was working at Paul Hoefle's saloon in Canadian, a scant two hundred yards from the Santa Fe Railroad depot. Two strangers entered the saloon. Kirkham said both were small men with black mustaches and wore overcoats. He briefly visited with one of them. Later, after those two men had been arrested, he was able to identify them. That's when he learned their names: Joe Blake (brother of Will "Tulsa Jack" Blake) and Jim Harbolt.

★ ★ ★

When the Santa Fe station agent, A. B. Harding, learned that there was a large shipment of money scheduled to arrive that night on the eight o'clock train, he sent for Hemphill County sheriff Tom T. McGee. McGee was the first sheriff of the newly formed (1887) Hemphill County. Prior to that McGee had been foreman of the PO Ranch in unorganized Hemphill County since the ranch's establishment in 1884. McGee was highly respected and was remembered as "honest, fearless, and of a kindly disposition."[3] Sheriff McGee arrived at the depot before the Santa Fe train got there and went into the Wells Fargo Express office, where Harding was waiting for him.

By chance the Texas Panhandle's most famous and feared lawman—acclaimed as its "first and greatest peace officer"—happened to be in Canadian that same day.[4] His name was George Washington "Cap" Arrington.

Cap Arrington was a battle-scarred veteran of the Civil War, having gained notoriety as a scout and spy for Confederate colonel John Singleton Mosby. After his service with Mosby's Rangers he migrated to Texas, where he joined the Texas Rangers as an enlisted man in 1875. During his first assignment, he and a handful of other rangers were assigned duty in the chaotic Rio Grande Valley, where, during one month in 1877, they succeeded in arresting twenty-six men, including seven for murder and three for horse theft, without suffering a casualty.

As Texas Ranger field reports attest, for the next five years, as the Texas frontier slowly advanced westward, the Frontier Battalion of the rangers, although badly undermanned, fought continuous battles against outlaws, marauding Indians, and renegades of all types while protecting the settlers and their property.

Meanwhile, Arrington's fearlessness and leadership qualities were soon recognized, and he quickly rose through the ranks. In 1879 he was promoted to the rank of captain. While Arrington was respected for his courage, audacity, and effectiveness, he had a volatile temper that flared when anyone crossed him. He also imposed rigid discipline on his men, earning him the reputation of being "the iron-handed ranger."[5]

Arrington resigned from the Texas Rangers on August 31, 1882, to take advantage of ranching opportunities in the Texas Panhandle, but his reputation as a hard-edged and effective lawman caused pioneers in Mobeetie, beleaguered by scores of gamblers, saloon keepers, and prostitutes, as well as cattle rustlers and other outlaws, to practically draft Arrington as sheriff of the newly formed Wheeler County. At that time fourteen other as yet

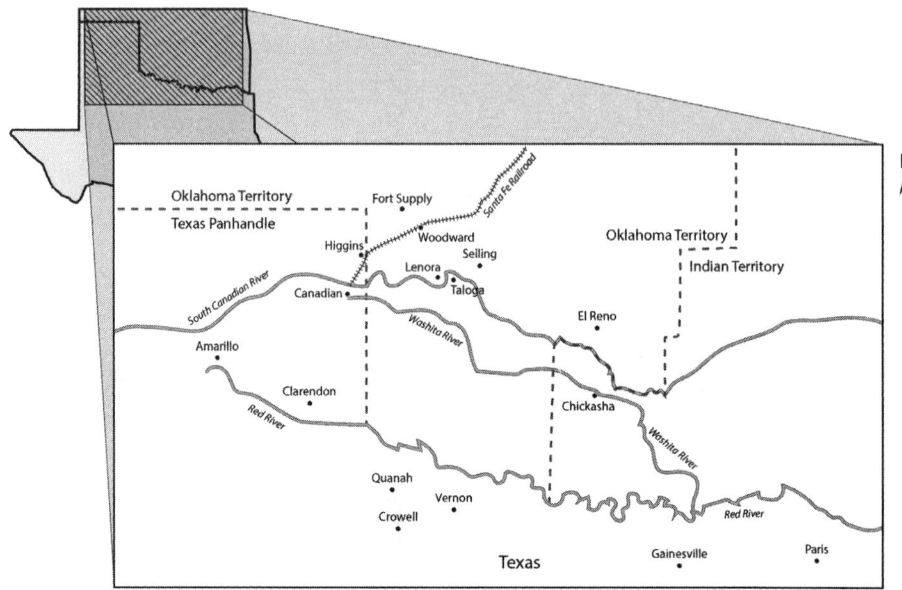

Map 1. Where It All Happened

unorganized counties in the Panhandle were attached to Wheeler County. Together those fifteen counties covered more than half of the Texas Panhandle, and Cap Arrington was their sheriff beginning January 1, 1883. He served for eight years, having been reelected to three more two-year terms.[6]

When his eight-year stint as Wheeler County sheriff ended, Arrington tried once again to enjoy private life on his ranch. But soon he would be called back to duty as a Panhandle lawman.

That fateful evening—November 23, 1894—Cap Arrington was in Canadian intending to board the westbound Santa Fe train when it departed the depot. His destination was the small town of Panhandle, Texas, some hundred miles to the southwest.

The train arrived right on time at eight o'clock. A small man disembarked. His name was George Isaacs. However, instead of going to the Wells Fargo office to claim his money packets, George began walking away from the depot "at a brisk pace" in search of a local hotel. He needed to find one, quick. Strange as that must have seemed, it was also curious that George chose to send his phony money packets to himself at a small village where he didn't even know the location of a nearby hotel.

George Washington "Cap" Arrington, frontier Texas lawman, about 1920. He was commander of Company C of the Frontier Battalion of the Texas Rangers and later sheriff of Wheeler County and still later sheriff of Hemphill County, Texas. 425/649, reprinted by permission of Panhandle-Plains Historical Museum, Canyon, Texas.

Will "Tulsa Jack" Blake, here shown after his death in April 1895, was a member of Bill Doolin's gang of Oklahoma Territory outlaws. He was indicted as a coconspirator in the November 1894 attempted robbery of the Wells Fargo Express in Canadian, Texas, when Sheriff Tom T. McGee was murdered. Tulsa Jack Blake's brother, Joe Blake, was also indicted. Rose 2014, reprinted by permission of Western History Collections, Oklahoma University Libraries.

As George was swiftly striding south away from the depot, he encountered Cap Arrington, who was walking north toward the depot, intending to catch the train. George stopped Arrington and asked him for directions to the nearest hotel. Although Arrington had known George Isaacs from several years back when George cowboyed for the T Anchor Ranch, he didn't recognize him in the dusk. In answer to George's inquiry, Arrington simply pointed back north across the railroad tracks to the nearest hotel, the Fay Hotel. But to get there George would have had to turn around and walk back north toward the depot, and then cross the railroad tracks. George didn't want to do that. So he ignored Arrington's directions and kept striding south away from the depot until he reached the Sutherland Hotel, where he secured a room.[7]

By now it was dark. The Santa Fe train had come off the main track on the south side of the depot and entered the house track on the north side, where the Wells Fargo Express car was uncoupled. Then the train reentered the main track. Before the westbound train pulled out of the station, Cap Arrington got on board. The train carrying Arrington departed, but Cap Arrington would soon return—before the next sun, in fact.

Meanwhile, Sheriff Tom T. McGee was inside the Wells Fargo Express office visiting with station agent Harding. As soon as the Wells Fargo Express car was uncoupled and the train had departed, Harding exited the depot and entered the express car, where he retrieved George Isaacs's money packets.

About that time the four long riders approached the depot. At least, three of them did. The fourth rider—the tall, light-complected man—stayed with the horses at the stockyards just north of the depot, behind and out of sight.

A. B. Harding noticed the strangers as he got off the express car with the money packets. In the station lights he got a clear view of one of the outlaws. Later, Harding wouldn't hesitate to make a positive identification of that man: Jim Harbolt.[8]

The stage was set. The players were in place. And the curtain was about to rise on a tragic drama of far-reaching consequences. Before the curtain finally rang down on this incredible drama, there would be murders and murder trials in Texas and the Oklahoma Territory. And in between the murders and the trials the tale would take some mighty strange twists.

CHAPTER FOUR

SHOOTOUT AT THE CANADIAN DEPOT

SHERIFF MCGEE VERSUS THE OUTLAWS

Sometimes there comes a moment—maybe a second, maybe only a split-second, no matter—when a decision of such life-changing magnitude looms up so suddenly, so unexpectedly, and so dramatically that it is frozen forever after in time, etched indelibly in a man's mind and gut. Over and over again for the rest of his life he will replay that scene—the moment, the decision, and the result—but no amount of regret or second-guessing or rationalization can ever change its soul-searing impact. The moving hand of time, having once inked its writ, moves on, and neither a jot nor a tittle of the script can ever be erased or revised.

When Sheriff Tom T. McGee stepped out of the waiting room door onto the platform of the Santa Fe depot in Canadian, he almost ran into a small man with a dark mustache wearing a black overcoat and black hat—"a quick, nervous kind of fellow," the sheriff noted as the stranger kept walking away from him.[1]

"Hello! Where'd you come from?" the sheriff asked.

"From that light back there," the small man replied, pointing back north. But he kept walking south on the depot platform, moving away from the sheriff.

"Where ya going?"

The man never broke stride, nor did he answer. He just

pointed south in the direction of Paul Hoefle's saloon, still walking away from the sheriff.

"Hold on! I want to talk to you," shouted the sheriff.

Then the man suddenly turned back and faced the sheriff, each man sizing the other up. Time stood still—that frozen moment in time—and for each the moment of decision teetered precariously on the precipice of destiny. And doom.

Decision time. What to do?

The sheriff: Draw his pistol? Demand "Hands up!" Again demand an explanation? Or wait for an answer from the small man? Station agent Harding had already told the sheriff that he had encountered two strangers wearing black overcoats who were acting mighty suspicious when he got off the express car with the money packets. It also sounded mighty suspicious to Sheriff McGee. Likely they were outlaws. If so, the other outlaw or outlaws were probably lurking nearby in the darkness. What would they do if the sheriff drew his pistol? The sheriff hesitated and then elected to wait for an answer.

The nervous stranger on the platform: He had several options. He had committed no crime. He could make most any excuse, however lame, and walk away a free man. He could say he was going over to Hoefle's saloon for a drink—could say he missed his train and would have to wait overnight for the next one. Still, he and his companions had come on a mother-lode cash mission. A huge reward was almost within reach. But if he drew his pistol, should he shoot? Engage the sheriff in a gun battle? It was a big risk. What if he missed with that first shot? Or should he draw and demand, "Hands up!" Disarm the sheriff and force him into the depot? Make him open the safe and deliver the money packets? Too many options to consider; too little time to decide.

He drew his pistol and fired.

Inside the depot, Harding heard the gun battle erupt—heard ten or twelve shots ring out in quick succession. Then there was silence. Sheriff McGee staggered to the agent's door—it had a spring lock—and yelled, "My God, I've been shot." He hollered for someone to come open the door. When it was opened he staggered in and slumped down on a cot.

There was no sign of the outlaws. Strangely enough, even though the gang had incapacitated the sheriff, they did not attempt to enter the depot and complete their mission. Panic-stricken, they broke and ran, mounted their horses, and fled back to the Oklahoma Territory, leaving George Isaacs's money packets in the depot safe.

Harding summoned Dr. A. M. Newman, who raced to the scene and examined the wounded sheriff. McGee had been hit only once, but it was a fatal wound. The outlaw's bullet had entered McGee's body just above the right hip, the bullet's trajectory angling upward and forward until it finally lodged near the sheriff's navel. Two more bullet holes were found in McGee's clothing, but neither penetrated his body.

Although Sheriff McGee's wound would prove fatal, he was still conscious, and he was able to give Dr. Newman a detailed account of what happened as well as a description of the man who had shot him. It was that "nervous fellow" whom he had encountered on the platform. His description fit head to heel a man who would later be identified as Jim Harbolt—a small man, dark complected, with a dark mustache but no beard. Moreover, the sheriff told Dr. Newman that he had encountered that same man in Canadian earlier that afternoon and, thinking that he was a photographer, had asked him to show his occupation license. Apparently the sheriff was satisfied with whatever reply the fellow made and therefore didn't press the matter further.

McGee described the shootout to Dr. Newman. After he shouted, "Hold on! I want to talk to you," the small man turned abruptly and faced him. Each hesitated. Then the small man went for his pistol. When McGee saw the movement, he attempted to draw, but his pistol hung. The little man got off one or two shots and jumped off the northeast corner of the platform (a height of two and one-half feet) and continued firing. McGee's pistol finally cleared, and he returned fire.

Then the other two outlaws joined the battle, and he was hit just above the right hip and fell. McGee said he did not know if any of his rounds had hit their mark. Dr. Newman then had a sad duty to perform: he told Sheriff McGee that his wound was "necessarily fatal." They carried the sheriff to his home, where he was able to give his wife final instructions on how to wind up their affairs. And there he died the next morning.[2]

Meanwhile, back at the depot, shock and confusion reigned. No one was capable of taking charge or conducting an investigation—much less crafting a plan to capture the killers. Station agent Harding, however, wasted no time in firing off a telegram addressed to Cap Arrington at the next depot ahead of the westbound Santa Fe train at Panhandle, Texas. In the telegram Harding informed Arrington about George Isaacs's money packets and that

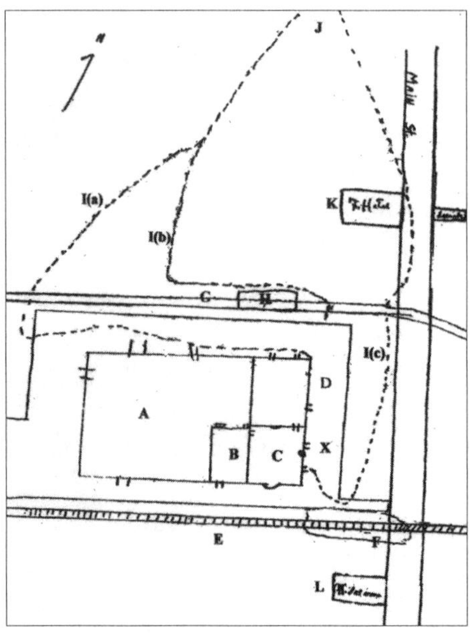

This crime scene sketch was introduced into evidence at the trial of Jim Harbolt for killing Hemphill County Sheriff Tom T. McGee at the Santa Fe depot in Canadian, Texas. X marks the location on the depot platform where Sheriff McGee was fatally wounded; A is the depot itself; B is the Wells Fargo office inside the depot; C is the depot waiting room; and D is the depot platform. E indicates the main Santa Fe track; F marks the location of the Wells Fargo Express car when it first arrived; G is the "house track" coming off the main Santa Fe track, and H is where the Wells Fargo Express car was parked after being uncoupled from the train. I-a, I-b, and I-c trace the paths taken by three of the four outlaws as they fled the scene of the murder and headed north to rendezvous with the fourth outlaw, who was holding their horses in the stockyards at J, north of the depot. From there, Ranger Arrington and his posse picked up the outlaws' trail. K is the Fay Hotel, and L is Paul Hoefle's saloon, where witnesses testified they saw Blake and Harbolt drinking late in the afternoon before Sheriff McGee was murdered. Letters A–L and X were added by the author based on evidence presented during the trial. *State of Texas v. Jim Harbolt,* Cause No. 647, Donley County District Court.

Canadian railroad depot (shown about 1887) where Sheriff Tom T. McGee was murdered in November 1894. 1974-152/14, reprinted by permission of Panhandle-Plains Historical Museum, Canyon, Texas.

George Isaacs had arrived on the same train that carried those packets. He also informed Arrington that Sheriff McGee had suffered a fatal wound during the ensuing gun battle. Cap Arrington then caught an eastbound Santa Fe stock train at the Panhandle depot at 3:00 a.m. and headed back to Canadian. He arrived before daylight and immediately took charge. Although Cap Arrington hadn't seen George Isaacs for several years—the period of time George had retreated to his Indian Territory lair—he was well acquainted with George's brothers, Sam, Will, and John Isaacs. All three now owned ranches in Hemphill County, as did Arrington. Therefore, when station agent Harding informed him that the crime apparently involved George Isaacs and the money packets, the first thing Arrington did was to send for Sam Isaacs, and when Sam arrived he asked, "Where's George?"

"In town."

"Find him and ask if anyone knew he was going to ship this money." Sam said he didn't know of anyone who knew about the money shipment. Then he left.[3]

At daybreak, Cap Arrington discovered the footprints of three men leading from the depot back north to the stockyards, where their horses had been held by a fourth man during the attempted robbery. Wasting no further time, he assembled a posse and was soon hard on the outlaws' trail. They picked up the trail of the four horses leaving the stockyards, the outlaws spurring hard and deep, racing back east along the Canadian River toward their sanctuary in Oklahoma Territory. Cap Arrington and his posse performed the herculean task of trailing the four criminals for about fifty miles along the Canadian River and then into Oklahoma Territory. Darkness overtook them near Dan McKenzie's farm. Pressing on in the dark, they arrived at the McKenzie homestead, where Arrington and his posse found McKenzie, his wife, his daughter, and Joe Blake, who had been living with the McKenzies. Behind McKenzie's cabin Arrington discovered a lathered sorrel horse resting in the corral. Several witnesses later testified that the horse belonged to Blake. Moreover, the horse's hooves matched one of the four hoof prints Arrington had followed from the scene of the killing. The other outlaws, it turned out, had departed shortly before Arrington's arrival. The next morning, after arresting Blake, Arrington took his men back up the trail to the point where darkness had overtaken them the night before. They were then able to track the four horsemen straight back to McKenzie's cabin. But, just before they got there, Arrington noted that a fifth horseman had joined the group and ridden with them to McKenzie's farm. Tracks were found showing the four horsemen had left the McKenzie farm sometime before Arrington and his posse had arrived the night before. Arrington and his exhausted posse did not pursue these four any farther but instead returned to Canadian with Joe Blake in custody.[4]

While Cap Arrington and his posse were on their chase-and-capture mission, and before they returned to Canadian with their captive, some very interesting events had taken place there. George Isaacs had heard the shootout from his room in the Sutherland Hotel that fateful Friday night, and the sun had not been above the horizon very long the next morning before he learned all the details. He was doubtless stunned when he learned that the Canadian sheriff had been killed in the debacle. But that news must have paled in his mind when compared with the rest of the story: his bungling outlaw sidekicks had failed to steal those phony money packets. George panicked. What to do? Those potentially incriminating packets could not be allowed to fall into the wrong hands.

Tom T. McGee, first sheriff of Hemphill County, Texas, about 1894. 1161/1, reprinted by permission of Panhandle-Plains Historical Museum, Canyon, Texas.

CHAPTER FIVE

STRUGGLING TO HIDE THE MONEY PACKETS

ENTER SAM ISAACS

By the time station agent A. B. Harding arrived at his Wells Fargo office that Saturday morning, everybody in town had already heard about the shooting of Sheriff McGee the night before. A man Harding had never seen before was waiting for him to open his office. The stranger was not alone, however. He was accompanied by someone with whom Harding was well acquainted: Sam Isaacs. Sam then introduced Harding to his brother George. (The fact that Sam Isaacs showed up with George Isaacs that morning shortly after the crack of dawn seemed very curious in retrospect, since both Sam Isaacs and his brother Will would later claim that they hadn't seen brother George for more than seven years and that George Isaacs had not even set foot in Canadian during that time.)

George wasted no time in getting down to the business at hand. He asked Harding to hold the money packets until Monday, explaining that he wanted to ship the money back to Kansas City in order to buy some cattle. Harding refused. George would have to receive the money packets. That being the case, George then told the agent that he would bring back some of the money the next day, Sunday. That wouldn't do either, Harding said. He would have to wait until Monday morning. Reluctantly, George accepted all five packets, signed a receipt acknowledging acceptance, and departed with Sam in tow. Then they took the packets to the J. A. Chambers mercantile store located on Main Street. Chambers, also, had never laid eyes on Sam's companion. After introducing George to Chambers, Sam asked permission to "put a little money" in Chambers's safe. Chambers agreed. Before leaving, Sam mentioned that they might want the packages back the next (Sunday) evening. Then they left the packets there unopened but locked away in the safe.[1]

That would prove to be a disastrous mistake. Why didn't George rip open those incriminating packets, stick the real five hundred dollars in his pocket, destroy the packets and the paper stuffing, then mount a fast horse, get the hell out of Canadian, Texas, and bolt for the safety of his Indian Territory refuge?

Locking up the money packets in Chambers's safe was obviously intended to shield the incriminating evidence from public discovery, but it had the exact opposite effect—it secured and preserved incriminating evidence that would later prove crucial to the state's case against George Isaacs. In fact, the prosecution's case against George Isaacs would have been dead in the water without those money packets—unless the state could have persuaded one of the four bandits involved in the attempted robbery to turn state's witness and finger George as a participant in the plot, but even then the prosecution would have had to produce some evidence to corroborate the accomplice testimony. That would have been a tall order indeed.

By Sunday morning everybody in the county was outraged by the news that the popular sheriff had been assassinated. Then, when it was learned that this outsider, George Isaacs, had sent some money packets supposedly containing $25,000 to himself at the Wells Fargo depot office, where some murderous thugs had mysteriously emerged out of the darkness just when the packets arrived and had shot the sheriff, well—everybody began to wonder. Somehow it all sounded very suspicious. Something was very wrong here.

A citizens' committee was quickly formed to investigate. D. J. Young, a cashier at the Canadian Valley Bank, was in charge. They soon discovered that George and Sam Isaacs had received the packets from the Wells Fargo office and had taken them to Chambers's store. That's where Young and his committee headed Sunday afternoon. However, before the committee arrived, Sam Isaacs learned what was afoot. He hastily collared brother George and beat the committee to the Chambers store. When they arrived about two o'clock that afternoon, Chambers wasn't present, but his clerk, a man named Jim Winsett, was there. Dick Brussells, a member of Young's committee, was also there, and Brussells later testified that he heard Sam demand that the safe be opened so they could remove the money packets and that he also heard Winsett refuse to do so. Later that afternoon, Young, Dick Brussell, and other committee members rounded up Sam and George Isaacs as well as Wells Fargo agent A. B. Harding and converged on Chambers's store. By now Chambers had also arrived. Young and the committee demanded that Chambers open his safe. In a classic understatement, Chambers would later testify, "Some parties came to me and asked me to keep out of the way as they wanted to examine the packages." Chambers complied.

If George had been nervous the night before, when his partners in crime failed to steal those packets, he must have been near hysteria waiting for the committee to open them and make the inevitable discovery. Even dull-witted George realized the jig was up. When he was shown the packages, George had to admit that they belonged to him, that his signature was on all five, that the sealing wax had not been broken, and that there had been no tampering with the packages.

Frozen in speechless terror, George Isaacs fidgeted nervously and sat on the edge of his chair tearing little bits of paper while D. J. Young opened each money packet and examined the contents in the presence of Sam and the committee. Each package contained only one hundred dollars in one- and two-dollar bills plus a lot of paper scraps. When done, Young announced that each packet was forty-nine hundred dollars short. George Isaacs made no objection or complaint about the count.

George then admitted his part in the scheme to defraud Wells Fargo, but he denied having anything to do with the murder of Sheriff McGee. That was definitely not part of the plan, he explained. Plus, he was asleep in the Sutherland Hotel when all the shooting took place. D. J. Young, leader of the committee, testified that after this mind-boggling discovery he gave the five hundred dollars in cash to Sam Isaacs and turned the other incriminating documents over to the authorities.[2] George was arrested and charged with the attempted robbery of the Wells Fargo office.

Meanwhile, lawmen and the Wells Fargo detectives continued their investigations. They sought positive identification of the four long riders who attempted to rob the Wells Fargo office—including that mysterious tall, light-complected fellow—and anyone else involved in the plot.

CHAPTER SIX

THE ISAACS BROTHERS

AND LIZZIE, TOO

As soon as they could mount a horse and draw a paycheck cowboying for frontier ranchers, the four Isaacs brothers—Will, George, Sam, and John—had left home and headed west.[1] They were the sons of Joseph C. and Mary Jack Isaacs, dirt-poor Alabama natives who had uprooted and moved to Bosque County in central Texas shortly before the outbreak of the Civil War. During the Civil War the father, Joseph, served as a captain in the Confederate army.

By 1883 the oldest brother, Will, age thirty-one, was riding for the Apple Company, a big operator that ran several thousand head of cattle on the open ranges located at the junction of Quartermaster Creek and the Washita River in the Indian Territory about sixty miles east of the Texas border. The two younger brothers, Sam and John, had remained down south not far from the family home. In 1878, when Sam was only fourteen years old, he got a job working for his brother-in-law, Alex Martin, on Martin's Half Diamond H outfit on Elm Creek in the Buffalo Gap country just south of Abilene in Taylor County, Texas. When his brother-in-law decided to move his cattle to New Mexico, Sam and his younger brother John decided to join Will in the land of the cattle barons. In 1884, Sam, then twenty years old, and John, eighteen, soon found work in the Oklahoma Territory—John riding for the Apple Company where brother Will was working and Sam scoring a job cowboying for William E. "Billy" Malaley and A. S. C. Forbes on the Cheyenne-Arapaho Indian Reservation adjoining Hemphill County, Texas, to the east.

Will, Sam, and John spent the next decade working for large cattle operations on the vast, mostly unfenced ranges of the Texas Panhandle, the Oklahoma Territory, and the New Mexico Territory. Somehow—with a heavy emphasis on the word *somehow*—by 1894 Will and Sam had managed, while drawing cowboy wages of thirty dollars per month, to acquire ranches of their own in Hemphill County near Canadian, Texas. And with newfound wealth came respectability in the community.

Meanwhile, George Isaacs started down the same cowboy trails that his brothers had ridden. He was a good cowhand, and in the early 1880s he was hired by the T Anchor Ranch, which at the time encompassed about 240,000 acres in the rugged Palo Duro Canyon country in the eastern part of Randall County in the Texas Panhandle south of Amarillo. In 1883 George was twenty-five years old, but like most of the young T Anchor hands he was full of life and vigor and eager for action. However, there was unrest among the ranks of the cowboys who worked for the large Panhandle ranches. Cattle ranching had become very profitable, and the owners of the big spreads were prospering. Cowboys, on the other hand, continued to be paid only thirty dollars per month plus board, while the wagon boss on each ranch was paid fifty dollars per month. The year 1883 became famous as the year of the cowboy strike. Demanding higher wages, about one hundred cowboys from the large Panhandle ranches, including six from the T Anchor, went on strike. But George didn't join the strike. He, another cowboy named Ed Beard, and the camp cook, Gus Lee, were the only T Anchor hands who elected to remain on the ranch payroll. The owners named young George Isaacs as the ranch foreman, a position he held until 1885, when the ranch ownership changed.[2]

Nothing much was heard from George for several years. Then, in about 1890 he resurfaced, living in that cabin along the Washita River near Chickasha in the Indian Territory. That was his residence at the time he showed up at the Kansas City office of Wells Fargo and initiated the twenty-five-thousand-dollar phony money packet scam. He had given up living the life of a thirty-dollars-per-month ranch cowboy and had cast his lot with the most notorious bands of outlaws in the territory.

George's close association with those outlaws would later cause one newspaper editor to classify George as being "the black sheep of the Isaacs family."[3] Subsequent developments in the George Isaacs story would cause others to wonder if George was really the only black sheep in that family.

Meanwhile, in 1890, while George Isaacs was living life on the wild side with his outlaw buddies in his Indian Territory hideout near Chickasha, George met the black sheep of another family. Born April 21, 1867, in Tishomingo County, Mississippi, Mary Elizabeth "Lizzie" Ellis was one of eight children born to William Rufus Ellis and wife, Mary Weton Horton Ellis, folks molded from the common clay of most poor, hardworking rural people of the time. They were apparently a respectable family; no reports of outlawry among the clan have been discovered, except, that is, for their third child, Lizzie, and Lizzie's older brother, John Ellis.

Lizzie was what was known in folk parlance of the day as a real "ring-tailed tooter." Nevertheless, during her youth, Lizzie, like George Isaacs, traveled the straight and narrow. By 1881 the Ellis family had left their Civil War–devastated homeland in Mississippi and migrated westward to the north-central Texas area around Gainesville in Cooke County. That land, just south of the Red River boundary of Indian Territory, was where, on November 7, 1883, sixteen-year-old Lizzie married her first husband, John L. Byrne, age twenty-six. Ten months later they had a son, Wiley Francis Washington Byrne. However, seven years of boring married life were about all Lizzie could stand. Sometime about then was when she met George Isaacs, and that's when she crossed over the Rubicon of respectability (that, geographically speaking, being the Red River in this case). George and Lizzie (apparently without bothering to get a divorce from John Byrne) were married on April 12, 1891, in El Reno, Oklahoma Territory. Then they returned to George's outlaw-infested cabin on the banks of the Washita River.

George and Lizzie had two sons: Richard "Dick" Isaacs, born April 16, 1892, and Roy Isaacs, born October 22, 1895.[4] Chicanery, feuds, romantic jealousy, barn burnings, violence, shootings, and killings ran in the family, and at one time or another each of the four members of the George and Lizzie Isaacs family would find themselves seated in the defendant's chair during a murder trial.

CHAPTER SEVEN

GEORGE ISAACS DECIDES TO DO THE RIGHT THING—SORT OF

CANADIAN, TEXAS, NOVEMBER 27, 1894

Wells Fargo Express detective Fred J. Dodge arrived in Canadian on the Tuesday after Sheriff McGee had been fatally wounded the previous Saturday evening. At that point George Isaacs had not been charged with murder, only with the lesser offense of conspiracy to commit robbery.

The first thing Detective Dodge did was to go to the Canadian jail and interview George. He told George that in his opinion the best thing for George to do was to tell the truth and clear this whole thing up. Dodge added that he couldn't promise George any favors, but that if he wanted to do the right thing he would reveal everything he knew about the debacle and name everybody who was involved. Finally, George agreed that he wanted "to do the right thing": fess up and come clean. He then told Detective Dodge the following:

The Wells Fargo scam really wasn't his idea in the first place. That notorious outlaw Bill Doolin and a fellow named Jim Stanley, whom he had never seen before, showed up one night at his cabin in the Indian Territory and proposed a scheme to swindle Wells Fargo out of a big bundle of money. There were two other men with them, but they stayed outside by his corral during the discussion and he never got a close look at them. He couldn't identify them and said only that they were small, dark-complected men.

According to George, Jim Stanley did all the talking. He wanted George to be the front man in the scheme since no one would recognize him as an outlaw. Stanley laid out the plan like this: He would give George a fairly small amount of money, and George would take it to the Wells Fargo Express office in Kansas City and put it in some Wells Fargo money packets but mark up the packets so that they purported to contain a very large amount of money. Then George was to have it sent by train to himself at Canadian, Texas. George was supposed to ride the train. Meanwhile, Stanley would put together a gang and rob the train and its passengers—including George—just before it got to Canadian. And, of course, they would relieve the Wells Fargo Express agent of the phony money packets. Then George would file his claim against Wells Fargo Express for the face amount stated on the money packets, and they would all split the spoils. George further claimed that he didn't know the identity of any of the four outlaws who attempted the Wells Fargo robbery the night Sheriff McGee was killed—except Jim Stanley. That statement must have seemed very suspicious to Detective Dodge. How did George Isaacs happen to know that this Jim Stanley fellow was among the four bandits, and how did he know that Bill Doolin wasn't among the four?

George told Detective Dodge that he really didn't want to participate in the scheme, but Doolin and Stanley had come back to his cabin several times and discussed the matter. Finally, he agreed to participate, but only, he explained, because he was "a poor man and didn't have any money." At that point George said he suggested to Stanley that it would look better if he took some cattle to Kansas City, sold them, and claimed that the money to be shipped via Wells Fargo was the proceeds from his cattle sales. Stanley agreed. Or so George claimed.[1]

It might have occurred to Detective Dodge that if the professional thieves really had twisted the arm of a reluctant amateur like George, then didn't it seem a bit strange that George came up with a refinement on their imaginative scam—a refinement like taking cattle to Kansas City and selling them in order to bolster the claim that the money came from a legitimate enterprise? The Doolin gang wasn't in the business of raising—or even stealing—cattle. George Isaacs didn't own any cattle. So whose cattle did George sell at Kansas City? There had to have been some other, as yet unidentified, player or players involved in the fraudulent scheme—a man, or men, who did own cattle. The question of the identity of the behind-the-scenes player or players would, for the time being, go unanswered.

Brother Sam Isaacs was not present when George gave his statement to Detective Dodge, but immediately afterward Dodge summoned Sam and had him listen to George's "confession." After hearing it, Sam expressed amazement and commented to the detective that he wouldn't have believed a word of it had he not "heard it from George's own lips."[2]

Detective Dodge once again pressed George for more background information on this mysterious Jim Stanley fellow. George claimed he didn't know any background information on Stanley. He described Jim Stanley as being a tall, light-complected man, weighing about 180 to 185 pounds, who had blue eyes. George again stated that there were two other men with Stanley and Bill Doolin when the plan was hatched, but he claimed he didn't get a good look at them and couldn't identify either. George, however, graciously agreed to assist Detective Dodge in learning the identity of these two men as well as obtaining more information about Jim Stanley if he could only get out of jail for a couple of weeks in order to go back to his cabin in the Indian Territory and do some undercover detective work of his own. He promised that he would then return and report his findings to Dodge.

Two days after Dodge's interview, G. W. "Cap" Arrington (who had been named as the interim sheriff of Hemphill County shortly after McGee was assassinated), Canadian lawyer H. E. Hoover, and Deputy Sheriff Vas Stickley also interviewed George in his jail cell. George reiterated his promise to help the officials identify and arrest the gang, if only they would release him for two weeks. Finally, the officials reluctantly agreed. George was released for two weeks in January 1895 after brothers Sam and Will Isaacs posted a five-thousand-dollar bond. He was to be confined again in the Hemphill County jail when he returned after concluding his undercover assignment.

Cap Arrington was more than a little skeptical about George's reliability as well as his intention to honor his promise. However, in agreeing to release George temporarily from custody, Cap Arrington wasn't relying solely on George's good intentions when George promised to return on schedule or to be a diligent undercover agent for the law. Recalling the report of Jake Hocker, deputy US marshal in Indian Territory, that Hocker had previously witnessed the worst stripe of territory outlaws hanging out at George's cabin, Arrington decided to hedge his bet. Accordingly, he notified Deputy

Marshal Hocker about George's temporary release and asked Hocker to keep George under close surveillance when he returned to his haunt in hopes of discovering the true identity of the mysterious Jim Stanley and his outlaw gang.[3]

George's mid-February deadline to return to his cell in the Canadian jail passed. No George. No undercover report from George—or Hocker. Cap Arrington waited three more weeks. Still, George was a no-show, and Arrington had received no reports. Finally, in March, Sheriff Arrington tracked George down in the Chickasaw Indian Territory, arrested him, and brought him back to Canadian. George Isaacs couldn't, or wouldn't, favor lawmen with a clue as to the identity of any gang members—including that of the mysterious Jim Stanley. This time the criminal charge lodged against George was soon upgraded from accessory to commit robbery to murder—the murder of Sheriff Tom T. McGee.

When Sheriff Cap Arrington incarcerated George Isaacs once again in the Hemphill County jail, he made a mistake. He locked George in the same cell with Joe Blake. Blake—boiling with rage at George for getting him locked up and charged with murder, all on account of George's cockeyed scheme to swindle Wells Fargo—took revenge on him by nearly beating him to death before officers could separate them. A felony charge of assault with intent to murder was filed against Joe Blake. That soon was reduced, however, to a charge of simple assault, and Blake was fined ten dollars.[4]

Cap Arrington would later testify that he didn't have any reason to believe that Bill Doolin or any of his gang (with the exception of Tulsa Jack Blake, Joe Blake's brother) was a part of the bumbling bunch that killed the sheriff. Further pressed on the subject, Arrington was asked: "Do you know that they (the Doolin gang) were not here?" Arrington answered, "I am well satisfied of it."[5]

In his biography of George Washington "Cap" Arrington, author Jerry Sinise made this comment about Arrington's involvement in the McGee murder investigation:

> Although the Doolin gang was suspect, Arrington didn't believe for a moment they were involved in the robbery attempt. George Isaacs lied, and Arrington knew it. Arrington knew the Doolin bunch—Bill Doolin, "Little Bill" Raidler, George "Red Buck" Waightman, George "Bitter Creek" Newcomb, Charles Pierce, Dick "Little Dick" West, Tulsa Jack Blake, Dynamite

> Dick and Arkansas Tom. The robbery just didn't have the feel of the Doolin gang. Tulsa Jack possibly free-lanced the Canadian robbery attempt, and was the only member of the gang involved. Six months following the Canadian shooting, Tulsa Jack was killed during a train robbery at Dover.[6]

Arrington's analysis that the Canadian debacle just "didn't have the feel of the Doolin gang" rings true. Had Bill Doolin been in charge, would he have sent an unknown like Jim Stanley—whoever he was—to lead the gang on a twenty-five-thousand-dollar robbery mission? And more to the point, once Sheriff McGee was wounded and immobilized, would Bill Doolin have spooked, mounted up, and raced away, leaving behind a jackpot of twenty-five thousand dollars that was within a few feet of his grasp? Arrington, who, as Sinise observed, knew well the members of the Doolin gang, also knew that this fellow Jim Stanley was not a member of Doolin's gang. Moreover, neither Arrington nor any other Texas or Oklahoma Territory lawman had ever heard of a man named Jim Stanley.

Meanwhile, Wells Fargo detective Dodge traveled to Kansas City, where he made some interesting discoveries. He verified that George Isaacs had, in fact, sold cattle in Kansas City, had sold them through the Drum-Flato Commission Company on November 21, 1894, and had received a check from Drum-Flato in the sum of $683.60. Obviously, George hadn't marketed a very large herd of cattle—whoever's cattle they were. In December 1894, cattle were selling for between $1.50 and $6.00 per hundredweight, depending on the quality of the animals. Thus, an average steer weighing about six hundred pounds would have sold for around $25.00.[7] George Isaacs probably sold only around twenty-five or thirty head of cattle in order to receive $683.60.

Detective Dodge also interviewed G. W. Fishburn, a cashier at the First National Bank of Kansas City. Fishburn identified George Isaacs as the man who presented the $683.60 Drum-Flato check to him, asking for cash. Fishburn said that he first gave George cash in twenty-dollar bills and change, but that George handed it back and demanded that he give him $500 out of the total amount in one- and two-dollar bills, explaining that he often traded with Indians back in the territory.

The information that Detective Dodge discovered in Kansas City further confirmed Cap Arrington's conclusion that the phony money packet debacle was not a Bill Doolin caper, but that it had all the earmarks of a plot concocted and executed by second-string amateurs. First, the mastermind behind the plot hadn't done his homework: Wells Fargo wasn't liable for a dime unless the plotters had allowed the Wells Fargo agent to count the money, seal the packets, and charge an insurance fee. Laying that legal defense aside, however, let's assume that the gang, as planned, really had robbed the train and taken those undocumented money packets and disappeared. Would Wells Fargo have simply opened its safe and handed George Isaacs $25,000 in cash? Definitely not. Wells Fargo would certainly have conducted some investigation, and beyond doubt Detective Fred Dodge would have wondered just how in the world some nobody—a poor boy like George Isaacs who lived in a shack in the Indian Territory—had come up with $25,000 in cash. Detective Dodge would have gone directly to Kansas City and interviewed express agent A. A. Rinehart, and Rinehart would have told him that George Isaacs explained that he got that $25,000 cash from selling cattle at the Kansas City stockyards. Fred Dodge would have immediately verified that George had indeed sold cattle at the Kansas City stockyards—twenty-odd head, for which Drum-Flato issued him a check for a whopping $683.60. Fred Dodge would then have invited George Isaacs to sit down and explain where he got the other $24,316.40.

And so the brilliant idea—whether it was George's idea or Jim Stanley's idea or someone else's idea—of taking a few head of cattle to Kansas City, selling them, and then claiming that the twenty-five thousand dollars was the proceeds of that sale was something less than brilliant. A lot less. Even had their plan turned out exactly as they expected, it was doomed to fail—the fools had rigged, baited, and set the trigger on a trap that was guaranteed to catch themselves—at least those who could be identified.

And, by the way, George, while you're at it, tell us all about your friend, this Jim Stanley fellow.

Up to this point, only two of the four desperadoes who were involved in the Canadian depot shootout had been identified: Joe Blake, whom Arrington and his posse had tracked to Dan McKenzie's cabin in the Oklahoma Territory, where they arrested him the day after the killing of Sheriff McGee, and Joe Blake's brother Will "Tulsa Jack" Blake, whom Doc Walton had recognized as one of the four long riders he had encountered the afternoon before Sheriff McGee was fatally wounded.

While Detective Dodge was conducting his investigation in Kansas City, Cap Arrington was conducting his own investigation over in that stronghold of the outlaws, D County, Oklahoma Territory, from whence had come the four long riders. That investigation eventually yielded the name of a third suspect: Jim Harbolt. Arrington arrested Harbolt in Taloga, the county seat of D County, on February 3, 1895, and brought him back to Canadian and jailed him. Harbolt was a small man, weighing about 140 to 145 pounds; stood five feet, seven or eight inches; was dark complected; and had a black mustache. He also had very small feet. For good measure, Dan McKenzie was also arrested in D County, as an accomplice to the gang, and was incarcerated in the Canadian jail with Joe Blake and Jim Harbolt.

That accounted for three of the four long riders. It left only one man unaccounted for and unidentified: the tall, light-complected long rider with the sandy sideburns—the man George Isaacs called Jim Stanley. Although Arrington conducted a thorough investigation that implicated Jim Harbolt as a principal in the murder of Sheriff McGee and implicated, as accessories, Dan McKenzie; Tulsa Jack Blake's brother, Sam Blake; and Tulsa Jack's running buddy, outlaw Bitter Creek Newcomb, Arrington could never find anyone on either side of the law who had ever even heard of a fellow called "Jim Stanley."

On May 20, 1895, a Hemphill County grand jury returned separate indictments against George Isaacs, Joe Blake, and Jim Harbolt for the murder of Sheriff Tom T. McGee. A joint indictment was also obtained against George Isaacs, Joe Blake, and Jim Harbolt as well as Dan McKenzie, Will "Tulsa Jack" Blake, Sam Blake, and George "Bitter Creek" Newcomb for the offense of conspiracy to commit robbery.[8]

Conspicuous by his absence in any of these indictments was the mysterious "Jim Stanley"—the man who never was.

CHAPTER EIGHT

THE MURDER OF A WELLS FARGO UNDERCOVER AGENT

TALOGA, OKLAHOMA TERRITORY, JANUARY 22, 1895

The moment that secret undercover agent Fred Hoffman dropped that letter into the mail slot at the Taloga post office, he sealed his own fate; he was a doomed man.

Of course he didn't realize that fact—not then or for the rest of the brief remainder of his life. He never realized that the letter addressed to Wells Fargo would never reach its destination, never realized that a man named Cicero Davis would intercept it before it ever left the post office, never realized that his cover as a secret agent had just been blown.

Fred Hoffman was a merchant in Taloga, the first treasurer of D County, Oklahoma Territory, and a US commissioner for the territory. Recently he had accepted a new position. Shortly after the attempted Wells Fargo Express robbery at the Canadian railroad depot in November 1894, Wells Fargo hired Hoffman as a secret undercover agent to discover the names of the perpetrators of both the attempted Canadian, Texas, depot robbery and the March 1894 Woodward, Oklahoma Territory, depot robbery.

Hoffman's investigation had yielded some valuable information.

The town of Taloga is located in what had been the Cheyenne-Arapaho Indian Reservation until the federal government opened it for settlement on April 19, 1892, and D County was established with Taloga as its county seat. Before that time only Cheyenne and Arapaho Indians were permitted to homestead tracts of land within the reservation. However, two Anglos who were destined to play important roles in this story—indeed, in D County history—were able to homestead tracts within the boundary of the reservation by taking advantage of a loophole in the tribal rules: they married Cheyenne women. Fred Hoffman was one of those who settled in D County while it was still a part of the Cheyenne-Arapaho Indian Reservation.

Fred was born Frederick Von Huffman in Germany about 1863. He and his brother, William, both received a good education in their home country, and Fred became well versed in the law before the family emigrated to America. Frederick Americanized his name to Fred Hoffman and enlisted in the US Cavalry. His sterling qualities—including his honesty and devotion to duty—were soon recognized, and he was promoted to the rank of sergeant during his four-year enlistment term. He was stationed in the Oklahoma Territory at Fort Supply and Fort Reno, where he met and fell in love with a beautiful Cheyenne named Crooked Woman Redeye. She had first attended school at the Darlington Agency in the Oklahoma Territory and later at the Carlisle Institute in Pennsylvania. When Hoffman met her she was serving as an interpreter for US officials at the Darlington Agency. Not only intelligent, she was also a beauty with long black hair, dark, sharp eyes, dark skin, and a quietness about her person that left Fred mysteriously intrigued. The couple married on March 27, 1890, and she became known as Florence Redeye Hoffman. Soon thereafter, Florence obtained a 160-acre allotment of land on the Cheyenne-Arapaho Reservation about four miles west of where Taloga is presently located, and when Fred's enlistment was up, he and Florence moved there and settled in—unfortunately, in a neighborhood where support for law and order was considerably less than robust.[1]

Fred Hoffman was not the first white man to homestead on the reservation. That distinction went to Big Jim Riley. James Riley was born in 1855 in Ireland and emigrated with his family to the United States in 1859. The family drifted westward and ended up in the Fort Reno area. Riley was well-educated for that era and found employment as a clerk for a trader named Connell at the Darlington Agency, and he later drove a stagecoach between the agency and Caldwell, Kansas. In 1886 he married a Cheyenne woman named Nina Livingbear.[2] Nina was a cousin of Fred Hoffman's wife, Florence Redeye Hoffman.

Nina Livingbear soon developed some serious second thoughts about

Fred Hoffman, a US commissioner, county treasurer of D County, Oklahoma Territory, and secret agent for Wells Fargo Express, was assassinated by outlaws near Taloga on January 22, 1895. He is shown here about 1887. Courtesy of Mrs. Robert E. King, Seiling, Oklahoma.

her marriage. The following fall while they were still living at the Darlington Agency, the Indians came back to the agency for their winter supplies. That's when Jim Riley came home one night and found that his wife was gone. Not only was his wife gone, but all of her clothes were gone as well as all of his furniture. He found her camped with the Indians. He took one look at Nina dressed in Indian clothes with her teepee filled with his furniture and went back home. But he returned shortly with a blacksnake whip, and he used it vigorously. Jim told Nina if he ever found her dressed like an Indian and living like one again, the whipping she had just received would "not be a circumstance" to the one she would get next time. Then he gathered up his wife and his furniture and took them home—but not before setting the tepee afire.[3]

In February 1886 Nina obtained a 160-acre allotment on the Cheyenne reservation, and Big Jim and Nina settled near Camp Creek a mile east of present-day Lenora and about four miles west of present-day Taloga. Their claim was located in a section of land adjacent to, and just north of, the section where Fred Hoffman and Florence Redeye later settled.

Riley and his Cheyenne wife made their home on the reservation some six years before it was opened for settlement in 1892, and he made good use of a golden opportunity. With no homesteading neighbors around to

Crooked Woman Redeye, a full-blood Cheyenne, about 1887. She became known as Florence Redeye Hoffman after she married Fred Hoffman in 1890. She was a graduate of Carlisle Institute in Pennsylvania and an interpreter for US government officials at the Darlington Agency in the Oklahoma Territory when she met Fred. Courtesy of Mrs. Robert E. King, Seiling, Oklahoma.

erect inconvenient fences, Big Jim had access to an open range on which to pursue his ranching enterprise. He was one of the largest ranchers in the area. Years later a Dewey County historian noted that Riley was the second largest cattle rancher in the county. (D County was renamed Dewey County in the general election of 1898.) As profitable as that enterprise proved to be, rancher Riley soon recognized and exploited another very lucrative sideline: he catered to the needs of outlaws, including the Bob Dalton and Bill Doolin gangs as well as lesser miscreants, and he continued to do so even after the reservation was opened for settlement.[4]

With its miles of rivers, deep canyons, and two separate blackjack oak–covered areas, the county was a haven for even the most heinous and hunted of villains. They operated with comparative ease in that isolated and thinly settled area. No roads existed—only a few trails. There were no railroads or major settlements within a hundred miles and no communication facilities. The reservation, and later, D County, was accessible only by foot or by horse. Western historian Homer Croy, in an article entitled "Where the Outlaws Hid," wrote, "One reason the Oklahoma outlaws were so hard to bring to their knees was the multitude of hiding places in which they could tuck themselves away for weeks at a time. The owners of many ranches welcomed the saddle boys. In fact, some of the owners were just a step above being outlaws themselves."[5]

Historian Croy went on to list several outlaw-friendly sites that were destined to figure prominently in this tale:

> 1. Jim Riley's ranch. Riley was a water-carrier; he tried to keep on good terms with both law and outlaw, a difficult balancing feat.
>
> 2. Amos Chapman's ranch, near where the town of Seiling is now located. Chapman had a wooden leg and also was married to an Indian woman. Sometimes he was a deputy upholding the law; sometimes he wasn't. Anyway, he was one of Oklahoma's early picturesque characters.
>
> 3. George Isaacs's cabin on the north side of the Washita River, four miles from Chickasha, Indian Territory. Timber came close to the ranch house; if the outlaws were disturbed they would rush into the timber, where no officer would be foolhardy enough to follow.[6]

It is apparent, however, that Big Jim Riley went a great deal further than reluctantly providing an occasional hideout for outlaws. A history of the families of D (later Dewey) County contains some revealing comments about Big Jim. After stating that he was the second largest cattle rancher in the county, the historian noted that "he also trained horses for outlaws, some of the horses being stolen out of Texas." The stolen horses were kept at the Riley Ranch and trained in Big Jim's large picket log corral. "The outlaws taught their horses to jump the settlers' barbed-wire fences by placing their coats on the wire and having the horse jump over at this exact spot."[7]

Another revealing tidbit about Jim Riley's character had to do with where Taloga, the county seat, was to be situated. Had Taloga been located on the north side of the South Canadian River, it would have been about the geographical center of the county. But, as noted by the county historian, Big Jim Riley didn't want it located north of the river. His ranch was located north of the river, and he wanted his ranch to remain as remote and as inconspicuous as possible, and therefore he used his influence to have the county seat located south of the Canadian River in order that it wouldn't, as the local historian phrased it, "interfere with his operations." Riley also took pains to see that nobody other than outlaws or outlaw-friendly settlers infringed on his territory. On that subject the Dewey County historian offered this coy understatement: "He . . . helped many people find their claims; he also kept some undisclosed claims to give his friends."[8]

That historian was not the only author to document Riley's exceptional hospitality to Oklahoma Territory badmen. The Bob Dalton gang, which at that time included Bob Dalton and his brothers, Grat and Emmett, as well as Bill Doolin, Bitter Creek Newcomb, Bill Powers, Dick Broadwell, and Charlie Pierce, planned its first train robbery in the territory while lounging around Big Jim's place in May 1892. Years later, Emmett Dalton wrote that the Daltons hid in their sod house sanctuary on the north end of Riley's ranch. Emmett's account described how the gang had established their headquarters on a high bluff where the cedar brakes slashed away from the river and the surrounding country could be viewed in any direction. In a red clay bank in the "squat-black," gnarled dwarf timber, they had excavated a dugout and had laid in a supply of canned goods, flour, coffee, bacon, and beans. In a little brush corral nearby, they kept their horses, "ready for flight or foray," and Riley always kept another twenty or thirty fine animals available on this remote fringe of his range. Emmett concluded by noting that Big Jim "was then, and always, one of our most loyal friends."[9]

After Bob Dalton's gang was decimated on October 5, 1892, during a foolhardy attempt to rob two banks simultaneously in a broad daylight raid in downtown Coffeyville, Kansas, one of Dalton's surviving gang members, Bill Doolin, picked up the crown and formed his own gang. Doolin's gang continued to enjoy Riley's hospitality. (Meanwhile, Bill Doolin's sister and her husband, E. C. Kinney, homesteaded a tract in D County only a few miles south of Big Jim's ranch.)

When the Cheyenne-Arapaho Reservation in D County was opened for settlement in 1892, outlaws of whatever stripe or caliber—well known and unknown, professionals as well as wannabes—flocked to stake free homestead claims in that remote and well-camouflaged paradise of the lawless.

By January 1, 1895, known outlaws and outlaw sympathizers living within a stone's throw of Fred Hoffman's claim in D County included Dan McKenzie; the infamous Blake brothers, including Doolin gang member Will

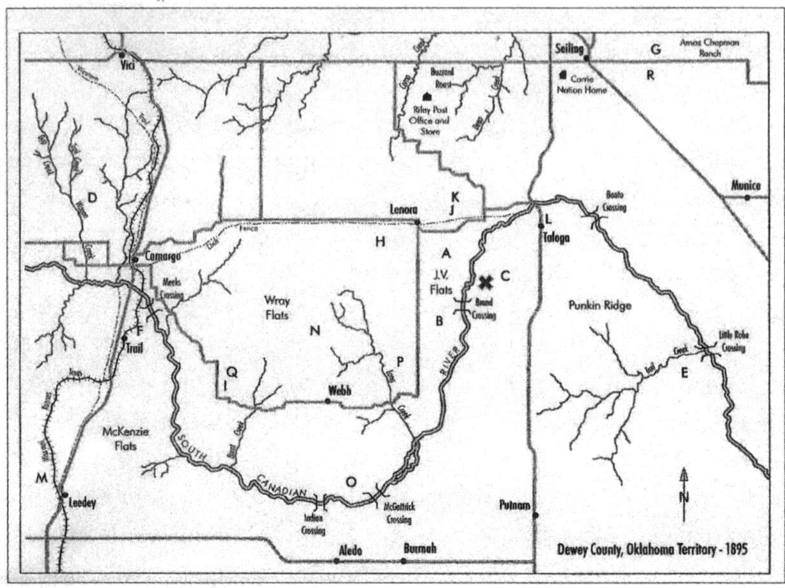

Map 2. D County (later Dewey County), Oklahoma Territory about 1895. On the morning of January 22, 1895, Fred Hoffman mounted his horse and left home just southeast of Lenora (A) en route to his office at Taloga. He rode south for a short distance then crossed the South Canadian River at the Brand Crossing (B) and turned north on the river road heading for Taloga. He was ambushed and killed shortly thereafter at a spot marked by the X, which was only a short distance from a well-known hideout of the Dalton and Doolin gangs (C). Dewey County's rough terrain, remoteness, and lack of law enforcement made it a favorite haven for outlaws in the late 1800s.

Many of Hoffman's neighbors were known outlaws and outlaw sympathizers. Their homes and hideouts, and other locations, are indicated on the map with corresponding letters: (D) Blake brothers Tulsa Jack (Will), Joe, and Sam, and their half-brother Charlie Pierce; (E) Jim Harbolt; (F) Dan McKenzie;(G) Alfred Son; (H) William F. "Little Bill" Raidler; (I) Joe Beckham; (J) Roy Daughtery, aka Arkansas Tom Jones; (K) Big Jim Riley; (L) town of Taloga; (M) brothers Bill, John, and Charlie Edwards; (N) Dutch Anderson; (O) Levi Moors Smith; (P) E. C. Kinney, married to Bill Doolin's sister; (Q) Nannie Wray, Joe Beckham's mother-in-law; and (R) Lee Son, aka Lee Moore, brother of Alfred Son, cousin of Bailey Son, and son-in-law of Amos Chapman. Taloga residents or regular visitors of the town included newspaper editor and lawyer Grant Pettyjohn, Probate Court judge O. L. McClung, County Attorney George Sexton, Deputy Sheriff Bert Sexton, saloon owner M. K. McFadden, Charlie Smith, George "Red Buck" Waightman, brothers Will and John Shumate, and Bailey Son, cousin of Alfred Son and Lee Moore.

Note the routes of the Western (Texas) Cattle Trail and the Wichita Falls & Northwestern Railway (later the Missouri-Kansas-Texas Railroad) traversing the county from north to south along the western edge. Although a number of D County towns are depicted on the map, the only established towns in 1895 were Taloga, Lenora, (old) Camargo, and the Riley post office and store. The railroad had not yet been constructed in 1895. The north boundary line of D County prior to 1892 was the south boundary of the Cherokee Strip and the north boundary of the Cheyenne-Arapaho Indian Reservation. Author's collection.

"Tulsa Jack" Blake, his brothers, Joe and Sam Blake, and their half-brother Charlie Pierce; Jim Harbolt; Big Jim Riley (who employed Joe Blake); and a host of other outlaws, including other Doolin gang members.[10]

George E. Black, who served as D County attorney from 1897 to 1898, in his memoirs recalled that during the 1890s "outlawry was rampant" in the county. The county historian added, "About all of those [Oklahoma Territory outlaws] operating during the period 1885–1901 came through Dewey County or lived here. The Daltons filed on lots in Taloga under assumed names. They also had a dugout hideout about five miles SW of Taloga near the [South Canadian] river."[11]

It was a dugout hideout that was destined to attain historical infamy on January 22, 1895.

However, not everyone who rushed to claim homesteads in the county was a criminal or a sympathizer with criminals. Many were poor but honest and hardworking Americans in pursuit of the American dream of owning their own piece of land and controlling their own destiny.[12]

Still, as time passed and the outlaw presence became more open, brazen, and pervasive, the law-abiding "nesters" became more and more resentful of their surly and overbearing neighbors. Years later one of those early settlers, Charles K. Cary, wrote his memoirs and recorded this revealing anecdote highlighting the official arrogance of Taloga leaders. In December 1895 the homesteaders kept hearing rumors that two or three outlaws were in town and were planning to rob Milt Shultise's general merchandise store (the Shultise and Alderdice store). The gang, led by the notorious killer Red Buck Waightman, had spent the previous night with outlaw sympathizers Will and John Shumate. (John Shumate had previously served as a deputy US marshal.) Some of the more daring settlers decided to arm themselves for the purpose of defending the store. Aware of what was afoot, D County deputy sheriff Bert Sexton intervened; he collected almost every gun in town and took them to the dugout home of his father, County Attorney

George Sexton, for "safekeeping," explaining that he was doing this for the safety of the townsfolk, since he feared that these untrained citizens might start shooting and accidentally injure or kill someone. As feared, the Shultise store was robbed that night. Cary's concluding sentence in describing the incident was this: "We learned in time that the Sextons and Shumates were hand in glove with the outlaws."[13]

By 1895, known outlaws with sizable bounties on their heads casually walked down the streets of Taloga and frequented the McFadden Saloon, their favorite watering hole, owned by M. K. McFadden. Taloga was also the home of desperado sympathizers Grant Pettyjohn, editor of the *Taloga Tomahawk*; county probate judge O. L. McClung; County Attorney George Sexton; Deputy Sheriff Bert Sexton; and Will and John Shumate. Many of these D County outlaws and their friends later became involved in the Sheriff Tom McGee murder trials in Texas—either on trial themselves or as alibi witnesses for their Oklahoma Territory compadres.[14]

Even though Fred Hoffman's 160-acre homestead was surrounded by the claims of some of the worst killers, thieves, thugs, and criminal facilitators, and even though his hardware store in Taloga put him in daily contact with known criminals who walked the streets in front of his business, Hoffman was not intimidated. As noted above, in addition to his other duties he had recently accepted that secret assignment as an undercover agent for Wells Fargo, tasked with learning the identity of the robbers who stole the army payroll at the Woodward depot and the would-be robbers who killed Sheriff McGee at the Canadian depot.

Fred Hoffman's investigation quickly led to results. Sometime in mid-January 1895, Hoffman told Wells Fargo officials T. M. Cook and Thomas Smith that he was directing his efforts toward eighteen-year-old Alfred Son and his "near relatives." Alfred Son (also referred to as Al Sohn and Alford Son) had only two near relatives in the area at that time: his cousin Bailey Son, who hung out with hardcases around Taloga, and his older brother, Lee Moore, who, for reasons of his own, had unofficially changed his name before showing up in D County. Lee Moore, son-in-law of and ranch foreman for the famed army Indian scout Amos Chapman, was not, by any stretch, a supporter of law enforcement. He was one of the Oklahoma Territory alibi witnesses who would later testify for the defendants in the Sheriff McGee murder trials in Texas, and the Chapman Ranch was one of the Doolin

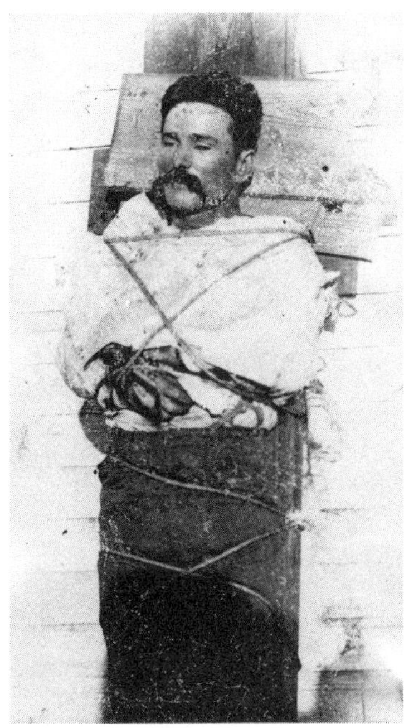

George "Red Buck" Waightman, the worst of Bill Doolin's outlaw gang and a "stone cold killer" for hire, shown here shortly after being killed in a shootout with Oklahoma Territory officers in March 1896. Phillips 3174, reprinted by permission of Western History Collections, University of Oklahoma.

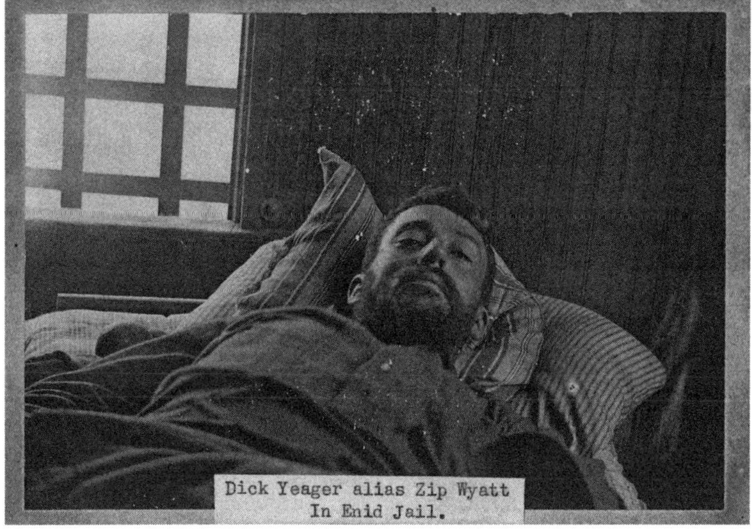

Zip Wyatt's real name was Nelson Elsworth Wyatt, but this Bill Doolin gang member went under several aliases, including Dick Yeager and Wild Charlie. He was indicted for the assassination of Fred Hoffman, but shortly thereafter he himself was killed. This photo was taken as Zip lay dying in the Enid, Oklahoma Territory, jail in August or early September 1895. Ferguson 813, reprinted by permission of Western History Collections, University of Oklahoma.

The McFadden Saloon in Taloga, Oklahoma Territory, was a favorite hangout of outlaws in the 1890s. In this photo famous Oklahoma Territory defense lawyer Temple Houston, son of Texas icon Governor Sam Houston, is shown (third from left) in the company of unidentified friends. Ferguson 515, reprinted by permission of Western History Collections, University of Oklahoma.

gang's favorite retreats. In fact, Moore even had a cabin (still standing to this day) moved onto a remote part of the Chapman Ranch on the North Canadian River about three miles east of Seiling for the sole purpose of hosting outlaws on the dodge. Young Alfred Son worked as a cowboy for his older brother, and he also took up with the outlaw element.[15]

Apparently Hoffman had developed even more damning information, and presumably he had reported this information in the letter addressed to Wells Fargo—the letter that D County official Cicero Davis, an outlaw sympathizer, intercepted at the Taloga post office in mid-January 1895. The interception of that letter sealed Fred Hoffman's fate. As would later be revealed, it contained incriminating information about at least two men (and perhaps more) who could not afford to be unmasked as outlaws.

On the morning of January 22, 1895, just two months after the attempted Canadian heist and the murder of Sheriff McGee, Fred Hoffman mounted his horse at his homestead about a mile southeast of Lenora and headed for his office in Taloga. He rode a short distance south, then crossed the Canadian River at the Brand Crossing and turned north along the river road leading to Taloga. Shortly thereafter, Hoffman, who was unarmed, was ambushed. The outlaws shot him first through the heart and then in the mouth—just in case somebody missed the intended message. The latter shot was fired at such close range that it left powder burns. For good measure, they also shot and killed Fred's horse. Both bodies were discovered several days later in a sandy "blowhole" near the riverbank. The killing site was a few hundred yards from the famous Dalton-Doolin outlaw hideout: a dugout in the rugged hills a short distance east of the river road and about five miles southwest of Taloga—a dugout that earned historical infamy that day.[16]

On April 25, 1895, a D County grand jury indicted Alfred Son for the murder of Fred Hoffman. Also included in that indictment were Bailey Son, Dick Yeager (alias Zip Wyatt), Grant Pettyjohn, and Dan McKenzie.[17] However, before Alfred Son's trial was called, the scene shifted back to Texas for the first of the Sheriff Tom T. McGee murder trials. On May 20, 1895, a Hemphill County, Texas, grand jury indicted Jim Harbolt, Joe Blake, and George Isaacs for the murder of Sheriff McGee. The case against George Isaacs was called first, and it was slated to begin on October 20, 1895, on a change of venue to the Hardeman County District Court in Quanah, Texas.

But before the Texas justice system could deal with George Isaacs for the killing of Sheriff Tom T. McGee, his "ring-tailed tooter" of a wife, Lizzie, earned a murder indictment of her own.

CHAPTER NINE

LIZZIE ISAACS UPSTAGES HUSBAND GEORGE WITH A MURDER OF HER OWN

CHICKASHA, INDIAN TERRITORY, MAY 30, 1895

After George was jailed in Canadian, Texas, for the McGee murder, the rambunctious Lizzie retreated to the couple's known outlaw hideout cabin on the banks of the Washita River near Chickasha in the Indian Territory. Her brother, John Ellis, soon joined her there. The siblings then fenced off a small tract around their cabin and there pastured a few head of cattle. They had neighbors—Sterling and Mollie Elder—who fenced off an adjoining tract and turned out several cows of their own. Both families used a common gate to reach an access road to their properties. Frequent disputes soon developed over cattle trespassing onto each other's grass and the use of the common gate. On the morning of May 30, 1895, John Ellis and his hired hand were driving a few cows, apparently intending to pass through the common access gate. Sterling Elder spied them, rushed out of his cabin, and confronted them. They began quarrelling. The argument became more heated. John Ellis ran back to his cabin and returned with a Winchester rifle. Lizzie, meanwhile, never one to miss out on a good brawl, stormed out of the cabin with a pistol and a buggy whip. That's when Mollie Elder showed up also brandishing a pistol. She gave the pistol to her husband and then tore into Lizzie. A shouting match between the women soon escalated into a knock-down drag-out, hair-pulling, screaming, cussing, scratching catfight. Finally, Mollie Elder seemed to be getting the better of it. She threw Lizzie to the ground. (It should be noted here that Lizzie was then about four months pregnant.) At that point, brother John Ellis abruptly ended the fight. He unlimbered his Winchester rifle and shot Sterling Elder dead.

John Ellis was indicted for murder. Sister Lizzie was indicted for being an accessory to the murder. John Ellis's case was scheduled for trial in the US District Court just south of the Red River in Paris, Texas. Lizzie's case was set to be tried in the US District Court in Chickasha, Indian Territory, in what the local newspaper, the *Chickasha Express*, would later headline as "the most important case ever tried" in the US District Court for that part of the Indian Territory.[1]

However, the trials of John Ellis and Lizzie Isaacs were postponed for almost three years, in which time Lizzie had to yield center stage back to her husband, George. He was slated to meet his judicial fate on October 20, 1895, in Quanah, Texas for the murder of Sheriff McGee.

Lizzie Ellis Isaacs, shown here in the 1880s, was the black sheep of the Ellis family. She left her first husband, John L. Byrne, and married the black sheep of the Isaacs family, George Isaacs. Murder ran in the family. Courtesy of Carol Morse.

CHAPTER TEN

THE MURDER TRIAL OF GEORGE ISAACS: "JIM STANLEY WAS THERE"

QUANAH, TEXAS, OCTOBER 20, 1895

A murder trial is a whole lot more than just a murder trial—at least it was in any small West Texas town before the turn of the twentieth century. Life-and-death courtroom dramas were pageantry like no other in that time and place before movies, television, or radio—even better than rodeos, political speeches, circuses, or old-fashioned hellfire-and-brimstone tent revivals. Yet dispensing courtroom justice was only a part of the attraction that drew folks to town from miles around. For them it was also an exciting, festive social event and a vacation from their dull, rural, daylight-to-dark workaday world; a chance to visit with old friends, meet new settlers, exchange gossip, pitch horseshoes, have horse races, sing hymns, and attend dances in the evening.

In 1895 the town of Quanah—named for the famous Comanche chief Quanah Parker—with a population of less than one thousand souls was hardly more than a dot on those gently rolling, virtually treeless and windswept plains that sprawled about eight miles south of the Red River and then on north from there into the Oklahoma Territory. The town had sprung up from almost nothing only a few years earlier when, in 1887, the Fort Worth & Denver City Railroad laid tracks through the tiny village, linking it to the rest of the world.

Gathering each evening about six o'clock at the railroad depot to witness the arrival of the train had become a community ritual. In fact, the spectacle of the mighty iron monster in those horse-and-buggy days when nobody had even seen an automobile was a great source of entertainment. In addition, it freighted not only mundane supplies but also hints of exotic and faraway places that common folks of that time could never hope to visit; plus there was always the chance of glimpsing the face of some important traveler through a curtain briefly parted.[1]

But the folks of Quanah were in for a considerably more exciting spectacle than the arrival of the evening train when the murder trial of George Isaacs was gaveled to order on October 20, 1895. Judging from accounts in the local weekly newspaper, the weather before and during the Isaacs murder trial must have been perfect for outdoor games, music in the park, and other festive activities. The crisp, clean air of that mellow October had dispelled the sweltering heat of the summer in West Texas and held in abeyance the coming frigid northers of January. Out-of-towners had indeed flocked to Quanah in anticipation of the trial. Not a room was left vacant in Quanah's only hotel, and latecomers had to camp in the park or on the outskirts of town.[2]

Concerned, law-abiding citizens from Canadian, as well as friends and family of the popular Sheriff McGee, descended on the frontier town from the Texas Panhandle. Adding to the crowd, the prosecution subpoenaed scores of witnesses, including the Wells Fargo clerks and investigators and its chief station agent, A. A. Rinehart, all from Kansas City; the chief Wells Fargo detective, Fred Dodge; and former Texas Ranger and Panhandle sheriff G. W. Arrington. But the defense, bankrolled by the defendant's brothers, Will and Sam Isaacs, was not to be outdone. According to the Quanah weekly newspaper, the defense subpoenaed more than two hundred witnesses from D County, Oklahoma Territory, the stronghold of the outlaws.

The October 24, 1895, edition of the *Quanah Tribune* reported, "A number of the Wells Fargo boys, assisted by a portion of the Quanah orchestra, made some good music the other evening." Musical concerts notwithstanding, time hung heavy on the hands of all those witnesses while they waited for their turn to testify. They proceeded to solve that problem in a most innovative and entertaining fashion. The opposing witnesses—the laws and the outlaws—chose up sides and challenged each other to a series of baseball games on the courthouse lawn. The Quanah weekly duly noted that the two teams "gave good account of themselves" but, unfortunately, failed to give any scores. Outside the courthouse the carnival atmosphere continued unabated.

The scores of witnesses may have had plenty of leisure time for music and baseball, but the local weekly newspaper editor, Harry Koch, was burning the candle at both ends trying to cover the trial as well as reporting what went on outside the courtroom—plus harnessing his beleaguered back shop crew of printers to crank out the latest special edition. Koch and his printers were up late one night struggling with the press when an old newspaper friend of Koch's named Ben wandered into the office uninvited and drunk (or, as editor Koch later reported in the coy euphemism so beloved by country reporters of that day: "pretty well 'organized.' "). Ben soon became very "bothersome," and in an effort to get rid of him editor Koch gave him an assignment: go interview George Isaacs over at the county jail. Ben thought this was a prize assignment and a wonderful opportunity to break a sensational story. He immediately hot-footed it over to the jail in the middle of the night. Fortunately for Ben, the jailer was well acquainted with him and raised no objection to being jerked out of bed. In fact, he took Ben upstairs to the cell where George Isaacs was confined. Then he locked them both up and went back to bed.

Late the next morning Ben showed up at the newspaper office, "blue around the gills," complaining at length to Koch "about the disgrace that had befallen his blue Kentucky blood" on account of his enforced and prolonged incarceration with such a lowlife criminal. Toward the end of Ben's lamentations, editor Koch was beginning to feel sorry for him. But about that time he was startled when Ben pulled $1.50 out of his pocket and handed it over.

"What's that for, Ben?"

"Oh, I got that murderer to subscribe to your paper."[3]

In his last pretrial story, Koch brought his readers up to date on a couple of interesting historical developments: "Two of Isaacs's pals have since [the murder of Sheriff McGee] been killed by other officers while resisting arrest and one of the remaining, Jim Harbolt, has been shot in a row and his bond forfeited, the Isaacs brothers [Will and Sam] being on the bond."[4]

It was, in fact, true that "two of Isaacs's pals" had been killed before the Isaacs, Harbolt, or Blake cases were called for trial. Joe Blake's brother, Will

"Tulsa Jack" Blake, and George "Bitter Creek" Newcomb had both come to violent ends as pressure on the Doolin gang mounted. Tulsa Jack was killed on April 4, 1895, by a Chris Madsen–led posse that overtook the Doolin gang while it was fleeing from the scene of yet another train robbery (a Rock Island train near Dover, OT), and Bitter Creek Newcomb was ambushed in his sleep and killed on May 1, 1895, by Bee Dunn, a former friend turned bounty hunter. The same turncoat later collected the munificent sum of thirty-six dollars for helping US Marshal Heck Thomas ambush and kill Dunn's former compadre, Bill Doolin, on August 25, 1896.

Years later, in a reflection on the George Isaacs trial, editor Koch recalled that George Isaacs "had two rich brothers who spared no money in getting him clear, and a battle royal was the result." Sam and Will Isaacs must have come up with a tub full of cash, because when George came to court he was represented by no less than seven lawyers. The heavyweights were the famous Amos J. Fires of Childress, Texas, and W. B. Plemons of Amarillo. No one could read a jury better than Amos Fires, nor was anyone better attuned to the times and the pulse of the plebeians from whom the jury pool was drawn. Defending those accused of murder was his specialty, and during his long career in the trenches of the criminal courts he represented 123 murder-indicted defendants, of whom only 4 left the courthouse in shackles. But the lead attorney in the George Isaacs murder trial was W. B. Plemons. Plemons and his partner, John Veale, were then the foremost criminal defense attorneys in Amarillo. Plemons had served the entire Civil War in General Stonewall Jackson's famous corps and was wounded three times. He was with General Robert E. Lee at Appomattox when Lee surrendered. Later in his career he served as the first county judge of Potter County in Amarillo and still later was elected district judge of the 47th Judicial District Court. He was elected to the Texas legislature in 1894 and served one term. Yet he was best known as an almost unbeatable criminal defense lawyer. A fellow attorney once remarked that Plemons "glorified in agitation and dispute" and "was never excelled in repartee." The pugnacious Plemons believed there were two sides to every question—his side and the wrong side.[5] Interestingly, Plemons and Veale were later hired by Sam and Will Isaacs to defend Jim Harbolt.

The prosecution also had two heavy hitters on its roster to assist the local assistant district attorney, G. W. Walters. Sitting first chair on the state's side

W. B. Plemons, about 1900. This fiery defense lawyer from Amarillo defended both George Isaacs and Jim Harbolt in their murder trials for the killing of Sheriff Tom T. McGee. 581/1, reprinted by permission of Panhandle-Plains Historical Museum, Canyon, Texas.

as the lead attorney was Jim Cowan of Fort Worth, a rising star in the Texas legal community who frequently represented the Texas Cattle Raisers Association in high-profile prosecutions, and he was ably assisted by the highly respected H. E. Hoover of Canadian.

Promptly at nine o'clock on the morning of October 20, 1895, the Honorable J. M. Standee, special district judge of the 46th Judicial District Court in Hardeman County, Texas, banged his gavel and called the court to order, and the predicted "battle royal" got under way. The drama-starved audience would not be disappointed. Judge J. M. Hurt, one of the judges on the Texas Court of Criminal Appeals in Austin, would later comment that the George Isaacs murder case was "one of the most important prosecutions ever had in Texas both from the facts and the law involved."[6]

The prosecution conceded that George Isaacs was not the man who fired the shot that killed Sheriff McGee. (The state believed that Jim Harbolt was the triggerman.) The state also conceded that George was not even present when the fatal shot was fired; he was in his room at the Sutherland Hotel in Canadian when the gunfight erupted. Still, under Texas law the state contended that George was guilty of being an accessory to the murder because he was part of the criminal conspiracy to rob the Wells Fargo Express office and that the sheriff had been killed by one of George's fellow conspirators during the course of the attempted robbery.

The state called witnesses who provided the jury with a chronological account of the failed robbery and the murder of the sheriff.[7] G. W. Fishburn, cashier of the First National Bank of Kansas City, testified about cashing George Isaacs's $683.60 check from the Drum-Flato livestock commission company. A. A. Rinehart, the Wells Fargo Express agent at the Union Depot in Kansas City, identified George Isaacs as the same man who sent the five Wells Fargo money packets via the Santa Fe Railroad, addressed to himself at Canadian, Texas. Rinehart also testified that the second time George Isaacs came to his office—the time he returned with the stuffed packets—there was another man with him who stayed in the background. Rinehart added that he had never seen that second man before or since. That tidbit of Reinhart's testimony seemed insignificant at the time. Later it would prove to be very significant in fitting all the pieces of the puzzle together.

Called as the next state witnesses were the four Canadian locals who had witnessed the four long riders approaching Canadian from the direction of Oklahoma Territory the afternoon before Sheriff McGee was fatally wounded that evening. Dr. A. M. Newman told of attending Sheriff McGee after he had been shot and hearing the sheriff's account of what had happened. Agent Harding also testified that immediately after the shooting he had wired the news to Captain G. W. Arrington, who was then aboard the Santa Fe train headed for the next depot. When Arrington returned to Canadian later that night, he secured the crime scene, and at daylight he tracked the footprints of three of the bandits back to the stockyards north of the depot, where the fourth bandit had apparently been holding the horses. Then Arrington organized a posse and tracked the four long riders back east to Dan McKenzie's cabin in the Oklahoma Territory, where he arrested Joe Blake. Arrington testified that he returned to the Taloga area in January 1895, where further investigation led him to conclude that Jim Harbolt was one of the three smaller, dark-complected bandits involved in the Canadian depot shootout. He then arrested Harbolt and jailed him in Canadian.

Next the jury listened with rapt attention as the prosecution unfolded the story of the desperate struggle by Sam and George Isaacs to prevent those phony money packets from falling into the hands of the determined, self-appointed citizens' committee: the lies Sam and George told agent Harding in a futile effort to persuade him to hold on to the packets until Monday morning, when George could ship them back to Kansas City *unopened* so he could buy some cattle; the lies they told Chambers in order to persuade him to lock up that incriminating evidence in his store safe; the futile effort the next day to persuade Chambers's clerk, Winsett, to open the safe and surrender the packets when Sam learned that the citizens' committee was hot on their trail; and finally, the arrival of D. J. Young and his avenging angels followed by the inevitable collapse of George Isaacs's house of cards while George and Sam helplessly watched in despair.

During the trial, George Isaacs elected to exercise his Fifth Amendment right not to testify. However, Fred J. Dodge, chief detective for Wells Fargo Express, did testify, and he repeated the partial confession that he had obtained from George during his jailhouse interview. During his statement to Dodge, George Isaacs downplayed his role in the whole affair, contending that Jim Stanley had talked him into participating in the fraud. He said that Stanley and his gang were supposed to rob the train between Higgins, Texas, and Canadian but instead for some reason decided to wait until the train pulled into the Canadian depot and then rob the Wells Fargo Express agent. He emphasized that the only bandit he knew who participated in the attempted robbery was Jim Stanley. It was at that point that he told Detective Dodge that if the officers would only release him from jail for a couple of weeks he could go back home and "find out in a week or so" the names of the other outlaws in Stanley's gang—a pledge that George Isaacs failed to keep.

The prosecution called two surprise witnesses. The first was Dan McKenzie. Initially, McKenzie had denied knowing anything about the robbery or the killing or who had been involved in either. However, he was subsequently named in one of the resulting Hemphill County indictments for conspiring to commit the Canadian robbery, and later he was jointly indicted in D County, Oklahoma Territory, with Alfred Son, Zip Wyatt, Bailey Son, and Grant Pettyjohn for the murder of Fred Hoffman. While it is doubtful that lawmen really believed that Dan McKenzie took an active role in either crime, still he was an outlaw-friendly associate who undoubtedly knew all the guilty players as well as the details of both crimes. As events played out in Hemphill County, Texas, and D County, Oklahoma Territory, it became clear that dirt-poor, ignorant Dan McKenzie had become an unwitting and unwilling player caught between the lawmen and outlaw factions, and, in another bizarre twist to this unlikely tale, McKenzie would also soon find himself caught in the middle once again—and he was indicted as the principal in yet another criminal episode. Both sides found Dan McKenzie to be a handy and useful pawn in their tactical maneuvers.

As time for the George Isaacs murder trial approached, Dan McKenzie began to feel the heat, and to save his own skin he elected to turn state's evidence and testify for the prosecution. He swore to tell the truth, the whole truth, and nothing but the truth. In the end he kept his oath to tell the truth, but he did not quite tell the whole truth. He testified that the gang that attempted the Canadian Wells Fargo robbery had indeed gathered at his home the evening of Sunday, November 25, 1894, immediately after they returned from Canadian. He named the gang members: Joe Blake, Will "Tulsa Jack" Blake, Jim Harbolt, and Jim Stanley. Another outlaw, Bitter Creek Newcomb, soon joined them. Then another Blake brother, Sam Blake, arrived still later that night with news that the Canadian sheriff had died of his wounds. At that point all the outlaws except Joe Blake mounted up and fled, but not before threatening McKenzie that they would "shoot him down like a wolf" if he divulged any incriminating information to lawmen.

McKenzie volunteered another interesting tidbit of information: he said that he had had a conversation with Tulsa Jack Blake (apparently sometime in January or February 1895) during which Tulsa Jack showed him a letter he had received from George Isaacs stating that Isaacs had gotten out of the Canadian jail temporarily to return to his cabin on the Washita River and find out the names of the three bandits who accompanied Jim Stanley. In George Isaacs's letter to Tulsa Jack, he assured Tulsa Jack that he "hadn't given anything away." According to McKenzie's trial testimony, he said that during that conversation Tulsa Jack told him that he had offered George three hundred dollars to go to Canadian and "swear his brother, Joe Blake, out of jail." During his testimony Dan McKenzie also admitted that he knew Bill Doolin and had known him since 1892 and that he had seen him on different occasions with Tulsa Jack and Bitter Creek Newcomb.

All of Dan McKenzie's testimony seemed to have a ring of truth to it—at least until he got to the part about Jim Stanley. After having testified that he knew Bill Doolin and all the other outlaws and stating that Jim Stanley was one of the four bandits who attempted the Canadian heist and who had returned to his cabin the following evening, Dan McKenzie suddenly turned evasive. He was unable to provide any clue as to the real identity or whereabouts of Jim Stanley. The best he could do—or was willing to do—was to describe Jim Stanley as a "man six feet tall, small sideburns, light complected, light blue eyes, and a sandy mustache."

The prosecution saved its bombshell for last, and what an eye-opener it was. When George Isaacs made his jailhouse semi-confession to Wells Fargo detective Fred Dodge, George portrayed himself as an unwilling and reluctant conspirator in the fraud—almost an innocent bystander—claiming that the whole thing was Jim Stanley's idea, contending that he was just a "poor man who didn't have any money" and insisting that it was that overbearing rogue, that rapscallion Jim Stanley, who had bullied him into participating and then had dictated his role in the scam. However, when the state called Deputy US Marshal Luther J. Smith to the stand, that witness painted an entirely different portrait of poor, cringing George Isaacs. Smith testified that he had been a deputy US marshal in the Indian Territory stationed at Chickasha since 1890 and was well acquainted with George Isaacs.[8] According to the deputy marshal, George had twice solicited his participation in a scheme to defraud Wells Fargo Express. At Chickasha in the early spring of 1893, George outlined his plan to Smith: he would go to Kansas City, ship a few cattle, get a little money, then ship the money to himself by Wells Fargo but mark up the money packets to a large sum, and he would then get one or more of his friends to rob the train above Chickasha. According to George's script it was at that point that Deputy Smith was to play his role. He was to enlist the support and participation of another deputy US marshal, and Deputy Marshal Smith and his fellow lawman would then pursue the train robbers but would conveniently lose their trail. Then George would sue the express company, collect the amount shown on the money packets, and they would all divide the spoils. Smith, however, rejected George's generous offer. Later, at the Duncan store in Chickasha, George again approached Smith with the same proposal, but once again the deputy marshal declined.

When the state rested, George's battery of defense lawyers took over. They called Sam Isaacs to the stand. Sam denied that he had gone to Chambers's store that Sunday afternoon before Young's committee arrived and had attempted to persuade Chambers's clerk, Jim Winsett, to open the safe so he could make off with George's phony packets and thus prevent a discovery of the scam. Sam testified further that he was present when George made his jailhouse confession—or at least a partial confession—to Wells Fargo agent Fred Dodge, but he claimed that Dodge had coerced that confession by warning George that there were fifty enraged men outside who would tear the jail down and mob him if he did not confess. (Later, during the state's rebuttal testimony, Fred Dodge denied coercing George by making any such threat.)

It was at that point that the defense unleashed its horde of Oklahoma Territory character witnesses, each one testifying that the state's turncoat witness, Dan McKenzie, was a notorious liar whose testimony could not be believed. Next came an onslaught of alibi witnesses, headlined by D County officials including Judge O. L. McClung, Deputy Sheriff Bert Sexton, County Attorney George Sexton, *Taloga Tomahawk* editor Grant Pettyjohn (one and the same Grant Pettyjohn who was then under indictment in D County for the murder of Fred Hoffman), brothers Will and John Shumate, A. G. Wolley, and a host of other luminaries and plebeians, all of whom swore that they had personally witnessed Jim Harbolt, Joe Blake, Will "Tulsa Jack" Blake, and George "Bitter Creek" Newcomb walking the streets of Taloga on the day Sheriff Tom T. McGee was killed some 125 miles distant in Canadian, Texas. In reporting the events of the trial itself, *Quanah Tribune-Chief* editor Harry Koch took a rather dim view of the defense's two hundred-plus witnesses from the Oklahoma Territory: "There was a great deal of perjury among the witnesses of the defense, which caused Prosecuting Attorney Jim Cowan to exclaim in his argument that for rottenness and general viciousness, these witnesses were the vilest scum he had ever met, which was received with snickers by the men thus alluded to."[9]

Back in Hemphill County the *Canadian Record* editor W. S. Defibaugh also took a very dim view of the truth and veracity of the Oklahoma Territory witnesses, adding, "Even his 'Hon.' Judge McClung is noted for his prevaricating qualities." Some two decades after the trial, the *Tribune-Chief* editor would reflect that the army of defense witnesses constituted "the finest collection of horse thieves and perjurers that ever congregated in any small town."[10]

It seemed somewhat pointless for the defense team to mount any alibi defense for two of George Isaacs's pals—George "Bitter Creek" Newcomb and Will "Tulsa Jack" Blake—since both had been killed before George's murder trial. Still, defense attorney Plemons probably felt that for the sake of Jim Harbolt and Joe Blake, he needed the jury to believe that none of the four desperadoes was anywhere near the Canadian depot that night or that they had anything to do with the attempted robbery.

Finally, after the last of the raucous Oklahoma Territory defense witness parade had exited the stage, the state called a few rebuttal witnesses, primarily for the purpose of attacking the credibility of a number of the defense witnesses by pointing out that they had been charged with theft and other criminal offenses. Then the arguments began.

Even though the prosecution conceded that George was not present when McGee was murdered, still that didn't get him home free—not by a long shot. Two Texas laws applied in this case. First, any murder committed during the course of a robbery or an attempted robbery is classified as a first-degree murder. Second, any person who participates in the robbery in any way, including aiding, assisting, or conspiring with the actual robbers to commit a robbery, is also guilty of any murder that occurs during the course of the robbery. And that rule still applies even if none of those involved contemplated that a killing would occur during the course of the robbery. Plus, the penalty for being an accessory to a murder was the same: life in prison or death by hanging.

In view of the state's evidence, including George's confession that he was a part of the Wells Fargo heist conspiracy, that didn't leave George's defense team much wiggle room. Even so, George's veteran warhorse of a defense attorney, W. B. Plemons, forcefully argued a two-pronged defense. The first line of defense was that the state failed to prove that any person with whom George had conspired to rob the Wells Fargo Express office was actually present at the depot that fateful night. Plemons once again made the point that George was not present when the shootout occurred, that he had no part in it, and that he never contemplated or even condoned any killing in furtherance of the scheme. Although George had admitted to Wells Fargo detective Fred Dodge that he, together with Bill Doolin and Jim Stanley, had previously plotted the Wells Fargo scam, still Plemons argued for the defense that the state had failed to prove that George had conspired with any of the four outlaws who actually attempted the robbery during which the sheriff was killed. The prosecution, however, quoted George's own words that he uttered during his semiconfession to Detective Dodge when he told Dodge that he didn't know any of the men who were involved in the robbery attempt "*except Stanley*." George, perhaps believing that he was just too clever by half, must have figured that by giving up the name of a nonexistent person—and one who was not even joined in the murder indictment—it wouldn't count against him. But what clueless George didn't realize was that the fourth member of the long rider gang—that tall, light-complected fellow who held the horses for the other three during the shootout and who had gone under the name of Jim Stanley—was a real person. And whatever his real name was, he was a coconspirator. And he was one of the four outlaws who attempted the robbery that backfired and resulted in the murder of Sheriff McGee.

George's second line of defense did have some logical—if very little "gut-justice"—appeal. Plemons argued that George could be found guilty of being an accomplice to the crime of murder (as an admitted coconspirator to the crime of robbery) if, and only if, the murder had occurred *during the course of the robbery*. But, Plemons contended, the murder had occurred *before* the contemplated robbery commenced. And, in fact, the outlaws had abandoned their plan to rob the Wells Fargo office before the first shot was fired. Therefore, no robbery had ever occurred or was even attempted.

The jury was not impressed with either of those technical points. It took them only a few minutes to return with a guilty verdict and a life sentence. At least George had escaped the noose.

It also did not take the Texas Court of Criminal Appeals very long to dismiss both of George Isaacs's two technical points of alleged error when it considered his appeal. The court made short shrift of George's first argument by citing George's own words when he let it slip that he knew his coconspirator "Stanley" was among the foursome who killed Sheriff McGee. Neither did the appellate court buy into the Plemons argument that, at worst, the events amounted to only a pre-robbery murder and not a murder committed during the course of an attempted robbery. The court made short shrift of that contention with these words: "Four men had ridden 80 to 100 miles, armed to the teeth, well prepared for traveling; surrounded the depot for no other purpose on earth than to rob the agent of the money shipped by appellant [George Isaacs] to Canadian. When the deceased [Sheriff McGee] stepped to the door and asked one of them to stop . . . he was fired upon from all different directions, and killed."[11]

The appellate court thus found that defendant's interpretation of the events was a bit too strained for its taste. The conviction was affirmed, and poor George was destined to spend the rest of his life in prison.

Or so it would have seemed.

Meanwhile, back in Quanah, the Hardeman County grand jury met to consider the testimony offered during the George Isaacs trial by his army of Oklahoma Territory character and alibi witnesses—the "finest collection of horse thieves and perjurers that ever congregated in a small town." The grand jury agreed with editor Harry Koch's assessment and returned several perjury-related indictments. Grant Pettyjohn, a practicing lawyer and editor of the *Taloga Tomahawk* weekly newspaper, was indicted for suborning perjury by bribing defense witnesses A. G. Wolley, Bert Sexton, and John Shumate to commit perjury. Shumate and Sexton were indicted for actually committing perjury during the Isaacs trial.[12] The going price for perjury, according to the indictments, appears to have been one hundred dollars per witness.

CHAPTER ELEVEN

GETTING RICH ON THIRTY-DOLLARS-A-MONTH COWBOY WAGES

AN OPEN-RANGE MYSTERY

In 1884, when Sam Isaacs was twenty years old and brother John was eighteen, they saddled up and left their central Texas home country and headed north—Sam riding a borrowed horse and leading a packhorse upon which they had strapped all their earthly possessions—seeking cowboy jobs in the land of the big cattle operations in the Texas Panhandle and the western Oklahoma Territory.[1] They followed the trail of their older brother Will, who, a year earlier, had succeeded in finding employment and was then working as a cowboy for the Apple Company, an outfit that ran thousands of cattle on the sprawling Cheyenne-Arapaho Indian reservation adjoining Hemphill County, Texas, on the east. John soon got a job with the Apple Company, and brother Sam was hired by W. E. "Billy" Malaley, another cattle baron in the Cheyenne-Arapaho reservation.

Throughout his long career, Malaley gained an unchallenged reputation for extreme honesty. During the Civil War he served with the 11th Indiana Calvary. Afterward, he migrated to the West, where he first pursued a career in law enforcement, soon gaining an appointment as a deputy US marshal for the northwest part of the Oklahoma Territory in the Fort Supply and the

Darlington Indian Agency area. There, Malaley met and became a friend and protégé of Major John D. Miles, the Cheyenne-Arapaho Indian agent, who persuaded Malaley to become involved in the cattle business.

In about 1875, Malaley resigned as deputy US marshal and devoted full time to the cattle business. In the early part of January 1883, the principal chiefs of the Cheyenne-Arapaho Indians directed Indian Agent Miles to enter into a contract to lease the 4,300,000-acre Cheyenne-Arapaho reservation to cattlemen for a ten-year grazing lease. Miles complied and partitioned the leases to seven cattlemen, one of whom was William E. Malaley, who obtained a lease covering 570,000 acres. These cattlemen soon stocked the reservation with a total of 210,000 head of cattle and devoted considerable capital to clearing and fencing their pastures. Malaley took on a junior partner in his venture, a "jolly young Englishman" named A. S. C. Forbes, and they did business under the name Malaley and Forbes, also known as Toros Cattle Company. Cattle prices were good, and the cattle barons prospered—until 1885.

In the summer of 1885, President Grover Cleveland abruptly, and unexpectedly, ordered all of the big cattlemen (including W. E. Malaley) who were running cattle on lands they had previously leased in the Cheyenne-Arapaho reservation in the Oklahoma Territory to remove all their cattle from the reservation within forty days. The result was chaos and catastrophe for the cattlemen. Where to go with those 210,000 head of cattle and how to move them within such a ridiculously short time frame was a question with no easy or reasonable answer. Many, if not most, of the ranchers ended up dumping thousands of head of cattle on markets already saturated with the normal amount of cattle being marketed. When these thousands of additional head were pushed into the market, the result was predictable. The cattle market crashed and collapsed.

As devastating as was President Cleveland's gut punch to the Oklahoma Territory cattlemen, it was followed by another devastating gut punch—this one landed by Mother Nature. The 1885–86 winter was the worst in many years. During that winter one blizzard followed another and kept the prairies coated with frozen snow and ice for about two months.[2] Thousands of starving cattle died.

W. E. Malaley was ruined financially, and he was never able to recoup his lost fortune. The year of 1893 found Malaley and his wife, Katie, living in the small town of Hennessey, Oklahoma Territory, where he was reduced to eking out a living by owning one-half interest in a livery stable—a humble conclusion to an otherwise auspicious career.[3]

Nevertheless, during those years from 1886 to 1894 when W. E. Malaley suffered the loss of a considerable fortune, Will and Sam Isaacs somehow managed to amass a considerable fortune. When brother George Isaacs was tried in Quanah, Texas, in 1895 for the murder of Sheriff McGee, the hometown newspaper editor informed his readers that George Isaacs "had two rich brothers [Will and Sam Isaacs] who spared no money in getting him clear, and a battle royal was the result."[4] Thus, the question that begs for an answer is, How did two dirt-poor country boys get so rich so quick? Typically, during that time, cowboy wages were thirty dollars per month. From 1884 until Hemphill County sheriff Tom T. McGee was murdered in November 1894, there is no record that either Sam or Will had a source of income other than their cowboy paycheck. Sam later claimed that he worked for W. E. Malaley for nine years, ending in 1893. The claim that he worked for Malaley after 1886 is highly questionable, since Malaley went broke about 1886.

Although Texas became a state in 1845, for the next thirty years no permanent settler dared stake a claim in the Texas Panhandle or South Plains—the Llano Estacado: millions of acres of real estate, enough to swallow the whole of New England. It was the exclusive domain of the fierce Comanche and Kiowa warriors until the conclusion of the Red River War in the spring of 1875, when the Indians were consigned to Oklahoma reservations. Soon immigrants began to arrive. The first cattleman to put a hoof on the Texas Panhandle was Charles Goodnight, who, with his trail boss, Leigh Dyer, in the late fall of 1875 drove sixteen hundred head of longhorns down from Colorado. Soon other cattlemen followed, turning their herds loose onto the vast free-range prairies carpeted with lush, protein-rich grama and buffalo grasses.[5]

A lot of other men viewed the same prairies from a different perspective and recognized a different opportunity; they saw the unique advantage of taking residency in this wild and lawless land. With no lawmen or courts for more than two hundred miles in every direction, and no roads, no railroads, no transportation or communication facilities, it was a made-to-order outlaw heaven. During the late 1870s and all through the 1880s scores of outlaws of every denomination arrived, including killers, thieves, hucksters, and "wanted men" from back in the East riding in under a "consumed name" (that's what they called it in Old Tascosa in those days), as well as gamblers, saloon keepers, bums, drifters, drunks, and prostitutes.[6] Cattle thieves in particular discovered that this sprawling, unfenced, cattle-infested land offered a rare bonanza—a field of low-hanging fruit ripe unto harvest. With more than half a million cattle wandering free across those unfenced plains, the pickings were rich and easy.

In 1879, Texas Ranger captain G. W. Arrington, then in command of Company C of the Frontier Battalion, was ordered to establish the first Texas Ranger camp to patrol the Panhandle and South Plains. In compliance, Arrington and twelve of his men set up headquarters in Blanco Canyon on the headwaters of the Brazos River in Crosby County, and from there he and his men made wide-ranging tours through Northwest Texas and on north to the Canadian River in the Panhandle and then on to eastern New Mexico and back south into the South Plains country while backing up the infant law enforcement community. Once in 1880, in Tascosa—a place the iconic Texas Panhandle pioneer rancher Charles Goodnight called "the most lawless place on the continent"—Cap Arrington was summoned to support Tascosa's first sheriff, Caleb Berg "Cape" Willingham, and that resulted in a memorable showdown with Jess Jenkins and his gang of hardcases. Jenkins, who strongly objected to the intrusion of any lawman on his territory, had threatened to run Willingham out of town or kill him. Arrington agreed to leave two of his rangers in Tascosa, but first he went directly to Jenkins and informed him he was assigning two of his men to help the sheriff. Then he told Jenkins this: "If you allow them to be hurt, I'll return with my posse and hang every damned one of you and won't leave one 'dobe [adobe brick] on top of another."[7]

Cap Arrington's men remained there for a time until some sort of order was established.

Yet cattle rustling was pandemic on the range, and the cowboy majority held fast to the notion that they had a divine right to swing a wide loop and scorch their brand on any dogie in sight. Moreover, even when well-known cow thieves were caught, indicted, and tried with overwhelming evidence of guilt, juries would not convict. "The country was full of perjurers who almost made a business of going from court to court, where, with the help of sympathetic or frightened jurors, they swore thieves from under convictions in spite of incontrovertible evidence."[8] Noted Panhandle historian Laura V. Hamner depicted this graphic portrait of lawlessness in the late 1870s through the early 1890s and of the dangers and vengeance honest lawmen, grand jurors, and judges faced in those days: "The outlaw element . . . declared war against officers. Those officers knew they were walking dangerous paths. A member of the grand jury occupied a position of great service and great danger. The foreman of the grand jury was blamed for every case brought against a man. The outlaws had a loose sort of organization in some parts of the Panhandle. They threatened the grand jurors with death. The honest grand juror was a marked man during the years when law was being slowly established."[9]

With the law in their pocket, as it were, cattle thieves became so blatant and thievery became so rampant that, as one historian put it, "the boys went to stealing as if it was going out of style."[10] Finally, a number of cattlemen took the lead in organizing an association for self-protection. On July 23, 1880, they met in Mobeetie and formed the Panhandle Stockmen's Association. Charles Goodnight was named as the first president. Initial membership was between twenty-five and thirty and consisted of most of the prominent men in the Panhandle.[11]

The association offered a $250 reward for anyone caught rustling cattle belonging to any member of the association. Yet despite the initial efforts of association members as well as early lawmen and judges, they were greeted by jeers and threats from the outlaws. On one occasion a known cattle rustler boldly confronted Goodnight and sneered, "What can you do? We have 300 and you [the Panhandle Cattle Raiser's Association] have but fifty. Why should we fear you?" Goodnight replied: "You are mistaken. We've got seventy-two now . . . and we'll be here when you —— will be gone." Sympathy with—and confidence in—the rule of law in this lawless land began to take root. But it would be a long and uphill battle. And before the rule of law could exist, order would first have to be established.[12]

Establishing and maintaining order, however, would be a larger problem than Goodnight and the cattle barons imagined, and combating rampant cattle thievery would be only a part of the task. By the early 1880s times were changing in the Texas Panhandle. The availability of water had always been a problem on the arid plains, but the ranches soon discovered an ocean of underground water, known as the Ogallala Aquifer, and wells were now being drilled and windmills erected to tap that source. Barbed wire had been invented, and the large ranchers began stringing up boundary fences. That, in turn, helped reduce cattle thefts—provided that the absentee owners had

Charles Goodnight, pioneer Texas Panhandle icon, in the 1920s. Goodnight drove the first herd of cattle (sixteen hundred head) onto the lush, unfenced, and uninhabited pastures in the Texas Panhandle in 1875 at a time when there were no settlements, no courts, and no lawmen for two hundred miles in every direction—a virtual paradise for men on the run from the law, cattle rustlers, and other outlaws. 1997.74.1.21.15, reprinted by permission of Panhandle-Plains Historical Museum, Canyon, Texas.

hired managers who were not in cahoots with the rustlers. It also permitted ranchers to improve the quality of their cattle herds by fencing in only high-quality animals of the same breed.[13]

As advantageous to large operators as were these innovations, they came with an unanticipated cost. Those same innovations were also available to settlers of modest means who were eager to earn their independence and livelihood by claiming what they considered to be their fair share of that fertile prairie. Thus, an increasing friction developed between the range aristocrats and the commoners, and it only intensified as more and more homestead seekers arrived. To further aggravate the problem, most of the big ranches laid Winchester claim to all acreage lying within their boundaries, including land that was still owned by the state of Texas. Yet nesters, and with good reason, feared vengeful retaliation if they dared to fence off homestead tracts inside those cattle kingdoms—even if they had purchased or leased that land from the state.

As time passed, the animosity between the two factions increased, and the large ranchers found themselves embattled not only against cattle thieves but also against an increasing tide of immigrant homestead seekers whom they perceived as intruders upon their domains. In the end, establishing order as a foundation for the establishment of the rule of law on the Llano Estacado proved more difficult and time-consuming than anyone had anticipated.

Meanwhile, out-of-state capitalists from back East and in England begin piling on the "beef-bonanza express," intoxicated by all those get-rich-quick stories circulating about how king-sized domains of lush grassland in the Llano Estacado could be had for giveaway prices. Their lack of knowledge about the cattle business as well as their loose management practices ended up presenting cattle rustlers with a beef bonanza of their own, exhibit A of which was the incredible story of the Rocking Chair Ranche.

The 152,320-acre Rocking Chair Ranche, along the eastern edge of the Texas Panhandle, was purchased in 1883 by English owners John Campbell Hamilton Gordon, seventh Earl of Aberdeen, and Edward Majorbanks, eldest son of Sir Dudley Coutts Majorbanks, first Baron of Tweedmouth. American settlers of modest means who were struggling to acquire homestead acreage in the Panhandle were less than impressed by such pompous foreigners, who, with their fancy titles and fat wallets, were gobbling up huge chunks of what the settlers regarded as their turf. These commoners sneeringly referred to the Rocking Chair Ranche as "Nobility Ranch." The owners, in turn, referred to their cowboy employees as "cow servants."[14]

The owners hired John Drew, an experienced cattleman, as comanager of "the Rockers." It was a bad choice. Drew may have been a seasoned cattleman, but he was also a corrupt, unscrupulous, wily, hard-drinking opportunist. Edward Majorbanks's younger brother, Archibald John Majorbanks, was named as the other comanager. Archibald, known as Archie or Marshie, knew absolutely nothing about the cattle business and could not have cared less. Although he was the heir apparent to his father's vast estate, he took little interest in learning the cattle business or involving himself in the daily affairs of the ranch. Marshie devoted his time to living the pampered life of an English squire (albeit relocated to the Texas Panhandle), including hunting wolves with his pack of hounds and in between the chases smoking cigars, drinking whiskey, and gambling away his salary in the saloons at Mobeetie. Together, Marshie and Drew made the most outrageous and improbable management team ever: Drew energetically setting about to make his fortune at the ranch's expense while Marshie obligingly kept out of the way and paid scant attention to what was going on. Marshie did notice, however, that settlers in the area seemed to be somewhat hostile toward them. He once wrote his older brother, Edward, back in England, remarking that "a great many of them seem to think it is their right; and [therefore] attempt to live on us."[15]

Meanwhile, the Rocking Chair became a prime target for rustlers—both outsiders and insiders, as it turned out. In its July 15, 1923, edition, the *Fort Worth Star-Telegram* described the ensuing debacle in an article entitled, "As Manager of Rocking Chair Ranch Honorable Archie Was a Good Dog Fancier." It read, in part:

> The boys "up the creek" mavericked the Rocking Chair cattle and made a joke of it, and the hardened co-manager [John Drew] mavericked 100 to the settlers' one. They stole from the Rockers. Rocking Chair money came in a steady stream, so why not? Archie did not care; apparently nobody cared. There were squatters on alternate sections of school land and there were nesters up on the Elm. They could always sell [cattle] to the Rockers and get paid in Coin of the Realm. They drove bunches down, counted them, delivered them [to the Rockers] and got their money. Then they drove the cattle over the hill and threw them into a pasture; another outfit took them, drove them around from the other side, sold them and got their money a second time. This process was sometimes repeated until the same bunch of cattle had been sold [to the Rockers] four or five times.

John Drew, and just about everybody else in the Panhandle (except clueless Marshie), knew that professional rustlers, rowdy cowboys, resentful nesters, and Drew himself were stealing the Rockers blind. The results of all the rustling and chicanery finally began to show up on the company's financial records back in England. Lord Aberdeen and Baron Tweedmouth decided to investigate. One day they showed up at the ranch unannounced and demanded to see for themselves how many cattle they owned. Although momentarily caught off guard, the wily John Drew quickly recovered and devised a plan. He gave his cowboys appropriate instructions. The next day he took the two Englishmen to a large hill on the ranch. Soon his cowboys appeared, driving a herd of cattle around the hill. They were counted and then the cowboys drove them around the far side of the hill. Soon the cowboys reappeared coming around the hill again with another herd of cattle. Actually, it was not another herd. It was the same herd but with another hundred head or so thrown in. This process was repeated over and over until an amount of cattle sufficient to satisfy the Englishmen's financial records had been "accounted for." Then the investigators left and went back to England.[16] Meanwhile, back at the ranch, the mismanagement and thievery continued. A subsequent investigation confirmed it.

That's when, in July 1893, the owners hired Cap Arrington to manage the ranch and sell it. Arrington's first act was to fire the comanagers, the corrupt John Drew and the clueless Archibald John Majorbanks. When Cap Arrington took the helm in 1893, company records listed fourteen thousand head of cattle on the books. When Arrington rounded up all the cattle on the Rocking Chair Ranche, there were only three hundred head.[17] The ranch was eventually sold to the Continental Land and Cattle Company in October 1896, and Cap Arrington returned to managing his own ranch near Canadian. From the time the English lords purchased the Rocking Chair in 1883 until Cap Arrington took over the management in 1893, that 152,320-acre spread was a rustler's paradise. And it was located in Collingsworth County, Texas, only thirty miles south of Canadian—the headquarters of Sam and Will Isaacs.

Meanwhile, wholesale cattle theft was not only taking place south of Canadian, Texas, but also to the east over in the Oklahoma Territory. By 1894, settlers in the Taloga and Watonga areas became so outraged by the outlaws' arrogant and flagrant banditry in stealing their horses and cattle and then driving them into the Texas Panhandle that they decided to take the law into their own hands. Each county organized its own Anti–Horse Theft Association and joined in a pledge to make horse and cattle thieves scarce, "even if we have to plant more trees to hang them all." Soon these citizen law enforcers began arresting and obtaining indictments against numerous offenders, including some prominent residents.[18]

Will Isaacs, a wealthy retired rancher and banker, died in Canadian, Texas, in 1934; Sam Isaacs, a wealthy retired rancher and banker, died in Canadian, Texas, in 1943. Two years after Sam's death, his widow was interviewed for an article that appeared in the 1946 edition of the *Panhandle-Plains Historical Review*. She told the author that Sam had told her before he died that after President Cleveland ordered all cattlemen to vacate the Cheyenne-

Arapaho reservation in 1885, two thousand head of William E. Malaley's cattle were driven to an open range in eastern New Mexico, where Sam was hired to take care of them, and four years later, in 1889, he "drove the herd back to the Canadian, Texas, area and located them on Red Deer Creek." Then, according to Mrs. Isaacs, her husband told her that he and Will Isaacs purchased those two thousand head of cattle at a forced public auction sale on the steps of the courthouse in Canadian in 1893. Seven years later the Isaacs family embellished their account from 1946 most grandly when in 1953 they told the tale to F. Stanley, who wrote a history of the town of Canadian. According to the revised version, both Sam and Will Isaacs prior to their deaths had claimed that at the 1893 public auction on the steps of the courthouse, they bought from their employers "Mullally [*sic*] and Forbes a 30,000-acre ranch and 4,000 head of cattle." That version of the story was carried forward in 1977 in *Cowmen and Ladies: A History of Hemphill County* and in 1996 in *The New Handbook of Texas*.[19]

There was indeed a public auction on the steps of the courthouse in Canadian in 1893, and Will and Sam Isaacs did purchase some cattle at the auction—apparently seventy-nine head. What is clear, however—as attested by an examination of the official records of Hemphill County—is that Will and Sam did not purchase a thirty-thousand-acre ranch at that public auction. In fact neither Will nor Sam purchased *any* land at that public auction or at any other time at any other public auction.[20] Furthermore, Hemphill County records show that William E. Malaley never owned any land in Hemphill County.

The Hemphill County District Court records reflect that the 1893 public auction was triggered by a default judgment obtained by Will Isaacs in a lawsuit he filed the previous year against William Malaley's wife, Kate, and against Indian agent John D. Miles's wife, Lucy. Although William Malaley and John D. Miles were joined as parties to the lawsuit, the allegations were made against their wives.[21] The allegations claimed that Kate Malaley and Lucy Miles agreed to pay Will Isaacs a total of $3,658 for "holding and branding a herd of cattle" and for gathering seventy-nine head of cattle in New Mexico and driving them to Hemphill County. There are a number of things about Will's lawsuit that reek of fraud. The alleged agreement Will relied upon was a "verbal contract," and since no answer to the plaintiff's allegations was ever filed, and since no trial was ever held, and since Will then obtained a default judgment against the defendants, no documents or records of trial testimony exist to substantiate any of Will Isaacs's allegations. Some question also arises as to whether any of the defendants were ever served with notice that they had been sued. The lawsuit, filed in late 1892, alleges that the Malaleys were residents of Caldwell, Kansas, but records show that in May 1893, William Malaley was living in the small town of Hennessey, Oklahoma Territory, where he owned half interest in the local livery stable.[22]

Moreover, the verbal contract Will Isaacs relied upon was, according to his pleadings, made by "a firm of Plumb and Hood," but according to Will Isaacs's petition, the firm of Plumb and Hood had subsequently sold that (unnumbered) herd of cattle to the defendants Kate Malaley and Lucy Miles, who had also allegedly verbally agreed to pay Will Isaacs the requested $3,658. Meanwhile, the firm of Plumb and Hood was not made a party to the lawsuit, and the record shows that no notice was ever given to Plumb and Hood that this lawsuit had ever been filed. Also, Malaley's junior partner, A. S. C. Forbes, was not made a party to the lawsuit.

That said, it brings us back to the original question: How did two penniless cowboys, who came to the big ranch country in 1884, manage on thirty-dollars-a-month cowboy wages to become so wealthy that by 1894 they had acquired their own ranches, plus being able to afford the staggering costs of financing the defense in George Isaacs's murder trial plus his appeal to the Texas appellate court in Austin—plus shouldering the burden of paying for the defense in more murder trials and appeals yet to come? What was the source of their considerable wealth? The answer to that question becomes clear when we consider that the only source of wealth available to Will and Sam Isaacs during the 1880s and early 1890s, except for their salaries as cowboys, was other people's cattle: those half million or so head of cattle that roamed the millions of acres of the Llano Estacado and the Oklahoma Territory. It was a time, as we have previously noted, when cattle theft was common both by settlers stocking their small claims and by professional outlaws who engaged in wholesale cattle thievery. It is also clear that for Sam and Will Isaacs to have accumulated their great wealth in such a short time, their cattle thievery had to have been on a considerably grander scale than that of some nester-squatter stocking a section or two of state-owned school land.

CHAPTER TWELVE

JAILBREAK!

THE SECRETS OF JIM HARBOLT

Jim Harbolt knew many secrets. Important secrets. Important enough, he reckoned, to buy himself a get-out-of-jail-free card. And maybe even important enough to let him get away with murder—the murder of a Texas sheriff.

For openers, he knew the true identity of his fellow long rider, the mysterious Jim Stanley. And he also knew the identity, or identities, of who else was behind the ill-fated Wells Fargo scam.

Back in 1888, six years before Sheriff McGee was murdered, Jim Harbolt killed Giles Flippin at the Duncan store in Chickasha.[1] But even by that time Harbolt had already earned a reputation in the Indian Territory as a notorious outlaw. As Giles Flippin lay dying in the street, Harbolt mounted and fled the scene. For the next year and four months he played tag with federal marshals until he finally surrendered to Deputy US Marshal Sam Brown. But when the federal court in Paris, Texas, called his murder case for trial on May 15, 1891, it had to be dismissed. The next day's edition of the *Dallas Morning News* summed up the proceeding with this terse, light-hearted report: "The murder case against the notorious James Harbolt was dismissed, as all the witnesses necessary to convict were not to be found, some being fugitives. The killing was a part of the Christmas frolic."

Harbolt came from a clan of the sorriest of the sorry Indian Territory outlaws. (The adjective "trashy" begs for print here.) The family's stamping ground was on Hell Roaring Creek on the

Comanche reservation in Indian Territory some twenty miles east of where Fort Sill is now located.

In 1889, the year after Jim terminated Giles Flippin, Jim's older brother, George E. Harbolt, and two companions killed Boone Marlow, the boyfriend of Susan Harbolt, the sister of Jim and George, near their home. A reward of fifteen hundred dollars had previously been offered by authorities in North Texas for the arrest of Marlow. George Harbolt and his companions, however, were too cowardly to attempt an arrest, so they fed Marlow a generous helping of arsenic while his attention was focused on courting Susan. After he died, they shot him twice in the head, then hauled his body to Texas to collect the reward money, claiming they had to shoot him in self-defense when he resisted their attempt to arrest him. Texas authorities were suspicious. They had an autopsy performed on Marlow's body and discovered the true cause of his death, and Marlow's girlfriend, Susan Harbolt, later confirmed it. George was indicted for murder. He was released on bond in March 1889, and his trial was scheduled for October, but it is unclear whether he was ever tried. (Years later, the dramatic story of the valiant fight for justice waged by Boone Marlow and his four brothers against North Texas officials and lawmen was told in book and film versions.)[2]

When D County, Oklahoma Territory, was opened for settlement in 1892, Jim Harbolt staked a claim in the southeast quadrant of the county (see Map 2, p. 46). His claim was located only a few miles east of the claim staked by the Blake brothers, Tulsa Jack, Joe, and Sam. On February 3, 1895, Harbolt was arrested in Taloga for the November 1894 murder of Sheriff Tom T. McGee, and in May 1895 a Hemphill County, Texas, grand jury indicted him for murder.

In June 1895, Harbolt, with the support of Will and Sam Isaacs, applied to the local district judge, B. M. Baker, for release on bond. After a two-day hearing, Judge Baker denied bail. Will and Sam Isaacs then hired W. B. Plemons of Amarillo, the same lawyer they had employed to represent brother George Isaacs, to appeal Judge Baker's adverse ruling before Judge J. M. Hurt of the Texas Court of Criminal Appeals in Austin. In September of that year Judge Hurt granted Harbolt's motion and set bail at fifteen hundred dollars, which Will and Sam promptly posted. Harbolt hit the ground running with no intention of returning to face a murder trial.

The *Canadian Record* editor, W. S. Defibaugh, publicly criticized Judge

Texas Rangers Company B in the 1890s. In January 1897 Captain W. J. (Bill) McDonald, commander of Company B, Frontier Battalion of the Texas Rangers at Amarillo, sent ranger private Jack Harwell (*standing, far left*) and another ranger to Canadian, Texas, to investigate the jailbreak of Jim Harbolt from the Hemphill County jail. Harbolt was awaiting trial for the murder of Hemphill County, Texas, sheriff Tom T. McGee. *Back row, left to right:* Jack Harwell, Sergeant W. John L. Sullivan, Bob Pease, Arthur Jones, Ed Connell, and Lee Queen. *Front row, left to right:* Billy McCauley, Bob McClure, Wes Carter, and — Owens. 1974-152/11, reprinted by permission of Panhandle-Plains Historical Museum, Canyon, Texas.

Hurt for setting such a "very light bond" for a man indicted for the murder of Sheriff McGee, especially considering "the reputation of the man and the neighborhood from which he came." Defibaugh's criticism was validated two months later when, on November 19, 1895, Harbolt failed to appear at a pretrial hearing. Judge Baker ordered that Harbolt's bond be forfeited. (Sam and Will hired Plemons to contest the forfeiture and later prevailed on a procedural technicality.) An arrest warrant was issued for Jim Harbolt, but by then he was long gone—headed west, seeking refuge in the familiar haunts of his childhood home in the Indian Territory.[3]

On June 22, 1896, one year after Harbolt had jumped bail, Deputy US

Marshal A. A. "Gus" Bobbitt came across Jim Harbolt asleep in the woods near Pauls Valley, Indian Territory. Bobbitt quietly leaned his Winchester rifle against a tree, got out his handcuffs, and before Harbolt became sufficiently awake to realize what was going on, had slipped the handcuffs on the fugitive and effected an arrest. Harbolt was extradited back to Texas and lodged in the jail in Fort Worth for safekeeping until his trial date approached.[4]

At that point the Harbolt story took another strange turn. Harbolt was locked up in the same Fort Worth "run-around" cell with none other than George Isaacs, who had been convicted the previous November in Quanah, Texas, for the murder of Sheriff Tom T. McGee and sentenced to life imprisonment. George appealed his conviction and was cooling his heels in the Fort Worth jail while waiting for the Texas Court of Criminal Appeals in Austin to make up its mind. George must have been stunned that day—June 28, 1896—when he looked up and saw a prison guard ushering a long-lost friend into his cell.

George and Jim had another visitor that day. This one, however, was not a prison inmate. He was an enterprising reporter from the *Dallas Morning News* who apparently was on good terms with the Tarrant County sheriff. He had been alerted that George Isaacs and Jim Harbolt would be paired in the same cell and, knowing the background of the McGee murder, realized that it would be a news reporter's dream come true to score an in-person interview with this notorious and unsavory duo. Actually, he might have milked a better story out of them had he interviewed them separately. The newsman informed his readers that the "accidental" jailhouse meeting of the two had, during his interview, been "characterized by an indifference which lent admirable enchantment. They were strangers in every sense of the word to each other."[5] Each claimed that they had met only once before—a brief encounter several years earlier. George, of course, expressed confidence that the appellate court would see the light and liberate him soon. Harbolt expressed confidence that he would be acquitted when his trial was called if only he could get a fair and impartial jury. He explained that he had "jumped bond" only because he knew that "a bunch of lies" would have been told about him if he had been tried shortly after his arrest, and therefore he "wanted to remain away until matters had cooled down," at which time he had intended to return and stand trial. With that enlightening announcement, the correspondent closed his notebook and departed.

In December 1896 Harbolt was returned to his cell in the Hemphill County jail in Canadian to await his murder trial. And that's where the Jim Harbolt story got really peculiar.

To understand just how peculiar, a bit of background needs to be reviewed. After Sheriff McGee was murdered in November 1894, Cap Arrington was appointed as the interim sheriff of Hemphill County. Arrington never believed George Isaacs's claim that Bill Doolin was somehow behind the Wells Fargo plot. Arrington suspected that brothers Sam and Will Isaacs were somehow involved behind the scenes, and he was determined to get to the bottom of the mystery. The brothers were well aware that the tenacious Arrington was on their trail. As a result, when Arrington came up for election in November 1895, Will and Sam Isaacs found themselves another candidate—a much less hostile, a much more pliable candidate—to back for election as the next sheriff of Hemphill County. Their candidate's name was W. R. Boyd, and with the generous support of Sam and Will Isaacs, Boyd defeated Arrington for sheriff and took office in November 1895 almost a year to the day after Hemphill County's first sheriff, Tom T. McGee, had been murdered.

Cap Arrington wasn't the only Hemphill County citizen who suspected that Sam and Will Isaacs were attempting to cover up their role in the Wells Fargo affair, whatever it might have been. The district judge, B. M. Baker; banker D. J. Young; W. S. Defibaugh, editor of the local weekly newspaper, the *Canadian Record*; and other locals shared Cap Arrington's suspicion.

On December 10, 1896, shortly after his defeat in the November sheriff's race, Cap Arrington wrote this letter to Texas adjutant general W. H. Mabry, who was head of the Texas Rangers:

> I would ask that you appoint me as Special Ranger without pay as I believe I can be of considerable aid to this State in certain criminal matters, besides being a protection to myself. The attached letter from Judge Baker will explain the matters alluded to.
>
> Yours truly, G. W. Arrington[6]

District Judge B. M. Baker, by a letter to Adjutant General Mabry also dated December 10, 1896, joined Cap Arrington's request, and he told Mabry this:

Capt. G. W. Arrington was defeated for Sheriff of this county by the influence of Bill Isaacs the wealthy brother of George Isaacs who put up the Express Car robbery resulting in the assassination of Sheriff McGee three years ago. Capt. Arrington has persisted in working up the prosecution against the murderers and has much left yet to do. I wish you would appoint him a Special Ranger without pay. He is too well known to you to need my recommendation and this is written to show the reason for the appointment.

Most respectfully, B. M. Baker

P.S. Since writing this I have learned that the Court App. [the Texas Court of Criminal Appeals] has affirmed the George Isaacs case, but two others [Jim Harbolt and Joe Blake] are left untried and I count much on the aid of Capt. Arrington.[7]

Adjutant General Mabry honored the request of Cap Arrington, as seconded by Judge Baker, and so appointed Arrington as a nonsalaried special Texas Ranger.

Sometime about the middle of December 1896, a man named Gilliland was arrested on a misdemeanor charge and placed in the Canadian jail with Jim Harbolt, where he remained until sometime during the first part of January 1897. When he was released he told W. W. Owens, a Hemphill County pioneer who operated a hotel in Canadian, that Harbolt had saws in his possession inside his cell and was planning to break out of jail. Owens told Sheriff Boyd, who later reported that he had searched Harbolt's cell but could find no saws or other tools of escape, adding that he presumed that Gilliland was just lying about the matter "so as to create a sensation."[8] Shortly thereafter, Sheriff Boyd left Canadian, stating that he needed to see about renting a farm he owned in Oklahoma. He left a deputy named Fred Rathjen in charge of the jail.

It was a dark and stormy night. It was the night of Monday, January 18, 1897. Lots of snow fell during that night, and by nine o'clock the next morning, when Deputy Rathjen arrived at the jail with the prisoner's breakfast, the snow had already covered Jim Harbolt's tracks—the tracks he had left during his nocturnal sprint for freedom.

Defibaugh reported the details in the *Canadian Record.*[9] Sheriff Boyd, the editor noted, was still in Oklahoma the night Harbolt escaped. Harbolt was the only prisoner in the jail. It was obvious that some person or persons had slipped tools to Harbolt, including a heavy five-foot crowbar, a chain, and a saw. Harbolt had used the saw to partially cut through the cell bars and then used the chain and crowbar to break them loose. Then Harbolt had ripped up his canvas cot from which he fashioned a rope by which he lowered himself to the ground. Apparently his accomplice had also thoughtfully furnished Harbolt with a horse, but the horse tracks had also been obliterated by the snow.

Defibaugh ended his account of the jailbreak with an editorial raising the burning issue of the day: Who helped Harbolt escape? Without making a direct accusation, it was clear his suspicion was focused on Sheriff Boyd and Boyd's principal supporters: Sam and Will Isaacs. The editor ended his ruminations thus: "We sincerely hope that Sheriff Boyd will be able to clear it up, and it is the duty of all good, law-abiding citizens to give him every aid in their power by which to do so. It has been said that the Almighty never lends his aid to a wrong, which he appears to have done in this case by covering the tracks with a snow, but who knows but what it might have been for the purpose of bringing to light other crimes."[10]

Soon, however, the Almighty appeared to have switched sides. Five days later, Harbolt—sick and half starved to death—showed up back in Canadian. The first day of his escape he had managed to get across the Canadian River and hide in an empty house, but the storm was so severe that he was unable to travel farther. Afraid of being discovered in the old house, Harbolt left the next day and spent the next three days outside huddled in a crevice along Dry Creek without food. Meanwhile, his physical condition worsened and turned into pneumonia. He concluded that he had to have help, so he made his way back to Canadian seeking shelter and food. But he didn't return to the jail. Instead, he made his way to Will Isaacs's barn, where Will discovered him Saturday evening. We are left to wonder what kind of reaction that triggered in Will. Very likely it was a hot potato that Will wanted to divest himself of immediately—or sooner. After a hurried conference with Harbolt, Will sent his wife to the sheriff's office, where she notified Sheriff Boyd that Will was detaining Harbolt at their home. Sheriff Boyd showed up and marched Harbolt back to his cell.

Upon being questioned about his escape, Harbolt refused to tell who furnished him the tools for his jailbreak, saying only that none of the county officers were in any way implicated. In his next news story, Defibaugh informed his readers about the recapture of Harbolt, observing that this bizarre turn of events left the editor "very badly mixed." He concluded with this comment: "We are free to confess that it is a deep mystery to us yet. . . . We wait in patience for time to tell the story."[11] The escape and return of Harbolt might have left Defibaugh puzzled, but it precipitated a bitter and angry split between the Judge Baker–Cap Arrington faction and the Sheriff Boyd–Will Isaacs faction in Hemphill County. Both sides began soliciting names on petitions. Judge Baker solicited signatures on a petition addressed to Adjutant General Mabry in Austin requesting that he send Texas Rangers to Canadian to investigate the mystery of Jim Harbolt's escape. Meanwhile, the Sheriff Boyd–Will Isaacs faction was busy collecting names on a petition addressed to Texas Governor Charles Culberson urging him *not* to send Texas Rangers to Canadian, informing him that they had "utmost confidence" in the ability of their local county officers to solve the mystery.

On January 23, 1897, Judge Baker sent a Western Union telegraph to Adjutant General W. H. Mabry reading as follows: "Solicited by many best citizens I request ranger force at Canadian at once. Harbolt charged with assassination of Sheriff McGee delivered from jail. Want of confidence in presiding sheriff expressed to me by best of citizens. B. M. Baker—Judge 31st District."[12]

On the same date, the Sheriff Boyd–Will Isaacs faction fired off the following petition to Adjutant General W. H. Mabry's boss, Governor Charles Culberson:

> On Monday night, Jan. 18th, a Prisoner, the only one in our County Jail, was liberated. Presumably by outside assistance and we wish to inform you that a petition is now being circulated asking for state Rangers and an investigation by the Attorney General. And said petition also states that things are in a deplorable condition, and that Life and Property is [*sic*] in great danger. Which we state is emphatickly [*sic*] not the case. And as further evidence to you that we have the utmost confidence in our county officers to take care of the case, and knowing as we do that they are using every endeavor to apprehend the guilty parties, we the undersigned taxpayers and Citizens and property holders herewith affix our names.

The petition was signed by thirty-seven citizens, including Sheriff W. R.

Boyd, Will Isaacs, Sam Isaacs, John Isaacs, County Judge Richard Brussell, District and County Clerk O. R. McMordie, precinct no. 1 commissioner D. M. Hargrave, former county judge E. E. Polly, and twenty-nine others.[13]

Despite the objections of the Sheriff Boyd–Will Isaacs faction, Adjutant General Mabry ordered Captain W. J. (Bill) McDonald, commander of Company B of the Frontier Battalion of the Texas Rangers, with headquarters at Amarillo, to investigate the Harbolt escape. Captain McDonald complied by dispatching two privates, John "Jack" Harwell and Ed Donley, to Canadian on January 22, 1897. On January 24, Judge Baker wired Mabry informing him that Rangers Harwell and Donley had arrived in Canadian, adding this cryptic note to the telegram: "satisfaction confidence of the people."[14] Unfortunately, the two ranger privates were rookies who had very limited briefing on the background of the tense and complicated situation then existing in Hemphill County.

Apparently the Boyd-Isaacs faction, realizing that further protest against Texas Ranger involvement in the investigation was futile, adopted an alternative strategy—cooperation with the two rangers. At least they feigned cooperation. At first, when Harbolt was recaptured and returned to the Canadian jail he had refused to divulge the name of his accomplice in the escape. But when interrogated by the two rangers, Harbolt readily volunteered that it had been Dan McKenzie who had slipped the saw, chain, and crowbar to him. Apparently the two rangers simply took Harbolt's word for it. Without further investigation or verification they arrested McKenzie and then caught the next train back to Amarillo. Case closed.[15] McKenzie, however, stoutly denied any involvement.

An examining trial on the criminal charge against McKenzie was held a few days later, and it raised serious doubt as to Harbolt's assertion. The February 4, 1897, edition of the *Canadian Record* reported the substance of the examining trial:

> Dan McKinzie [*sic*] was arrested last Friday evening on the charge of having assisted Jim Harbolt to escape from the jail, and an examining trial was had before Justice Montgomery Monday. The only evidence against him was that of Harbolt's who swore that the crowbar and chain was passed in to him on the night of the 27th of December [1896] by a man who gave his name as Dan McKinzie. The owners of the crowbar and chain, however, swore that the articles were in their possession on the 4th of January [1897]. McKinzie's bond was placed at $750, which was promptly given and he was released.

Three glaring problems with Harbolt's testimony are apparent. First, the part about the tools being slipped to him "by a man who gave his name as Dan McKinzie" is ridiculous. Harbolt was well acquainted with Dan McKenzie: they were neighbors, living within a few miles of each other in D County; Harbolt was positively identified as one of the four long riders who rode to Canadian that fateful day; he was positively identified as being in Hoefle's Saloon, a stone's throw from the Canadian depot, the afternoon before the fatal shootout; Cap Arrington tracked Harbolt's horse back to McKenzie's cabin after the shootout; and, finally, McKenzie's testimony at the George Isaacs trial identified Harbolt as returning to his cabin after the shooting.

Second, the owners of the breakout tools—the crowbar and chain—testified without equivocation that they had possession of these tools as late as January 4, 1897, contradicting Harbolt's testimony that McKenzie slipped them to him on December 27, 1896.

And third, the *only* evidence that Dan McKenzie had anything to do with the breakout was Harbolt's unsubstantiated testimony, and Jim Harbolt's credibility was somewhere between feeble and nonexistent. Needless to add, McKenzie was never tried on the charge of helping Harbolt escape the Canadian jail.

Harbolt's assertion that Dan McKenzie was the man who slipped him the escape tools seems preposterous for other reasons as well. What possible motive could McKenzie have had for assisting Jim Harbolt? Just prior to the George Isaacs murder trial in November 1895, McKenzie had flipped, turned state's witness, and testified for the prosecution, thereby implicating not only George Isaacs but also Jim Harbolt and Joe Blake in the Wells Fargo scam. And he was scheduled to testify for the state again when Harbolt's case was set for trial in February. (He did so and again implicated Harbolt.)

On the other hand, how convenient was it for Harbolt to shift the blame from his real accomplice to McKenzie? Plus, it was a satisfying payback for McKenzie's betrayal of the outlaw faction, and it assured Harbolt of further support from his undercover cohort or cohorts.

Meanwhile, quiet was restored in Hemphill County, and, strangely enough, Judge Baker made no further demands for a more thorough investigation by the Texas Ranger force. The Sheriff Boyd–Will Isaacs faction had played its hand masterfully, thereby adroitly deflecting—at least for the time being—accusations of involvement not only in the jailbreak but also in the Wells Fargo plot and the murder of Sheriff McGee. And how clever it had been to suggest to Jim Harbolt that he lay all of the blame on Dan McKenzie.

Once again, the hapless McKenzie had served as a handy pawn in the ongoing battle between the laws and the outlaws.

Nevertheless, there remained a yet unanswered question—one that didn't quite pass the smell test. Why did the sick and starving escapee, Jim Harbolt, turn to Will Isaacs for help in his time of need?

But there was still another and more puzzling question that remained to be answered. Jim Harbolt, Joe Blake, and George Isaacs, all penny-ante crooks, had no means with which to hire a lawyer or post a bail bond. It was understandable that Will and Sam Isaacs might rally to support brother George, even if he was the "black sheep" of the family. It was also understandable that Will and Sam Isaacs might have decided to come to the aid of brother George's accomplices—Jim Harbolt and Joe Blake—fearing that if they had refused to do so, either outlaw might have been tempted by a lucrative offer from the prosecutor to accept a lenient sentence in exchange for flipping and turning state's witness against brother George. In fact, tight-fisted as were brothers Will and Sam Isaacs, they had nevertheless already parted with a substantial sum in fighting all the way up to the appellate ladder to persuade the court to set a bail bond to free Jim Harbolt pending his trial, and then spending yet another substantial sum in another court battle when the state sought to forfeit their bail bond after Harbolt had immediately hit the ground running and disappeared into the Indian Territory.

Meanwhile, brother George had been tried, and in December 1896 the Texas Court of Criminal Appeals had overruled his appeal.[16] Nothing more could be done to help or hurt George's judicial fate. He was locked securely behind prisons walls for the rest of his life. Now, some two months later, Harbolt (who had finally been recaptured) was set to go on trial in February 1897. The question was, would Will and Sam Isaacs waste another hefty bankroll hiring a very expensive battery of lawyers to defend that penny-ante outlaw, Jim Harbolt, in his upcoming murder trial? And, if so, why? What possible motive did they have?

Perhaps it was because Jim Harbolt knew many secrets—many very important secrets that, if disclosed, would incriminate some very prominent people in the Wells Fargo scam that resulted in the killing of Sheriff McGee.

CHAPTER THIRTEEN

THE TRIAL OF JIM HARBOLT: TURNING GOLD INTO DROSS

CLARENDON, TEXAS, FEBRUARY 1, 1897

Even though George Isaacs's conviction for the murder of Sheriff McGee had become final after his appeal was denied, Jim Harbolt needn't have worried about whether Sam and Will Isaacs would finance his defense. Although they denied it, Sam and Will hired the same expensive battery of top-notch lawyers to represent Jim Harbolt that they had hired to represent brother George. Once again, W. B. Plemons of Amarillo was the lead defense attorney.

The prosecutors were D. E. Decker, district attorney of the 46th Judicial District of Texas, assisted by G. W. Walters and by special prosecutors H. E. Hoover of Canadian and Jim Cowan of Fort Worth. Cowan headed the prosecution team.

District Judge G. A. Brown gaveled the court to order on February 1, 1897, in Clarendon, Texas, thus opening the trial of Jim Harbolt. Both Harbolt and Joe Blake had been indicted in Hemphill County for the murder of Sheriff Tom T. McGee, but owing to the outrage that the senseless killing of the popular sheriff had ignited, the Hemphill County district judge, B. M. Baker, wisely ordered a change of venue in both cases: the Jim Harbolt case transferred to Clarendon, county seat of Donley County, some 80 miles south of Canadian and about 50 miles southeast of Amarillo, and the Joe Blake case transferred to Vernon, county seat of Wilbarger County, approximately 120 miles southeast of Clarendon.[1]

To a large extent the Jim Harbolt trial was a replay of the George Isaacs trial, and the state relied on the same cast of witnesses to prove its case.[2] The state's star witnesses in Harbolt's (and later Joe Blake's) trial were express agent A. B. Harding, Cap Arrington, and Dan McKenzie, the defendant's erstwhile accomplice turned state's witness.

The state called a number of impartial eyewitnesses who nailed Jim Harbolt and Joe Blake to the crime. J. W. Conaster, one of the locals who had met the four long riders coming to Canadian from the Oklahoma Territory earlier that fateful day, identified both Jim Harbolt and Joe Blake. Another, Doc Walton, identified Harbolt and also Tulsa Jack Blake (whom he had previously met) as being two of the four long riders. Saloon patron John Kirkham identified Jim Harbolt and Joe Blake as being two fellow imbibers at Hoefle's Saloon (located less than a hundred yards from the Canadian depot) during the afternoon before Sheriff McGee was fatally wounded later that evening. Station agent A. B. Harding, who met Jim Harbolt that evening as Harding exited the Wells Fargo Express car en route to his depot office with the money packets, made a positive identification. Plus, the dying sheriff lived long enough that night to give a detailed description of the man who drew his pistol and fired the fatal shot, and his description fit Jim Harbolt exactly.

To ice the cake, the prosecution called on its turncoat witness, Dan McKenzie. He was followed by his wife and then his thirteen-year-old daughter, Stella, both of whom confirmed Dan's testimony. They testified that Joe Blake was living with them when these events occurred, that Blake left home on the Monday prior to the attempted robbery and the killing of Sheriff McGee the following Saturday night, and that Blake did not return to their cabin until Sunday night. When he returned, Joe Blake was accompanied by Jim Harbolt, Tulsa Jack Blake, Bitter Creek Newcomb, and the mysterious Jim Stanley. When the third Blake brother, Sam Blake, arrived later that Sunday night with news that the Canadian sheriff had died of his wound, all except Joe Blake saddled up and fled.

All McKenzie would say about Jim Stanley was that he was tall, with a light complexion, and had auburn sideburns and mustache. At least the physical description matched the description given by an independent and impartial witness—J. W. Conaster, one of the locals who witnessed the four long riders approach Canadian on the day of the fatal encounter. McKenzie did verify that all three of the Blake brothers as well as Harbolt were small men with a dark complexion. McKenzie admitted that he knew Bill Doolin and verified the fact that Jim Stanley was not Bill Doolin. Thus, the real identity of Jim Stanley remained cloaked in a conspiracy of silence.

When it became the defense's turn at bat, Harbolt's lawyers claimed it was all a case of mistaken identity: both Jim Harbolt and Joe Blake, they contended, were actually in the Taloga community when McGee was gunned down. The defense even summoned the same cadre of Oklahoma Territory witnesses who had testified for George Isaacs to prop up the alibi. In addition to their role as alibi witnesses, each also testified that they knew Dan McKenzie's reputation for "truth and veracity" and that it was "bad."

The surprise witness for the defense was none other than Will Isaacs. He also testified that Dan McKenzie's reputation for truth and veracity was bad. Going even further, Will contended that Cap Arrington had offered Dan McKenzie a thousand dollars if he would turn state's evidence and give perjured testimony that would help convict brother George Isaacs and the other defendants. On cross-examination Will admitted that he and Sheriff Boyd had approached McKenzie before the George Isaacs trial with an affidavit setting out Arrington's alleged thousand-dollar offer as well as the specific facts McKenzie was supposed to testify to. He admitted that McKenzie had refused to sign the affidavit. Will Isaacs also admitted that he had talked with McKenzie only once before the trials, and that was the time he had approached McKenzie with the previously prepared affidavit.

That gave prosecutor Cowan a wonderful target for further cross-examination. If, as Will Isaacs had just admitted, he had talked with McKenzie only once, and that was the time that he and Sheriff Boyd presented him with the prepared affidavit stating all the specific facts about Arrington's supposed offer of a thousand dollars, then how could he possibly have already prepared that affidavit? Had Will invented his own brand of perjury that he wanted McKenzie to repeat? Will dodged that bullet by saying that it was really Mrs. McKenzie who had previously told him all about Cap Arrington's supposed thousand-dollar offer for perjured testimony.

Then Cowan fired another bullet. He forced Will to admit that he knew all about Cap Arrington's alleged attempt to bribe Dan McKenzie *before* brother George Isaacs's trial and realized that this would have been important evidence favorable to his brother's defense, yet he didn't take the stand to reveal this to the jury during George's trial. Why? Will, lamely, shrugged off the question, saying that, well, he just wasn't called by the defense lawyers—this despite the fact that he and Sam hired those defense lawyers. (There was, however, a more plausible answer to the question of why Will Isaacs did not testify in brother George's murder trial—one that would surface when Will took the stand and was questioned again on the same subject in the upcoming trial of Joe Blake.) The cross-examination of Will Isaacs ended with Will's denying that he was paying for Jim Harbolt's lawyers in this trial. That also had a distinct, off-key ring of deception, since he and Sam had hired those same lawyers to represent the penniless Harbolt at a bail bond hearing, then to appeal the district court's decision to deny bail, and had thereafter posted bond for Harbolt's release.

Jim Harbolt exercised his right not to testify and did not take the stand in his own defense. Both sides rested.

The army of lying alibi witnesses from Oklahoma Territory didn't impress the Clarendon jurors any more than they had the Quanah jurors in the George Isaacs case. On February 12, 1897, the jury found Jim Harbolt guilty and sentenced him to life imprisonment.

Wrapping up his story on the Harbolt trial, the *Canadian Record* editor had this to say: "During the trying ordeal Harbolt displayed no emotion whatever with the exception of twisting and turning a toothpick which he held between his fingers in a decidedly nervous manner. . . . He accepts his conviction philosophically, but asserts his entire innocence of the crime for which he is to remain behind prison walls for the balance of his life."[3]

Fortunately for Jim Harbolt, however, the editor's gloomy prognosis proved to be premature. Harbolt's lawyers appealed the jury's decision, and the Texas Court of Criminal Appeals overturned the conviction and sent it back to the trial court for a retrial. And just what was the reversible error? In Harbolt's trial the district judge gave written instructions to the jury thus providing it with the choice of finding the defendant not guilty or guilty of first-degree murder or guilty of second-degree murder. The court further instructed the jury that the *penalty for first-degree murder was life imprisonment or death*, and the *penalty for second-degree murder was imprisonment for any number of years, not less than five*. When the jury returned, they found the defendant "guilty as charged in the indictment, and *assess his punishment at confinement in the penitentiary for life*" [my emphasis].

The jury's verdict seems simple and straightforward. But it wasn't good enough to suit the Texas Court of Criminal Appeals. According to the appellate court, the jury's fatal mistake was not stating specifically in the verdict whether it found Harbolt guilty of first-degree murder or second-degree murder.[4] It would seem obvious to anybody not afflicted with a case of terminal legalitis that the jury must have found Harbolt guilty of first-degree murder since it fixed the punishment at life imprisonment instead of a term of years in prison. Nevertheless, on that hypertechnical point (so typical of the legal hair-splitting common to Texas appellate courts in criminal cases at that time), the higher court overturned Harbolt's conviction and ordered a retrial.

CHAPTER FOURTEEN

THE TRIAL OF JOE BLAKE: THE JAILHOUSE LETTERS

VERNON, TEXAS, MARCH 1, 1897

In a jailhouse letter to Dan McKenzie dated August 11, 1895, Joe Blake wrote: "Dan, you asked me what I would swear. I will tell you what I have told them and that is what I will swear on the witness stand if it suits you and if it don't, let me know by return mail and what you will swear. . . . Dan, I want 'straight goods' about this, or there will be hell when I do get out."[1]

They called Lorenzo Dow Miller "the cowboy lawyer." He was much more akin to the former than the latter. Lorenzo Dow himself was the author of a withering judicial remark that became a classic among the frontier legal community. He once became infuriated when an adverse witness skipped glibly from one lie to another with effortless ease while dodging every attempt by Miller to pin him down. "Gentlemen of the jury," Miller fumed, "I could take that witness and prove to you that Jesus Christ runs a hog ranch on the North Fork [of the Red River]—yes sir, a hog ranch on the North Fork!"[2]

Somebody employed Lorenzo Dow Miller and three other Panhandle lawyers to represent Joe Blake in his murder trial. It couldn't have been Joe Blake. He was penniless—as were all of his relatives. Yet somewhere out there Joe Blake, like Jim Harbolt, had a supporter who wished to remain anonymous.

On a change of venue from Hemphill County, Texas, the trial

commenced on March 1, 1897, in Vernon, Wilbarger County, Texas. The same prosecution team that had represented the state in the George Isaacs and the Jim Harbolt cases was on hand for the state. Jim Cowan, special prosecutor, headed that team. Again, H. E. Hoover of Canadian, also a special prosecutor, sat second chair for the state.

The Joe Blake trial was not the first time H. E. Hoover and Lorenzo Dow Miller—those two pioneer Panhandle courtroom gladiators—had jousted. Wise and impressive as he was, Hoover once met his match—and more—when he crossed legal swords with the eccentric and often outrageous Lorenzo Dow Miller. Their classic encounter happened sometime in the late nineteenth century in a remote Panhandle county before a justice of the peace who rarely let judicial matters interfere with business. This JP owned and operated a two-story establishment, the upper floor of which His Honor euphemistically referred to as his "hotel." (Strangely enough, his second-story hotel guests always seemed to be females.) The bottom floor was a saloon, and the backroom of the saloon was where he held court—as soon as he could clear out all the poker players. That was where Hoover and Lorenzo Dow Miller locked horns. It wasn't long before a learned discussion of the legal issues deteriorated into a fist-pounding shouting match. Hoover vehemently insisted that the law was on his side. Miller exploded with even more vehemence, insisting that he had the law on *his* side. Meanwhile, His Honor, clueless, drummed his fingers on the poker table, taking in all this flow of legal lava. Finally, Lorenzo Dow Miller pulled out his fee in the case—a ten-dollar gold piece—and slammed it down on the poker table in front of the judge. He said, "Here's ten dollars to back up what I say is the law. Now, Hoover, put up or shut up!" Of course there wasn't a law book within sixty miles, whatever good that would have done. Besides, Hoover only had two dollars in his pocket. Puffing up with an air of affronted dignity Hoover pontificated that this was no way to resolve a serious legal issue, and furthermore, he insisted this was an insult to the majesty and intelligence of the court. His Honor, meanwhile, solemnly contemplated all this, still drumming his fingers on the poker table. Finally, he announced his decision, a judicial solution worthy of Solomon himself: "Well, Mr. Hoover," he said, "money talks. Ya got to ante up or drop out of the game. If'n ya ain't got the nerve to kivver his ten, I reckon ya wrong, and the court goes agin' ya." Hoover lost his case. Lorenzo Dow Miller won the case but lost his ten-dollar attorney's fee. Court costs, of course.[3]

★ ★ ★

The Joe Blake trial tracked closely the Jim Harbolt trial.[4] The state called essentially the same witnesses to prove the crimes of attempted robbery and the murder of Sheriff McGee. Again, the defense relied upon mistaken identity—Joe Blake was really in Taloga at the time of the crime—and again paraded the same army of Oklahoma Territory alibi witnesses to bolster that assertion. But there were three dramatic departures from the Harbolt trial. While Harbolt's lawyers had elected to assert Harbolt's right not to testify when presenting his defense, Joe Blake's lawyers put Blake on the stand.

Blake testified that he and Dan McKenzie had gone to Taloga on the Wednesday before McGee was shot the following Friday night, and that he, Dan McKenzie, Big Jim Riley, and the saloon keeper, M. K. McFadden, did some heavy drinking, rode a bronc, and rolled dice at the saloon until late Wednesday night. He and his friend Jim Riley slept in the saloon. The next day they bought more whiskey and eventually headed back to Dan McKenzie's place, where they spent Thursday night. They stayed in that area doing odd jobs Friday and Saturday and ended up in Dan's cabin that fateful Sunday night when four horsemen arrived. Joe Blake identified them as his brother Tulsa Jack, Jim Stanley, "little George," and a fourth man he knew only as "Mexico." Joe Blake contended that Tulsa Jack was the only one that he knew, although he admitted that he "had seen Stanley before." Later that evening his brother Sam Blake showed up with news that Sheriff McGee had been killed in the shootout, and then all five of the visitors saddled up and rode off. The next morning Cap Arrington arrived and arrested him and took him to jail in Canadian. He claimed that the lathered sorrel horse Arrington found in McKenzie's corral belonged to his brother Sam.

The courtroom drama ramped up considerably when the prosecutor, Jim Cowan, took Joe Blake on cross-examination. Cowan had a bombshell of a surprise in store for the defendant. He reached into his briefcase and pulled out several letters that the defendant and Dan McKenzie had exchanged in August 1895 while both were in the Canadian jail. (The letters were all written prior to the time that McKenzie turned state's witness.) Unknown to Joe Blake, the jailer eventually discovered the letters and delivered them to the prosecution. The primary thrust of the letters was an effort by Joe Blake and McKenzie to concoct and coordinate lies and alibis as to where they both had been and what they were doing before, during, and shortly after the Canadian crimes. Blake also demanded to know what McKenzie and his wife had told authorities, meanwhile assuring McKenzie that he "hadn't given anything away." He added this ominous threat: "Dan, I want 'straight goods' about this, or there will be hell when I do get out, for I am doing this all for you."

As to part of the coverup story, Blake told McKenzie that he had told authorities this: "I told them that little fellow with blue eyes and stubby mustache [obviously referring to Jim Harbolt] and that big fellow with sideburns [obviously referring to the fictitious Jim Stanley] were there the week before and got dinner but you were at the cedar brakes." Apparently "Jim Stanley" had also been going under yet another alias among the outlaws, that being "Tom Brown," because at another place in his letters to Dan McKenzie, Joe Blake said, "Tell me what was said about that Tom Brown? Who do they think he is? What do they say about him?"

It was also apparent that at that point in time, August 1895, Joe Blake was not able to employ his own lawyer and didn't yet know that Lorenzo Dow Miller had been hired to represent him. Blake wrote: "Tell me what you know about my lawyer. Whether he is employed or not." It was clear that Joe Blake expected some deep-pocket source would hire a lawyer to represent him—had better hire a lawyer to represent him. When prosecutor Cowan showed Joe Blake the jailhouse letters, Blake at first denied he had written them, said that he hadn't seen them before, and had no idea who had written them. Later, however, Blake admitted he had written the letters, claiming that he had just forgotten all about it. When Cowan questioned him about his prior criminal record, Blake admitted that he did "get into one or two little scrapes in Missouri," but denied that he left Missouri because there was a robbery indictment pending against him there.

The mystery of "Jim Stanley," aka "Tom Brown," continued to deepen—not only the question of who he was but also the reason why these Oklahoma Territory outlaws were so determined to shield his true identity. Meanwhile, they seemed to have no qualms about discussing known outlaws such as Bill Doolin, Bitter Creek Newcomb, Tulsa Jack Blake, and others and calling them by name.

The most dramatic twist in the Blake trial occurred when the defense called Will Isaacs as a witness. Will was called primarily to attack the character and credibility of both Dan McKenzie and Cap Arrington. First, Isaacs testified that McKenzie's reputation for "truth and veracity" was bad in the community and so his testimony was not worthy of belief. Then he testified that McKenzie's wife had told him that Cap Arrington had offered to pay

H. E. Hoover (here about 1900), prominent pioneer lawyer of Canadian, Texas, assisted Jim Cowan of Fort Worth in the prosecution of George Isaacs, Jim Harbolt, and Joe Blake for the murder of Hemphill County sheriff Tom T. McGee. 1977-137/14, reprinted by permission of Panhandle-Plains Historical Museum, Canyon, Texas.

McKenzie a thousand dollars to volunteer false and incriminating testimony against George Isaacs, Jim Harbolt, and Joe Blake. (Later, the prosecution would recall Mrs. McKenzie, Dan McKenzie, and Cap Arrington to deny this assertion.)

On cross-examination by the state, Will Isaacs was forced to admit some very revealing facts. Will admitted that he and Sam had executed Jim Harbolt's fifteen-hundred-dollar bail bond, allowing him to be released pending his trial. He also admitted that he had previously testified in Jim Harbolt's trial and made the same accusations against Dan McKenzie and Cap Arrington. Although Will admitted that he knew this was very material and damaging testimony against prosecution witnesses McKenzie and Arrington, he was at a loss to explain why he did not appear as a defense witness for his own brother, George Isaacs, at his earlier trial in Quanah and make these accusations. Why? Well, Will shrugged, he just wasn't called as a witness—this even though he and Sam had hired George's defense attorneys.

Although that admission by Will must have sounded rather weak to jurors, the next admission prosecutor Cowan pried out of Will was a real stunner. Will admitted that he was in Kansas City the same day (November 22, 1894) that brother George showed up at the Kansas City Wells Fargo Express office and sent those phony money packets to himself. Will, however, denied that he knew that George was in Kansas City that day, denied that he was the man who accompanied George to the Wells Fargo office in Kansas City, and contended that he hadn't even seen George in the previous eleven years.

Nevertheless, the key question remained unanswered: If, as Will contended, he was not the man who had accompanied George to the Wells Fargo office that fateful day when George posted the phony money packets, then why didn't he take the stand in brother George's trial and attack the credibility of Arrington and McKenzie—as he did later during the trial of Jim Harbolt and now during the trial of Joe Blake?

Later, during the telling of this tale, when we fit all the pieces of the puzzle together, we will discover the truth, the whole truth, and nothing but the truth, illuminating the real reason that Will declined to take the stand and testify during his brother's trial. And what a stunner that will be.

It didn't take the Clarendon jury very long to ignore Joe Blake's defense and find him guilty of murder and sentence him to life in prison. He appealed. The Court of Criminal Appeals, as it had done in the Harbolt case, reversed the conviction and sent it back to the district court for a retrial.[5]

What was the fatal flaw in Blake's conviction? In furtherance of Blake's alibi defense, he called a number of live witnesses from Oklahoma Territory to testify that he was elsewhere at the time of the shooting. In addition, Blake's defense lawyers had taken pretrial depositions (via written interrogatories) of three of his buddies to be introduced into evidence at the trial. Those three defense witnesses included D County attorney George Sexton, Lenora rancher Big Jim Riley, and Taloga saloon keeper M. K. McFadden. However, during the trial the prosecution objected to the admission of these written interrogatories into evidence because the state contended that there was a technical defect in the taking of them. The trial court ruled for the state, and they were excluded.

The appellate court agreed with the prosecution that there was a defect in the taking of these interrogatories, but it held that the trial court erred in granting the prosecution's motion to exclude them because the state had not raised its objections in a timely manner. The appellate court held, in effect, that the state had unfairly "laid behind the log" and thus ambushed the defense by waiting until the day of trial to make its objection. Therefore, the case was reversed and a retrial ordered.

The Retrials of Jim Harbolt and Joe Blake

Both cases were retried and achieved identical results: not guilty. Harbolt was acquitted August 14, 1897; Joe Blake, February 25, 1898. Why? By what strange alchemy did the defense transform the prosecution's gold into the dross of defeat? How did the prosecution manage to lose what appeared to be two easy convictions? How could any jury fail to give due credence to the eyewitness testimony of a host of disinterested witnesses who saw the defendants riding into town, drinking at Paul Hoefle's saloon, and then arriving at the depot moments before the shootout? How could they ignore identifications made by the depot agent? Ignore the dying sheriff's statement? Ignore Cap Arrington's testimony? Ignore the corroborated testimony of Dan McKenzie and his wife? Ignore the damning incrimination in Joe Blake's own handwritten letters?

Perhaps the prosecution's defeat was, in part at least, due to overconfidence; likely the prosecutors believed they had a lay-down hand; likely they didn't go full-throttle in presenting their case; likely they didn't pursue the same slash-and-burn cross-examination of those sleazy alibi witnesses this time. But there was more to it than that.

The defense had obviously beefed up its "alibi" defense considerably. In preparation for the retrial of Jim Harbolt and Joe Blake, both Plemons and Miller had journeyed to the Taloga community and cultivated more impressive alibi witnesses. In addition to the usual platoon of ordinary Oklahoma Territory witnesses, they enlisted alibi witnesses with impressive credentials (at least "impressive" to Texas jurors who were not familiar with Taloga's outlaw saturation and tolerance). The witnesses included John Shumate, a former deputy US marshal, as well as three D County, Oklahoma Territory, officials: Bert Sexton, deputy sheriff; his father, George Sexton, county attorney; and O. L. McClung, probate judge, all four being residents of Taloga. It will be recalled that John Shumate and Bert Sexton had been indicted (though never tried or convicted) by the Hardeman County, Texas, district court for committing perjury in the George Isaacs trial. Years later, Charles Cary, a pioneer Dewey County homesteader and later a teacher and, still later, a Taloga attorney, recalled that the Sextons (George and Bert) and the Shumate brothers (Will and John) "were hand in glove with the outlaws."[6] In any event, Deputy Bert Sexton, County Attorney George Sexton, and Judge O. L. McClung all testified that they saw Jim Harbolt, Joe Blake, and Dan McKenzie (contrary to the latter's testimony) in Taloga on November 22,

1894, the day before Sheriff McGee was murdered. If true, then it would have been impossible for them to ride horseback some ninety miles or more to Canadian, Texas, the next day and arrive there during the afternoon.

It was at this point that the defense unveiled a surprise—a surprise that caught the prosecution flat-footed, evidence that lent credence to the testimony of all those Oklahoma Territory alibi witnesses who claimed that they clearly remembered Harbolt and Blake being in Taloga on November 22, 1894, the reason being that it was the day that a theft case was being tried in the D County Probate Court, presided over by Judge McClung. And, they claimed, County Attorney George Sexton prosecuted the case and George Sexton's son, Bert Sexton, deputy sheriff, was acting as the bailiff. Moreover, Jim Harbolt had testified as a witness, and Joe Blake and Dan McKenzie were present in the courtroom. They referred to D County probate court records to verify their claims. The defense lawyers, however, didn't deem it necessary to actually produce those court records for the prosecution and the jury to inspect.

Although not produced for the jury to examine, the probate court docket entries purported to show that a Lew Herring and a William Kopp were tried on November 22, 1894, in Taloga for the theft of barbed wire and timbers of the value of ten dollars.[7] However, these same court records so heavily relied upon by the defense, had they been produced at the trial, would have made a liar out of County Attorney George Sexton. He testified during the retrials of Blake and Harbolt that *he* had prosecuted the wire theft case. However, the docket entries plainly state that George Sexton did *not* prosecute the case; that in his absence the court appointed a substitute counsel to prosecute the case, the substitute being none other than editor/lawyer and outlaw-friendly Grant Pettyjohn—the same Grant Pettyjohn who had been indicted for suborning perjury during the George Isaacs trial. The records would also have disclosed that George Sexton told another lie. He testified in the retrial of Jim Harbolt that Harbolt had appeared as a witness in the wire theft case in Taloga. The docket book lists all witnesses appearing for both the Territory and the defense, and Jim Harbolt's name does not appear on either list. Neither do the names of Joe Blake or Dan McKenzie.

The prosecution contended that these official records must have been altered, since the trial actually occurred a month later on December 22, 1894. But Judge McClung, George Sexton, and Bert Sexton all stoutly denied that the books were cooked. Nevertheless, even if the records were correct, still, had the prosecution produced them, they would have clearly discredited George Sexton's testimony and cast serious doubt on the testimony of the other alibi witnesses.

Caught by surprise while the trial of Jim Harbolt was already underway and after the prosecution had rested its case, there was not sufficient time, in those days when transportation and communication facilities were so limited, for prosecutors to subpoena and produce those distant, out-of-state court records as well as the custodian of the records, whose testimony would have been necessary to authenticate them. Consequently, the juries in both the Jim Harbolt trial and the ensuing trial of Joe Blake were never able to view those official court records or to hear the cross-examination of their custodian. Thus, both juries were left with only the representation of the alibi witnesses as to the content and authenticity of those records. Since the key alibi witnesses escaped impeachment, the jurors must have believed this array of D County officialdom, or at least the added weight of these "official" alibi witnesses buttressed by misrepresented official court records caused them to have a reasonable doubt of the guilt of the defendants. Result: Joe Blake and Jim Harbolt walked.

Upon further reflection as to the reason for the juries' seemingly inexplicable verdicts of "not guilty" during the second trials of Blake and Harbolt, yet another explanation for their verdicts appears at least possible. The retrials were both held in the same small frontier counties where the first trials were held. As sensational as were these murder trials, there is little doubt but that everyone in those communities was aware of the fact that the defendants had been tried and convicted and then that the appellate court in Austin had reversed those convictions. Unsophisticated as those rural pioneers were in matters of law, they may not have realized that those learned judges in Austin had reversed the convictions on procedural defects and not because the judges had weighed the evidence and thus believed that the defendants were innocent. Therefore, if those learned judges believed that Harbolt and Blake were not guilty—well then, they must not be guilty under the law, and so why should we jurors go through all this time-consuming courthouse nonsense again?

In the 1890s perjury was common, and liars came cheap in the Oklahoma Territory. US Marshal E. D. Nix was fired by the US attorney general when, in 1896, it was discovered that he was more than $100,000 short in his accounts. One report put the shortage at $850,000. A federal inspector was sent to investigate, and in his report Inspector Sheibley asserted that Nix had indeed defrauded the government out of large sums of money, had committed perjury during the investigation, had offered bribes to investigators, had solicited illegal kickbacks from government contractors, had overcharged the government by filing fictitious deputy vouchers, and had set up false bank accounts to hide his chicanery. Nix was removed from his post in Oklahoma Territory as a result of the investigation, but the federal investigator recommended that criminal charges not be pursued despite the overwhelming proof of guilt. It would not be practical to do so, he concluded, explaining, "Testimony in Oklahoma is cheap, many of the witnesses likely to be of service to the government are tainted or have already been impeached in prosecutions for perjury involving almost every land claim in the Territory. . . . Conditions existing in Oklahoma are different and more extreme than those existing in any other district of the United States."[8]

One of the written interrogatories that the trial court erroneously excluded during the first Joe Blake trial contained the testimony of the D County outlaw-friendly rancher Big Jim Riley. In his interrogatory, Riley had provided an alibi for Joe Blake, saying that on November 21 and 22, 1894, M. K. McFadden, Dan McKenzie, and he were all drinking at McFadden's saloon in Taloga. However, in an answer to a cross-interrogatory submitted by the prosecution, Big Jim Riley volunteered some information that may not have seemed particularly significant at the time, but that would later become very important in fitting together the pieces of one of the most intriguing puzzles in this story. Big Jim Riley remarked that he and Joe Blake were good friends and often drank together. Once in the fall of 1894, Joe Blake got drunk and fired off his pistol in Taloga. He was arrested and brought before Justice Shumate and fined; however, since he was still so intoxicated, he was turned over to his friend, Big Jim Riley, who took Blake to the Riley home to sober up. Big Jim Riley added that Joe Blake had worked for him at his ranch and lived with him in his home in August and September 1894. From then until Sheriff McGee was murdered on November 23, 1894, Joe Blake had lived with Big Jim Riley's close neighbor, Dan McKenzie.

Binding Joe Blake and Big Jim Riley together still closer to the date of the murder of Sheriff McGee was Blake's own testimony during his first trial. He testified that he and his friend Big Jim Riley had been on a binge at the

McFadden Saloon in Taloga just two days before the four local citizens spotted the four long riders (Joe Blake, Tulsa Jack Blake, Jim Harbolt, and the mysterious Jim Stanley, that tall, light-complected fellow with sideburns and a light mustache) riding toward Canadian on the afternoon before Sheriff Tom T. McGee was murdered.

CHAPTER FIFTEEN

THE FRED HOFFMAN MURDER TRIAL: TEMPLE HOUSTON'S MAGIC

EL RENO, OKLAHOMA TERRITORY, NOVEMBER 17, 1897

The prosecution's case against young Alfred Son for the cowardly assassination of D County treasurer and law-and-order champion Fred Hoffman looked for all the world like a slam dunk, an open-and-shut case.

The D County grand jury had indicted not only Alfred Son for Hoffman's murder, but also his cousin Bailey Son, Dan McKenzie, Taloga newspaper editor Grant Pettyjohn, and known outlaw Dick Yeager (alias Zip Wyatt). The case against Alfred Son was by far the strongest, and the prosecution elected to try him first. The trial was transferred from Taloga in D County to El Reno in Canadian County, Oklahoma Territory. Judge John C. Tarsney set the trial for February 1896.

In El Reno, away from the outlaws' stronghold in Taloga, the public was outraged at the cowardly nature of the assassination. That outrage was aggravated by the fact that the victim was not some Texas official; Fred Hoffman was one of them. Although the prosecution had no eyewitness to the murder, still, the aggregation of circumstantial evidence was damning. Given the formidable evidence against him, Alfred Son needed the services of a good defense lawyer. Actually, Alfred Son needed the services of a really great trial lawyer to slip the noose that dangled before him.

Alfred Son succeeded in getting a great lawyer. He got the best and the most eloquent, the most overpowering, and the most brilliant criminal defense attorney in West Texas and the Oklahoma Territory: Temple Lea Houston, youngest son of Texas hero Sam Houston. Born August 12, 1860, in the Texas governor's mansion in Austin, Temple became the youngest practicing lawyer in the state of Texas at age eighteen, and in 1882 he was appointed as district attorney of the newly formed 35th Judicial District in the Texas Panhandle, consisting of twenty-six as yet unorganized counties.

Temple Houston was a boozer and a rake to boot. But no one could deny that, in addition to his wild side and his eccentricities, Houston possessed a glib tongue. Before a jury he was a spellbinder without equal, liberally seasoning his arguments with quotations from classical literature and the Bible. In court, Temple cut a dashing figure. Standing six feet plus two inches, he was slender, with gray eyes and auburn hair that flowed in curling locks to his shoulders, all of which was accentuated by his flamboyant attire. Typically, he would appear in an extra long (Prince Albert) frock coat, black cravat, yellow-beaded vest, Spanish-style satin-striped trousers cut with a bell flare at the bottom, and boots of the finest leather. Plus, both in and out of court, he was never without Old Betsy, his pearl-handled .45 pistol. Old Betsy was not merely for show. Houston gained considerable renown as a crack pistol and rifle marksman.

With his famous Houston name, coupled with his native brilliance, charisma, and eloquence—well, politically speaking, the sky would have been the limit in Austin or Washington.[1] But Washington and Austin were much too civilized to suit Temple Houston; he craved the freedom, excitement, and adventure of the untamed wilderness. And, frontier folks took to Temple as much as Temple took to the frontier. When folks heard that "Old Sam's boy" was trying a case, they congregated from miles around to witness the show. The ever-inventive Temple Houston, in addition to his much-celebrated eloquence, usually had a dramatic trick or two up his sleeve. He once succeeded, in 1893, in winning an unwinnable murder trial in Enid with a strategy that had never been attempted before—and hasn't been attempted since, either.[2] He was defending a range cowboy who had been indicted for killing a respected rancher and, even worse, stealing the rancher's horse. Worse yet, during the trial Houston became aware that the prosecution had managed to pack the jury with several close friends of the deceased victim. There was no chance for an acquittal with that jury. Undeterred, however, Houston pressed on.

During his final jury argument, Houston lowered his voice and crept closer and closer to the spellbound jurors. Suddenly, Temple Houston pulled Old Betsy from his frock coat, pointed it directly at the jury, and began firing away—fired all six shots. The terrified jurors bolted from the jury box and joined the spectators in a mad stampede for the nearest exit. The judge dove under the bench.[3]

When order was finally restored and the jurors were reseated, Houston, feigning wide-eyed innocence, explained to the unamused judge that he had only been firing blanks in order to make a self-defense argument. The jury was also not amused and found his client guilty of murder. Undeterred, however, Houston immediately moved for a mistrial—and the judge had to grant it.

At the beginning of the trial the judge had sequestered the jury and issued strict instructions that for the remainder of the trial they were not to communicate or mingle with anyone except other jurors. As Houston pointed out in his motion for mistrial, the judge himself had witnessed the entire jury jump out of the box and mix and mingle with all the spectators. The judge, even more infuriated than ever, had no choice but to grant Houston's motion for a mistrial. Upon retrial, Houston was able to select a much more congenial jury and thus obtain an acquittal.

How did a lowly young cowpuncher such as Alfred Son manage to acquire the services of such a high-powered legal talent? Who bankrolled the attorney's fees? Was it Alfred Son's brother, Lee Moore? Amos Chapman? Big Jim Riley? Will or Sam Isaacs? Or maybe this was not the case at all. Perhaps the terrible plight of young Alfred Son caught Temple Houston's fancy; perhaps the brilliant yet eccentric Houston was lured by the challenge of a near hopeless case, which was enhanced by its inevitable hoopla and publicity.[4] For whatever reason, Houston undertook the defense of Alfred Son.

Defense attorney Houston did have one marked advantage in the Alfred Son trial: his courtroom opponent was an inexperienced D County pioneer lawyer named George E. Black, who was only twenty-one years old at the time. Nevertheless, Black was a bright young man who was not intimidated. D County also hired an older lawyer, Jake McKnight of Thomas, Oklahoma Territory, to assist Black.[5]

Prior to his murder, Fred Hoffman had reported to Wells Fargo officials T. M. Cook and Thomas Smith about mid-January 1895 that he was making

Temple Houston, son of Texas governor Sam Houston and premier defense attorney in turn-of-the-century Texas Panhandle and western Oklahoma Territory, shown about 1884–88. Temple Houston defended Alfred Son when he was tried for the murder of undercover Wells Fargo agent Fred Hoffman. Author's collection.

progress in his investigation of the Woodward and Canadian robberies and that his efforts were directed toward eighteen-year-old Alfred Son and his "near relatives." Alfred Son had only two near relatives in the area at that time: his cousin Bailey Son and his older brother Lee Moore.

Hoffman might have zeroed in on Alfred Son, believing that even if the naïve young cowboy was not directly involved in either robbery, he more than likely knew who the guilty parties were. Hoffman figured that if Alfred were pressured, he might confess his role, if any, or at least implicate the guilty parties. As further events demonstrated, however, this was an ill-conceived strategy; young Alfred Son was much more afraid of the outlaws than the law.

During Alfred Son's trial, prosecutors George Black and Jake McKnight proved that Fred Hoffman had been ambushed and killed on the morning of January 22, 1895, about four miles southwest of Taloga while en route from his home to his office in town—shot first in the heart and then in the mouth. The outlaws also killed Fred's horse. Fred Hoffman was unarmed when he was assassinated.

According to trial testimony, officers at the crime scene observed the tracks of a team and buggy leaving the river road and stopping at the rim of the sandy blowhole at the bottom of which the bodies of Hoffman and his horse were found.[6] Footprints indicated that two people had exited the buggy, walked over to Hoffman's body, and then returned to the buggy, which they drove back to the roadway. One of the sets of footprints leading up to the body was particularly distinct: the footprints were very small and made by a peculiar, sharp-heeled pair of boots. Also, about one hundred feet south of where the buggy stood, the officers discovered the tracks of two more persons leading into and then out of the blowhole.

By fortuitous happenstance, R. Burkhart, a homesteader, and his wife were repairing a fence approximately half a mile away at the time of the shooting. They testified that just before the shooting they had seen Hoffman ford the South Canadian River on his horse at the Brand Crossing and then turn north toward Taloga. They also saw a buggy come down the road from the opposite direction. About the time the parties met, they heard shots. Although they did not see the buggy again, they did see "a party on a gray horse" riding away from the shooting scene and going toward the river crossing that Hoffman had just forded. They were not close enough to identify the rider, however.

Other circumstantial evidence presented at the trial linked Son to the shooting. A few hours before Hoffman was killed, Alfred Son and a man who called himself Bert Collins were seen together in a Taloga saloon. Son became very drunk and shot his revolver into the air. He later bought a box of cartridges for his pistol. Afterward, he and Collins went to a livery stable, where Son rented two horses and a single-seated buggy. He was so drunk, however, that the stable owner attempted to take the buggy and horses back, and he would have done so if Bert Collins had not intervened and assured him that he would make sure the team and buggy were properly cared for. Collins was armed with a revolver and a Winchester rifle. The pair got in the buggy and left, leading a gray horse. They were observed heading southwest along the same river road that Hoffman was traveling toward Taloga. Hoffman was killed about the time he would have encountered Son and Collins on the same road, assuming that they all traveled at a normal pace. Moreover, the homesteader and his wife both identified the buggy that they saw on the day of the murder as the same buggy the livery stable owner testified he had rented to Alfred Son and Bert Collins. Still worse, when Deputy US Marshal Chris Madsen arrested Alfred Son, Son was wearing extra-small, sharp-heeled boots that perfectly matched the tracks observed near Hoffman's body. After the killing, Bert Collins disappeared.

The prosecution rested its case. Temple Houston grasped the baton and undertook Alfred Son's defense. It was based on "coincidence" and "lack of motive." It was just a coincidence, he argued, that Alfred Son happened to be in the vicinity of the killing when Hoffman was murdered by an unknown party—a murder with no eyewitnesses. Actually, Houston contended, Alfred Son was on a completely innocent errand at the time; he was traveling from Taloga to Lenora to retrieve his girlfriend, Minnie Shanholster, and return her to her home in Taloga. Houston produced a note from the young lady addressed to Son requesting that he come to Lenora and take her home, and so, according to Houston, he had rented the buggy on that fateful day to comply with her request. Besides, Houston pointed out, Alfred Son had no motive to kill Hoffman. (The jury was not informed that Fred Hoffman was an undercover agent for Wells Fargo and that his investigation had become focused on Alfred Son and his "near relatives.") The state's case relied heavily on those small, sharp-heeled boot prints observed at the scene of the killing that perfectly matched the boots Alfred Son was wearing when he was arrested.

This was the gist of the first Alfred Son trial. Son barely escaped conviction when the jury hung up at eleven to one in favor of a guilty verdict. The juror who held out for acquittal for three days before the judge declared a mistrial left the courthouse bruised and bandaged, having apparently endured considerable punishment at the hands of his fellow jurors. Straightaway after the trial he mounted up and departed, never to be heard from again in those parts. A question was thus left a-dangling: Did the holdout juror endure such punishment because of an extraordinarily unwavering certainty of conscience, or was he bought and paid for by the outlaws and knew beyond the shadow of a doubt that a much worse fate awaited him if he reneged on his Faustian bargain?

Meanwhile, Son confided to Houston that Bert Collins was the actual killer and that Collins was really the outlaw Red Buck Waightman, but for him to publicly finger Waightman, a notorious killer, would be a serious error in judgment. As Son put it to Houston, he would rather "take the rap than be six feet under." County Attorney George E. Black in his memoirs written years later described Red Buck as "the basest and most cruel outlaw to infest that area," and his rate as a killer-for-hire was well known: fifty dollars per man, cash up front, and no questions asked.[7] The event that followed lends credence to Alfred Son's remark. Prior to Son's trial, Houston received a message from the infamous outlaw himself that directed Houston to meet Red Buck alone and unarmed at night at a designated spot near Seiling, Oklahoma Territory. Houston kept that appointment, and sure enough, standing in the moonlight with a Winchester leveled at Houston was Red Buck Waightman, the auburn-haired, mustached, cold-eyed, gray-horse bandit. He told Houston that he had killed Hoffman and that he "didn't want another man taking credit for my crime."

However noble that sentiment might have sounded, though belatedly expressed, it was apparently not rooted deeply enough to cause Red Buck to come forward and publicly take the blame, thus saving Alfred Son. One wonders if Red Buck's message was really such as stated above, or more believably, a threat: "Don't implicate me—or else!" Houston assured him that his business was only to defend the innocent boy and not to point the finger of guilt at any other identified suspect. With that assurance, Red Buck simply faded back into the darkness.

Houston did keep the outlaw's confidence. He did not mention his rendezvous with Waightman until after Red Buck had been killed in a March 1896 shootout at his hideout near Canute in Custer County, Oklahoma Territory, by a posse led by Deputy US Marshal Joe Ventioner. In fact, before Alfred Son's second trial began in December 1896, the entire Bill Doolin gang had been decimated, the climax of which was the ambush killing of Doolin himself near Ingalls, Oklahoma Territory, on August 25, 1896.

In December 1896, Judge John C. Tarsney presided over Alfred Son's second murder trial at El Reno. The circumstantial evidence case against Son was even more damning this time. In addition to the evidence revealed during the first trial, the prosecution, over Houston's strenuous objections, was permitted to put the two Wells Fargo officials, T. M. Cook and Thomas Smith, on the stand and let them testify that just prior to Hoffman's murder, Hoffman had been employed by Wells Fargo to investigate the attempted robberies at Canadian and Woodward. And again, over Houston's objection, Cook and Smith were allowed to tell the jury that Hoffman had told them his investigation was focusing on the defendant, Alfred Son, and his "near relatives." The Wells Fargo witnesses admitted on cross-examination by Houston that few were aware that Hoffman was engaged in this undercover investigation and that Hoffman's investigation and its focus had never, to their knowledge, been communicated to Alfred Son. The prosecution's purpose in introducing this hearsay evidence (about Hoffman's focusing his investigation on the defendant Son and his relatives) was to demonstrate a motive for Son to kill Hoffman.

The impact of this evidence (when combined with all the other circumstantial evidence tying Son to the crime) was devastating, and the second jury had little difficulty finding young Alfred Son guilty. His punishment was fixed at life imprisonment, and he was sent to prison. Houston appealed to the Oklahoma Territory Supreme Court, and his primary point on appeal was that the trial court had erred in admitting Cook's and Smith's testimony. Houston contended that before the prosecution could attempt to prove that Son had a motive to kill Hoffman, it had the burden of proving that, prior to the killing, Son had knowledge of Hoffman's pending accusation. Otherwise, if Son didn't know of the investigation, how could it be argued that Son had a motive to kill Hoffman? The effect of this testimony was magnified because it called the jury's attention to the Wells Fargo heists at Canadian and Woodward as well as the murder of Sheriff McGee (when otherwise these crimes would have been irrelevant and thus inadmissible), plus it implicated Alfred Son in all the crimes.

The Oklahoma Territory Supreme Court agreed with Houston's argument and reversed the trial court in June 1897.[8] The case was remanded back to the court for yet another trial. Son was returned from prison that August and released on bond pending the third trial that was set for the November 1897 term of court in El Reno. The streets of El Reno were jammed and the courthouse was packed when the Alfred Son murder case was called for trial the third time.

This time, as a result of the appellate court's decision in the second trial, the prosecution was not allowed to inform the jury of Hoffman's investigation or introduce the damming testimony that Alfred Son was their prime suspect. That was the trial court's ruling because the prosecution was still unable to lay the proper predicate for this evidence by proving that Alfred Son, prior to the killing, was aware of Hoffman's potentially incriminating investigation. This omission allowed Houston to run wild in his jury argument, dramatically calling attention to the fact that the Territory had failed to prove any motive for Alfred Son to kill Fred Hoffman. He held the jury spellbound, and the jurors drank in every word. The following is a sample:

> Gentlemen, as I told you in the beginning, the Territory has shown no motive for the commission of such a crime; and we have given you a reasonable—a true—explanation of every act and utterance of the defendant—even for his trip in that fatal direction. He went only to woo-and-win one of the daughters of the land. . . .

> This brave boy asked me to say to you that, to him, honor is dearer than life, and as the old exemplar of purest patriotism thundered in the ears of his country's oppressors, he says in this, his hour of trial, "give me liberty or give me death!" He demands that you free him or inflict the death penalty. . . .
>
> Gentlemen, be just; heed not the perjured fiends who thirst for this boy's blood, and in the years yet to come, when the pall messenger summons you before the court where you shall be tried alongside the kings of the earth, each memorized hour of life shall come back to you with awful distinctness, then happily can you recall that when you judged here, you judged with justice, and in the very spirit of Him who said: "Even as you did it unto the least of these, so you did it unto me. . . ."
>
> He has a Texas home far across the southern prairies, where the skies are a deeper purple, where the dawn has a brighter glow and the sunset wears a softer gold; where midnight stars look down upon us in a more unspeakable splendor. His loved ones, like yours, are waiting—no! no! not like yours—for his life is darkened even now by the awful shadow of death; and who shall tell what he feels?
>
> Gentlemen, break the suspense; dry those tears; bind up these almost broken hearts, for now no power but you can do so. This noble duty done, each hour of your life thereafter will grow proud with this recollection![9]

It didn't take the jury long to acquit the defendant—the verdict was returned on November 17, 1897. It was greeted with wild cheering, and it was reported that, but for the interference of the judge, the crowd would have hoisted the defendant, the defense attorneys, and the jury on their shoulders and paraded them about in the street.

With the collapse of what had appeared to be its strongest case for a conviction in the pending trials for the murder of Fred Hoffman—*The Territory of Oklahoma v. Alfred Son*—along with the understandable reluctance of any D County witness to come forward and "bell the buzzards," the prosecution, deflated, dismissed the indictments against the others: Zip Wyatt (who, by that time, had been hunted down and killed by a group of Anti–Horse Thief Association vigilantes in a cornfield near Enid), Dan McKenzie, Bailey Son, and the ubiquitous Grant Pettyjohn.

While the flamboyant Houston's rhetorical tour de force mesmerized the El Reno jury, the evidence against Alfred Son failed to prove that he was Fred Hoffman's assassin or that he was even a knowing accomplice to the assassination. In the end, about all that the evidence against Alfred Son amounted to was that he was a drunken bystander. Local historians agree that Bert Collins was Red Buck Waightman and that Red Buck was, in fact, the killer. Thus, one of the mysteries in the Wells Fargo scam investigation had been solved: the assassin Red Buck Waightman killed Wells Fargo undercover agent Fred Hoffman. But solving that mystery only created another unsolved mystery: Who hired the assassin to kill Hoffman? That mystery would prove to be a lot more difficult to unravel.

In his memoirs penned years later, prosecutor George E. Black flatly stated: "Red Buck killed Fred Hoffman. Alford [*sic*] Son had no part in it, but was with Red Buck at the time. After Red Buck was killed, Son disclosed the true facts. His final acquittal and release was justified."[10]

However, if Alfred Son disclosed *all* the "true facts," they have not been recorded. Officers found four sets of footprints around the crime scene, indicating that at least two additional men were present. But nowhere is there a mention of the names of the other two parties. Some hints of what must have been going on behind the scenes, as well as the motive for Hoffman's murder, remain. Hoffman was killed, and the killer then took pains to shoot him again in the mouth—a clear message that he was executed not only to silence him but also to discourage anybody else who might get the urge to start wagging his tongue. Nevertheless, the primary motive for the killing was an attempt to cover up someone's involvement in the Canadian and/or Woodward robberies. But who had a motive to cover up these heists? In answering that question, perhaps, in a process of elimination, we should first ask who *didn't* have a motive to cover up his identity as an outlaw?

Bill Doolin, Zip Wyatt, Red Buck Waightman, Tulsa Jack Blake, Bitter Creek Newcomb, Charlie Pierce, and other Doolin gang members were already well known and had sizable bounties on their heads. In fact, they seemed to revel in their respective reputations as brazen outlaws or even in their participation in prior train robberies. For example, the two professional outlaws who relieved the Wells Fargo agent of the army payroll funds during the Woodward heist hadn't bothered to wear masks. These major outlaws didn't give a rip about a coverup of their identity as a known outlaw. Their principal concern was to outrun the posses and avoid bounty hunters. It would seem much more likely that the man in need of a coverup was a man not known as an infamous outlaw, one who was instead a man (or men) of some prominence who was involved behind the scenes as a mastermind or a facilitator, or even a disguised participant. Someone who, for instance, might have concocted the bizarre phony money packet scheme or furnished the cattle George Isaacs shipped to Kansas City, or someone who accompanied George to the Wells Fargo office in Kansas City. Or perhaps he was the fourth long rider, the one who rode behind the Jim Stanley mask the day Sheriff McGee was killed.

County Attorney George E. Black stated that shortly before Hoffman was killed, he had mailed a letter at the Taloga post office addressed to a Wells Fargo official. It contained additional incriminating information discovered during Hoffman's investigation, but it was a letter Wells Fargo never received. According to Black, a D County official named Cicero Davis saw the letter and stole it from the Taloga post office. Black further relates that Davis "took [Hoffman's letter] to a man who lived near Lenora, and he and a man who lived near Seiling together paid Red Buck $500 to kill Hoffman. Lee Moore paid this money to Red Buck, and there was an eyewitness to the payoff."[11]

"The man who lived near Lenora" is a thinly veiled reference to Big Jim Riley, a known outlaw colleague whose ranch headquarters was located about a mile east of Lenora, while "the man who lived near Seiling" is almost certainly a reference to Amos Chapman, whose ranch was located near Seiling. Lee Moore (Alfred Son's brother) was Amos Chapman's ranch foreman and son-in-law. Chapman, Moore, and Riley, close friends and business associates, provided both refuge and fresh horses for the Doolin gang and other outlaws, and they were partners in establishing Taloga's most active saloon, which later became known as the infamous McFadden Saloon, the outlaws' favorite watering hole. Court records reflect numerous charges were brought against Moore during this time for assault, receiving and handling stolen property, public intoxication, carrying a firearm in the city limits, and grand larceny. Although Moore was never convicted of any felonies, D County probate records further reveal that several months after the Fred Hoffman murder, Moore and his famous father-in-law, Amos Chapman, pled guilty to assaulting and pistol-whipping a man in Taloga.[12] County Attorney Black's cryptic report raises the question: What role, if any, did Big Jim Riley, Lee Moore, Amos Chapman, Sam Isaacs, or Will Isaacs play in the Hoffman and McGee murders and the Wells Fargo robberies at Canadian and Woodward?

One of the last questions that remains unanswered is whether the bandits who attempted the Canadian heist were the same ones who, a few months earlier, had pulled off the Woodward caper. Cap Arrington, who was in the best position to answer that question, was convinced that the robberies were the work of two separate gangs. The botched Canadian attempt had all the earmarks of an ill-conceived and sloppy raid executed by amateurs—B-grade wannabes at best. True, Tulsa Jack Blake was one of the four and was a member of Bill Doolin's gang, but he seems to have been the only one who was a real professional, and as Cap Arrington surmised, he most likely was drawn into the scheme by his brother Joe. The Woodward caper, on the other hand, had the earmarks of a professional robbery. It was well planned, carried out successfully with efficiency and dispatch, and without violence. And it netted substantial loot. Although the Woodward station agent had never met Bill Doolin, his description led lawmen to conclude that Bill Doolin was one of the two men who woke him up late that night and forced him to open the station safe.

A later report tended to confirm lawmen's belief that the Woodward robbery was indeed executed by Bill Doolin and company. George E. Black, the D County attorney from 1897 to 1898, later penned this entry in his memoirs: "During my term as County Attorney, Bell Lonnan committed suicide north of Jim Riley's homestead. He rode with the outlaws, unknown to his charming wife, and was in a saloon at Taloga when Red Buck, Bill Doolin and two other outlaws divided up the spoils from the Express robbery at Woodward."[13]

The four long riders from the Oklahoma Territory who perpetrated the Canadian robbery attempt and murder were Jim Harbolt, Joe Blake, Tulsa Jack Blake, and Jim Stanley, the man who never was. But who was the real man behind that mask? It couldn't have been either Sam Isaacs or Will Isaacs, because Will was in Kansas City and Sam was in Canadian during the time that Jim Stanley and the other three long riders were en route from the Oklahoma Territory to Canadian. And why was the D County outlaw community so determined to conceal his true identity at all costs? Nevertheless, bits and pieces of the puzzle were beginning to fit together and frame a portrait.

Meanwhile, back in the Texas penitentiary, dull-witted George Isaacs, the only poor soul who ended up doing time for any of these robberies or murders, was facing a decidedly bleak future, locked away for life behind prison walls.

But then one day George met a very imaginative fellow convict.

CHAPTER SIXTEEN

PARDON ME, PLEASE!

GEORGE ISAACS MEETS THE CONSUMMATE CON MAN

At the bottom of George Isaacs's prisoner intake form was this item: "Expiration of Sentence: ____." That's where the prison official in charge of inmate records filled in the blank with the bleakest of all notations: "Death." The form further revealed that George Isaacs, age thirty-nine, had been received at the state's penitentiary at Rusk, Texas, on August 11, 1897, to begin serving his life sentence, and that all avenues of appealing his conviction had been exhausted.[1]

It appeared to be the end of the line for George Isaacs; it looked for all the world like George was doomed to spend the rest of his life swinging a pick, making very small rocks out of very large rocks, and doing so at the warden's pleasure. There was, however, one last possibility of escaping such a dismal fate: a pardon from the governor of Texas. But what a remote possibility that seemed to be. George Isaacs was about the least appealing candidate for a pardon who had ever heard the Texas prison gate slam shut behind him—he who had been convicted of the unprovoked and greed-motivated murder of a popular sheriff. Besides which, he was also an admitted would-be swindler and a confessed coconspirator with the scum of Oklahoma Territory outlaws.

But then, as we shall soon discover, a lot of funny things can happen when it comes to the business of finagling pardons in the great state of Texas.

★ ★ ★

George Isaacs hadn't endured the harsh regimen of prison life for long when he became acquainted with a fellow inmate named J. W. Brown. Brown had arrived at the penitentiary about the same time that George had, and the two became friends. But what an odd pair they were: J. W. Brown appeared to be everything that poor, dull-witted George wasn't: intelligent, articulate, imaginative, and very audacious—at least when there arose an opportunity to make easy money. That inclination was the underlying cause of his present predicament. J. W. was serving a six-year prison term after having been convicted of swindling with a worthless check. Mr. Brown also had another very pronounced inclination—a fanatical dedication to do whatever it took to avoid any form of physical labor. None of that rock-busting stuff for him. Within a short time after his arrival at Rusk, Brown had talked himself into being classified as a trusty and was assigned a cushy job as bookkeeper in the prison's financial office.

Actually, J. W. Brown was not his real name. His real name was William J. Dent. It had seemed more prudent to introduce himself by a pseudonym when he arrived in the state of Texas in 1896, since under his real name he had previously been convicted of similar felonies in Colorado and Missouri—all by the time he was thirty years old.

William J. Dent was a consummate con man, and only his talent as a forger equaled his talent as a con artist. Those skills were activated and accentuated when fueled by a toddy or two. Folks who had witnessed his work would likely comment, "If you give Dent a drink and a little ink—well, just stand back! No telling what kind of devilment he'll get into."

As unbelievable as were some of Dent's past and future criminal shenanigans, an account of his background would like as not be dismissed by even the most credulous soul as improbable fiction were it not all true and documented. For openers, he was descended from Old South wealth and royalty. His father was a wealthy pioneer from Parkersburg, West Virginia; his first cousin was Confederate Civil War general Stonewall Jackson; as of 1899, one uncle, George W. Atkinson, was governor of West Virginia, and another uncle, John J. Jackson, had served thirty-eight years as judge of the US District Court for the District of West Virginia. His parents died when Dent was a small boy, and he and his two sisters were raised by their aunt, America Small, a very wealthy widow who was among the social elite of West Virginia. The three children received all the advantages that wealth could provide and were well educated, and when William came of age, he and his two sisters divided their father's valuable estate.

Meanwhile, William was a favorite of the social set even though, early on, he displayed a wild and reckless streak. Then, when he received his inheritance, there was no holding William J. Dent back. He went on a booze-fueled binge and an unchecked spending spree. From then on he got into one scrape after another with the law, usually for passing forged or worthless checks. Still, his wealthy aunt, his two sisters, and his uncle, Judge Jackson, in an effort to preserve and defend their esteemed family name from public scandal, stood behind him and bailed him out of all his brushes with the law by covering the worthless checks. At last, a prosecutor in Colorado succeeded in winning a felony conviction against Dent for a forged check, and he was sent to the penitentiary. Once again to salvage the proud Old South family honor, Judge Jackson rode to his rescue and prevailed on the Colorado governor to grant William Dent a pardon. No sooner was he released from prison than he rewarded Judge Jackson's generosity by forging the judge's signature on several thousands of dollars' worth of checks in Saint Louis. For that stunt he was sent to the Missouri penitentiary. Once again the long-suffering Judge Jackson used his influence to secure a pardon, this time from the Missouri governor.[2]

From there Dent was persuaded to return to his aunt's home and undergo treatment for his drinking problem. Another reason that his relatives were sympathetic to William was that he had received a severe lick to his head when a boy, and that had necessitated the insertion of a silver plate in his skull. The family believed that the lingering effects of the head injury, when aggravated by too much alcohol, caused him to become unhinged and go on another wild spree.

Therapeutic as the sedentary life of a reformed Southern gentleman might have been, it was not for William J. Dent. Lounging around the Magnolia-shaded plantation veranda, sipping mint juleps, and basking in the reflected family glory were just too boring. He was geared for life in the fast lane—even before fast lanes were invented. And so, without notice to any of his Old South supporters, he disappeared one day, abandoning his aunt's home of luxury, wealth, and refinement. Several days later, Aunt Small noticed that she was missing jewelry worth about $5,000 ($5,000 in 1890 dollars being worth approximately $128,000 in 2011 dollars). It was also discovered that William had departed in the company of a woman named Ida

Touston. The happy couple, celebrating their new wealth and freedom, fled to Chicago and got married.[3]

In 1896, William J. Dent surfaced in Fort Worth, Texas, sans his bride. (Apparently Aunt Small's jewelry proceeds had been depleted.) William J. Dent introduced himself to folks in Fort Worth as J. W. Brown. He immediately got down to business—funny business. W. J. held himself out as an accountant by trade, claiming that he had fifteen years of schooling in that field. Before long he talked himself into a position as secretary and treasurer of the Flurry Cattle Company.[4] Soon he began drawing sizeable drafts on the company, which, because they were paid, increased his credibility.

On August 26, 1896, he went into a Fort Worth jewelry store and bought a ring for $175. He gave the proprietor a check for that amount on a Missouri bank. Later in the day he came back to the jewelry store, returned the ring, and got his check back. But before he left he suddenly got interested in other jewelry and bought a diamond ring and pin for $500, giving the proprietor a check for that amount on the same Missouri bank. He showed the proprietor a $20,000 certificate of deposit in a Fort Worth bank in favor of the Flurry Cattle Company but explained that since that was firm money he'd prefer to give a check on his own account in the Missouri bank. Of course the check bounced, and W. J. was indicted for swindling. He was tried, convicted and sentenced to ten years in the pen. However, on appeal his conviction was overturned on a technicality.[5]

So W. J. Dent (still going under the pseudonym of J. W. Brown) went merrily upon his diamond-studded way—but not for long. Soon he tried a similar scam, but this time not only did a jury convict him, but the appellate court also got it right. On this appeal Dent had the audacity to argue that conviction should be reversed because he had signed the worthless check J. W. Brown and that was not his real name—so it didn't count. The appellate court, however, summarily disposed of this sophistic nonsense: "This view is too absurd for discussion."[6] And so on March 17, 1898, Dent was off to the state prison for six years, and that is where he met fellow inmate George Isaacs.

As soon as Dent had talked himself into the job as a bookkeeper in the prison's financial office, he immediately launched a vigorous campaign to get himself pardoned. And, as reflected in Dent's prison records (on file in the official Texas State Archives), W. J. pulled out all the stops. He enlisted the support of his illustrious Old South family members. Soon Texas governor

Joseph D. Sayers was being bombarded by letters urging him to pardon their poor, misguided relative.

It would seem that the "name" thing might have presented some problem: that is, urging the governor to pardon W. J. Dent when the prisoner in question had been convicted, and was serving time, under his pseudonym, J. W. Brown. But that was not much of a hill for a stepper like W. J. Dent to climb. Dent himself wrote a letter directly to Governor Sayers explaining that he had been going under the name J. W. Brown since he didn't want to besmirch the name of his honored family back in the Virginias. Yet at another place in the same letter he took a contradictory position, to wit, that he was actually innocent of any wrongdoing in the first place.[7] W. J. was also a couple of clicks shy of passable candor with the governor about another minor matter. Before assuming the pseudonym J. W. Brown and heading for Texas, he had been convicted of those felonies in Colorado and Missouri under his real name—colorful little adventures of which neither the governor nor the prison officials were yet aware.

Dent's plea to the governor was indeed a thing of beauty. He wrote on the official stationery of his boss, William G. Hill, who was the financial agent for J. S. Rice, the Texas prison system's superintendent. The letter itself was long, eloquent, and cleverly worded. He informed Governor Sayers that he had been orphaned at an early age and thus deprived of the "wise guidance and tender care, which a boy can only receive from a mother." He acknowledged that at times in the past he had been "wayward and dissipated" but assured the governor that he had learned his lesson well and was "no longer the careless, thoughtless boy of only a few years ago, but had become a man with a settled purpose . . . to devote the balance of his days to redeeming the follies of the past, to rehabilitating his good name . . . and becoming a respected and useful member of society." W. J. ended his plea for mercy with the following words (words that Governor Sayers would ruefully recall on numerous occasions in the future): "I most solemnly promise by those things which I hold most sacred and holy, by the honor of my family . . . that, should you find it possible to grant the executive clemency asked for, I will never, so long as I live, commit any action which might cause you to feel a pang of regret for having shown mercy which was undeserved. With inward trembling, but with great hope [etc.]."[8]

That accomplished, Dent sent the governor still another letter, this also being written on the stationery of his boss, William G. Hill, and purporting to have been signed by Hill himself. The letter stated that Hill was writing the governor on behalf of prison superintendent Rice, who was "absent." The governor was informed as follows:

> As per request from you, directed to Sup't. J. S. Rice, in regard to convict J. W. Brown, would state that said convict was transferred to my office as bookkeeper. His conduct has been first-class in every particular. He has proven very efficient and attentive to his duties. He evidently has good breeding, and he tells me that his correct name is William J. Dent, and that he abandoned his correct name because he had disgraced his family and name. I write you because Mr. Rice is absent. Brown has every appearance of, and his conduct is that of, a gentleman, and I learn that he has never given officials any trouble since he has been in prison.[9]

Governor Sayers next received two letters directly from Dent's uncle, US District Judge J. J. Jackson of West Virginia, who beseeched Governor Sayers to extend leniency to his nephew. His Honor conceded that Dent's career "has been a wild one," but attributed this to a head injury which, the judge explained, affected Dent's brain so that " the moment he takes a drink, it sets him crazy and his inclination is to be wielding a pen and trying to counterfeit names." Nevertheless, Judge Jackson assured Governor Sayers that Dent came from one of the finest families in the Virginias, that he was "naturally a very kind-hearted man," and that he had now learned his lesson. He added that Dent was seeking a full pardon so that he could "enlist in the public services under the call for soldiers for the Philippine War."[10]

The next luminary to weigh in on W. J.'s behalf was no less than the governor of West Virginia himself, the Honorable George W. Atkinson, who informed Governor Sayers that he had personally known Dent since childhood and attested to the fact that W. J. was "of good stock," being a member of the "the great Jackson family" and first cousin to the legendary Civil War general Stonewall Jackson. Although Dent had "good impulses" and had been "properly reared," Governor Atkinson lamented that Dent had "brought great disgrace to one of our most noted Virginia families." He also attributed W. J.'s "wild methods of living" to his head injury, which, Governor Atkinson speculated, was the cause of Dent's "weakness in forging names."[11]

Governor Sayers finally threw up his hands and yielded to this impressive barrage. On August 28, 1899, slightly more than one year after Dent's arrival at the prison, Governor Sayers granted William J. Dent a full and unconditional pardon.

W. J. was overjoyed when he heard the news of his impending release. But first he had some business to attend to. Dent saw a golden opportunity, and he didn't hesitate to exploit it. He sat down with his good buddy, George Isaacs, and let him in on the good news. By this time, we must assume that Dent had learned that his pal came from a relatively wealthy and supportive family. On the other hand, George was no doubt mightily impressed by Dent's demonstrated political clout. Dent expressed his sorrow that he would soon be forced to leave his dear friend behind. But suddenly it occurred to W. J. that perhaps he could use his political connections to do good old George a favor by also obtaining a pardon for him—all for a mere ten thousand dollars. (Dent probably explained that wheels had to be greased in Austin, since George wasn't descended from Old South royalty back in the Virginias.) In any event, a deal was struck. We may believe, however, with great assurance, that the Isaacs brothers back in Canadian had at least enough sense not to give Dent the ten thousand dollars until *after* the promised pardon was secured.

As soon as the prison gate swung open, Dent hit the ground running—headed straight for Austin. He paid a visit to the governor's office as well as to the office of D. H. Hardy, the secretary of state, but he did not personally appeal to Governor Sayers to pardon his good friend George Isaacs. Instead, assuming yet another fictitious name, he represented himself to be a wealthy Montana rancher and told officials he was interested in the case of another Texas prison inmate—a cowboy from Montana—who was seeking a pardon. He explained that he wanted to protest the granting of that pardon when a hearing was scheduled before the Pardons and Parole Board. Meanwhile, Dent proceeded to ingratiate himself with the secretary of state and other office personnel there and in the governor's office and spent several days sauntering about those offices becoming familiar with all the details and procedures of the pardoning process—as well as the signatures of Governor Sayers and Secretary of State Hardy. Next, Dent borrowed an official envelope from the governor's office addressed to the prison officials. He even secured a typewriter of the same make and with the same color ribbon as the governor used in writing pardons.[12] Finally, W. J. Dent sat down and composed an impressive pardon for George Isaacs and forged the names of Governor Sayers and Secretary of State D. H. Hardy on it. W. J. Dent's composition certainly was an impressive piece of work—of pure fiction, that is, laden with one outrageous whopper stacked on another. (He even revealed that the Texas "sheriff's association" had just passed a resolution demanding that George Isaacs be released since he was innocent, framed by that greedy Wells Fargo outfit.) W. J. Dent's masterpiece reads as follows:

The [Forged] Pardon

Proclamation—by the governor of the state of Texas. No. 5425

To all to whom these presents shall come: Whereas, at the November term, A.D. 1896, of the district court of Hardeman county, Texas, George Isaacs was convicted of the offense of murder and his punishment assessed at confinement in the state penitentiary for life, and whereas the said murder consisted in his being charged as an accessory to the commission of the crime of murder, and whereas Jim Harbolt and Joe Blake, who were indicted as principals in the commission of said crime of murder, were both tried therefore and acquitted, and whereas the person who was killed being at the time of his death sheriff of Hemphill county, made the statement on his death bed that the aforesaid George Isaacs was innocent of any participation in his murder or unlawful knowledge thereof, and whereas at a meeting of the sheriff's association of the state of Texas a resolution was passed by said association declaring its belief in his innocence of said crime of murder and instructing the secretary of said association to transmit a copy thereof to the governor of the state of Texas and on behalf of said association to ask for his pardon, and whereas the Wells-Fargo express company had a large pecuniary interest in his conviction, and it has been satisfactorily and clearly proven that said company, through its agents, was extremely active in securing the same, and whereas his conviction was secured wholly upon circumstantial evidence and there is grave doubt as to his guilt and, whereas the widow of said deceased has always expressed a strong belief in his innocence and has requested his pardon, and whereas the district attorney and sheriff of Hemphill county further state that it is absolutely necessary to have him pardoned, as the real perpetrators of the crime have been apprehended, and without the testimony of said George Isaacs it will be impossible to go into a trial of the cases now pending against them in the district court of Hemphill county, and whereas his pardon has been requested by many reputable citizens of Hardeman and Hemphill counties and has been recommended by the judge before whom he was tried, by the district attorney, by all members of the jury which tried him and by all the county officers of Hardeman and Hemphill counties, and whereas the board of pardons have unanimously recommended the same.

Now, therefore, I, Joseph D. Sayers, governor of Texas, do by virtue of the authority vested in me by the constitution and laws of this state, hereby, for the reasons specified, now on file in the office of the secretary of state, grant the above named convict a full pardon and restore him to full citizenship and the right of suffrage, and his competency to testify in courts of justice.

In testimony whereof, I have hereunto signed my name and caused the seal of state to be hereon impressed, at the city of Austin, this 26th day of September, A.D. 1899.

Joseph D. Sayers
Governor of Texas
D. H. Hardy
Secretary of State[13]

Dent then mailed his masterpiece to Superintendent J. S. Rice at the state penitentiary. The cover letter instructed Superintendent Rice to release inmate George Isaacs forthwith in compliance with the enclosed pardon.

Superintendent Rice received this missive, examined it, and since all appeared to be in order, he, on September 30, 1899 (only a month and two days after he had released Dent), recorded on the official prison records that George Isaacs had been pardoned by the governor and opened the gate. Joyous George, believing the pardon to be genuine (as did brothers Sam and Will Isaacs), hightailed it out of that prison and headed for his old haunts in the Indian Territory and the Canadian, Texas, area, where he openly bragged about his good fortune, proudly displaying his pardon from Governor Sayers. Some of the good folks around Canadian, Texas, were at first flabbergasted and then enraged by the temerity of Governor Sayers in freeing the only one of the outlaws convicted of the murder of their beloved sheriff and doing so after such a brief stint in prison. Their outrage soon reached the ears of the baffled governor, who immediately ordered an investigation.

George Isaacs's prison records were soon changed. The word "pardoned" was scratched out, and the words "Escaped September 30, 1899, by means of a forged pardon" inserted. A warrant was issued for the arrest of George Isaacs. But by that time George (or, more probably, one of his more astute brothers) had already detected the very foul odor of a decaying rodent and anticipated what was about to happen. Therefore, when the warrant for George's arrest arrived in the Panhandle, George was gone—long gone and gone for good. Texas Rangers, meanwhile, spurred on by exhortations from the enraged Governor Sayers, entered the name of George Isaacs in their Most Wanted book (the rangers called it their "Book of Knaves") and roamed far and wide in a frenzied search for long-gone George. Ignoring state boundaries, the rangers scoured eastern New Mexico, Kansas, and Nebraska but returned frustrated and empty-handed.[14]

Governor Sayers and his secretary of state were infuriated when they discovered that they had been bamboozled by some fellow posing as a wealthy Montana rancher. They were also baffled. Who was that guy? Nobody had a clue. Then one day about three months later Governor Sayers received a letter. It was from a woman. The letter began with these words: "If you desire to know all about the liberation of George Isaacs. . . ."[15]

William J. Dent had proved beyond dispute that he was very clever when it came to bamboozling governors, secretaries of state, prison officials, cattle company executives, jewelry store owners, and just about everybody else, but he was not very clever when it came to bamboozling girlfriends. At least not bamboozling them for very long. Apparently Dent's silver tongue had, at first, produced the desired amorous result when he successfully wooed Mrs. W. J. St. Clair in Colorado shortly after his career-crowning triumph in Austin, Texas. Then, in the crimson glow of romance, the lovebirds migrated to Arizona, where, in the afterglow, Dent's attention turned to other matters—or girlfriends. In any event, "hell hath no fury," thus Mrs. St. Clair's letter to Governor Sayers.

The letter was dated December 9, 1899, and posted from Tucson, Arizona. It led to the identification of William J. Dent as the wealthy Montana rancher poser. Plus, the final paragraph read as follows: "It would be well to guard all ports leaving this country for South America and Australia, as George Isaacs intends to sail for one of those places."[16] Texas officials were thus able to capture William J. Dent before he departed Tucson, Arizona. But by the time the Texas lawmen got to Tucson, George Isaacs had already departed. He neglected to leave any forwarding address.

Dent was extradited for a command performance in the Texas courts, where he was afforded the opportunity to explain the matter of the "funny" pardon. As ever, Dent was not at a loss for an explanation: It was not forged at all. Governor Sayers had actually signed it. The problem was that Governor Sayers was so drunk at the time that he just "disremembered" signing it—an explanation that, unsurprisingly, further infuriated Governor Sayers, who was already embarrassed far beyond irate.

Harry Koch was the pioneer newspaperman who owned, published, and edited the *Quanah Tribune-Chief* when, in 1895, George Isaacs was convicted of the murder of Sheriff McGee. Years later, in the February 17, 1931, edition of the *Quanah Tribune-Chief*, Koch wrote some memoirs, including his recollection of the George Isaacs murder trial as well as the ensuing flap about the forged pardon. After giving an account of the murder trial, Koch wrote about the forged pardon episode as follows:

> Dent stoutly maintained that the pardon was genuine, and that he got Sayers to sign it when the old governor was drunk. Judge W. B. Plemons [George Isaacs's defense lawyer] who told me about it said that it was whispered around Austin that Sayers did go on a "high lonesome" once in a while, and the Governor, knowing about such talk, was not a little incensed. He swore that if there was any law by which he could have Dent hung, he certainly was going to let him swing for it, and uttered a number of threats that amused Plemons greatly. While Dent was not executed, he did have to board in Huntsville for several years thereafter.

In a strange legal twist, William J. Dent was not indicted for forging an official governmental document (the pardon) as one might have expected. The district attorney obtained an indictment against Dent for being an accessory to murder—the murder of Sheriff Tom McGee in Canadian, Texas, in the foiled Wells Fargo robbery of 1894. This, even though Dent had nothing to do with the incident, nor was he ever, so far as we know, anywhere near Canadian, Texas, in his whole life. Most likely the district attorney went for the jugular in prosecuting Dent due to a little behind-the-scenes arm-twisting from Governor Sayers. The Texas statute then in effect upon which the prosecution relied (Article 86, Texas Penal Code) to indict Dent for being an accessory to the murder of Sheriff McGee read as follows: "An accessory is one who knowing that an offense has been committed, conceals the offender or gives him *any other aid, in order that he may evade* an arrest or trial, or the *execution of his sentence* [my emphasis]."

The punishment prescribed for being an accessory was the same as for the principal. The novel case was called for trial in the Cherokee County,

Joseph D. Sayers, governor of the state of Texas, 1898–1902. Sayers regretted the day in August 1899 when he granted William J. Dent an unconditional pardon and released him from the Texas penitentiary. PICB 07896, reprinted by permission of Austin History Center, Austin Public Library.

Texas, District Court, where W. J. Dent told his tale of the tipsy governor. Perhaps it was the setting (the cold, stern, sober ambience of a court of law being a most uncongenial setting for a con man's performance), but whatever the reason, W. J.'s flimflam artistry failed him. The jury, having considered the evidence, did not believe that Governor Sayers signed George Isaacs's pardon—drunk, sober, or anywhere in between—and so found Dent guilty and decided that since he had cheated the Texas justice system out of Isaacs's life sentence, he might just as well serve it himself.

Dent, of course, appealed. His main point on appeal was that the prosecution (for a purely vindictive motive) had overreached in attempting to stretch the legal definition of "accessory" to unconscionable lengths and considerably beyond the intent of the statute. Such a tortured interpretation of the accessory statute, he argued, resulted in a ridiculous result: that is, convicting Dent, a mere forger at worst, of the murder of a Panhandle sheriff way back in 1894 during an event in which he had absolutely no part. He didn't even know the deceased or any of the parties involved (including George Isaacs) until years afterward.

The appellate court wrestled mightily with this argument, but in the end (albeit in a split decision), it affirmed Dent's conviction.[17] Undoubtedly Gov-

William J. Dent, the consummate con man and forger, perfected his craft by concocting a forged pardon for George Isaacs in August 1899. January 23, 1900, edition of the *Galveston Daily News.*

ernor Sayers must have taken great delight in that result. And so, despite his heavy-hitter connections and famous relatives, William J. Dent was returned to his recently vacated prison cell, this time for life. And when the warden welcomed W. J. Dent to a return visit to the Texas inmate community, he completed a new prisoner intake form, and when he came to the blank following the "Expiration of Sentence" query, he made that same chilling entry he had previously entered on George Isaacs's form: "Death." Ironically, that left William J. Dent, who had never even heard of Sheriff McGee or Fred Hoffman, being the only mortal doing prison time—and a life sentence, at that—for the murders of either Sheriff Tom T. McGee or Wells Fargo undercover agent Fred Hoffman.

Governor Sayers and the prison warden figured that settled the W. J. Dent aggravation once and for all. Forever.

But W. J. Dent didn't see it that way.

The irrepressible Dent was not through just yet. He prudently waited until Governor Sayers exited the Austin stage and then applied to the new governor for a pardon, leaning once again on his long-suffering West Virginia royalty. In May 1911, ten years into Dent's life sentence, Governor O. B. Colquitt, for whatever reasons, granted Dent yet another pardon—even after the Texas authorities had finally learned of Dent's two prior felony convictions in Missouri and Colorado. One is tempted to speculate that Governor Colquitt might have concluded that a murder conviction, carrying an attendant life sentence, was just a bit much in view of the fact that the underlying violation of Texas penal law was the nonviolent forging of an

Flavor of the time. On the same page that the *Galveston Daily News* printed George Isaacs's forged pardon, two advertisements appeared revealing much about the society of that time and place: Dr. T. McGork's liquid "invigorator" tonic and Dr. M. A. McLaughlin's "Perfect Strength" magic electric belt. January 23, 1900, edition of the *Galveston Daily News.*

official document. Maybe he believed ten years of hard time was sufficient punishment for a forger despite Dent's prior record and despite the understandably bilious reaction of his predecessor, Governor Sayers. Whatever, Governor Colquitt's official statement of grounds for granting Dent a pardon read: "Whereas, it appears that Applicant has an Aunt residing in West Virginia, who raised him from an infant, who now pleads for his release on grounds that he has been sufficiently punished for the crime committed, and, if released, will take him to her home and do all in her power to make his reformation complete."

However, Governor Colquitt was somewhat more circumspect than Governor Sayers had been. He did not grant Dent a full pardon—only a conditional pardon, the principal condition being that "he shall go to his Aunt in West Virginia and remain outside of this State."[18]

Meanwhile, rumors persisted that George Isaacs had indeed taken permanent residence somewhere in South America.

Wherever he was, George Isaacs was never heard from again, and so

George (with a little help from his friends and relatives) succeeded in cheating the Texas criminal justice system and never served another day of his life sentence.

Therefore, insofar as the record shows, Texas finally got rid of both George Isaacs and William J. Dent. Perhaps Mr. Dent's "reformation was completed" in West Virginia among his esteemed relatives, and perhaps Mr. Isaacs began earning his livelihood through honest labor somewhere in South America.

Perhaps. Anything is possible.

CHAPTER SEVENTEEN

HERE COMES LIZZIE AGAIN

MORE MURDERS AND MAYHEM

Almost three years had lapsed by the time the US federal court in Chickasha finally called the trial of George Isaacs' wayward wife, Lizzie Isaacs, for being accessory to the murder of Sterling Elder back on May 30, 1895. Both Lizzie and her brother John Ellis had been indicted for shooting their neighbor, Sterling Elder, during a squabble about the use of a common gate between their properties. Lizzie, who was about four months pregnant with son Roy at the time, had gotten into a "fist and skull" catfight with Sterling Elder's wife, Mollie, when brother John ended the dispute by killing Sterling Elder.[1] John Ellis was indicted for murder; Lizzie was indicted for being an accessory to the murder. Both were to be tried in a US district court—Lizzie in Chickasha, Indian Territory, and brother John in Paris, Texas. Lizzie's case was called first, and her trial began on February 1, 1898.

Unfortunately, records of that court for that time frame are no longer available, all having been destroyed in a 1916 fire that burned down the courthouse in Paris, Texas. However, a brief account of Lizzie's trial appeared in the February 11, 1898, edition of the *Daily Oklahoman* and in area weekly newspapers, including the February 24, 1898, edition of the *Purcell Register*, reprinting a story carried in the previous week's edition of the *Chickasha Express* in which the editor commented that the

Lizzie Isaacs murder trial was "the most important case ever tried in this court . . . the verdict of the jury being 'guilty as charged.'" The article continued: "This meant death, but the jury recommended a life sentence. The case was ably prosecuted and ably defended. The verdict of the jury is considered by the outside public as proper, but rather severe. Mrs. Isaacs bore the incidents of the trial with remarkable fortitude, and walked firmly from the courtroom with her baby while a tear in the eye was the only indication of her emotions. The jury was out but a short time."

Lizzie's attorney filed a motion for a new trial. The next week's edition of the *Chickasha Express* reported that the court had granted Lizzie a new trial. She was freed on bond awaiting the new trial, whereupon Lizzie "departed for home."

Lizzie was never retried for the killing of Sterling Elder. An article discovered in the *Shiner (Texas) Gazette* dated October 24, 1900, reported that the Chickasha, Indian Territory, District Court was then in session and that on October 19, 1900, the court "called and dismissed" the case against Lizzie Isaacs. The same article, however, reported that the case against John Ellis for the murder of William Sterling Elder had been tried previously in the Paris, Texas, federal district court and that Ellis had been convicted "and is now serving his sentence." No further information was provided.

We know from official records, however, that John Ellis was not hanged, nor did he die in prison. Death records attest that John Ellis died on November 5, 1934, in Carter County, Oklahoma.

US census records show that in 1900 Lizzie and her two sons (Richard, born in El Reno on April 16, 1892, and Roy, born in El Reno on October 22, 1895) were living in Grady County near Chickasha. By 1910 Lizzie was forty-three years old, and her sons, Dick and Roy, were eighteen and fifteen, respectively. The 1910 federal census reported that they were residents of Custer County, Oklahoma. Rowdy and rambunctious though Lizzie had been, one would have thought that by 1910, after all the ordeals she had been through—that, plus parenthood and age—she would have mellowed. But not Lizzie: older, yes; wiser, maybe; but more mellow, never. Where Lizzie was concerned, epilogue would almost certainly mirror prologue.

Then Lizzie vanished. Nobody seemed to know where she went. If anybody in the Ellis family did know anything about her whereabouts or her subsequent adventures, they weren't talking. The Ellis family obviously felt about their black sheep daughter, Lizzie, the same way the Isaacs family felt about their black sheep brother, George: their scandalous escapades were an intolerable blight on the family name and best be swept under the rug and forgotten—or at least never mentioned in public.

Finally, years later in the 1990s one of Lizzie's descendants, Carol Byrne Morse, of Ardmore, Oklahoma, became determined to find out what happened to Lizzie after the 1898 murder trial in Chickasha. Morse is the great-granddaughter of Lizzie and her first husband, John L. Byrne. None of the older generation would answer any questions about Lizzie. Nevertheless, she had heard a muffled conversation about Lizzie—something about a man having killed Lizzie because she had burned down his barn.[2] That's when Morse checked out the 1900 and 1910 federal censuses of Oklahoma residents. But when she reviewed the 1920 federal census, there was no record of Lizzie or sons Roy or Richard.

At last Morse got her hands on the Ellis family Bible, where births, marriages, and deaths were conscientiously recorded. There was certainly no mention of Lizzie's divorce from John L. Byrne or her subsequent marriage to George Isaacs or her murder conviction or the births of Richard or Roy Isaacs. However, in the place reserved in the family Bible for deaths—the dates, places, circumstances of death, and burial places—Morse did find this brief entry: "Elizabeth, January 6, 191[illegible]." And that was all. The last digit in the date of death entry was blotched. It appeared to have been either a four or a six. At least, Lizzie did make it to the Ellis family Bible—barely.

Carol Morse spent several years conducting an exhaustive search of official records throughout the state of Oklahoma but found nothing—not even Lizzie's place of burial. Finally, in 2006, while I was conducting some historical research on a completely different subject in the small town of Crowell, Texas, thirty-five miles south of the Oklahoma border, a local historian, Mrs. Warren (Jo) Haynie, happened by pure chance to volunteer an unrelated tidbit of information. She remarked, "Yes, we had some pretty sensational killings around here in the early days. One woman caught her husband with another woman and so she burned down his barn to get even with him. That made him so mad he shot her."[3] What a jaw-dropper that remark was.

Subsequent research confirmed the fact that the deceased barn burner was indeed our long-lost Lizzie. She was killed by Thomas Sparks near Crowell on January 6, 1916.

That's when the whole story came unraveled.

Lizzie's youngest sister, Helen Gertrude Ellis, married Thomas N. Sparks on Christmas Day, 1903, in Carter County, Indian Territory. The Sparkses were a prominent and prosperous pioneer family, and several family members subsequently settled in and around the northwest-central Texas town of Crowell in Foard County. Thomas owned a farm several miles southwest of Crowell in the Foard City community. Apparently the marriage went well, and by 1914 Thomas and Helen were the proud parents of four children. But their marriage ended in tragedy when Helen, at age thirty-three, died on April 29, 1915, as a result of complications in childbirth. Their fifth child also died during the birth.[4]

Then along came Lizzie. She soon took up with Sparks and began living with him, going under the name Mrs. Jessie Sparks. She was forty-eight years old, and Sparks was thirty-six. A search of official documents in Texas and Oklahoma failed to uncover any record of a marriage between them or of a divorce between Lizzie and George Isaacs. Nevertheless, they presented themselves to the community as husband and wife. The fact that Lizzie called herself "Jessie" when she moved in with Sparks leads to the conclusion that she was trying to escape her checkered past and save the respectable Sparks family from any embarrassment.

Lizzie and Thomas Sparks did not live happily ever after. The union, whatever its exact nature, was not by any stretch a marriage made in heaven, and it certainly did not last long. On January 3, 1916, an enraged Lizzie burned down Tom Sparks's barn. (It must have been a huge barn, because Sparks had insured it for the enormous sum of four thousand dollars—and that was in 1915 dollars.)[5] What enraged Lizzie? According to Carol Morse, family legend (bolstered by the account of Mrs. Haynie, the local historian) has it that Sparks had exhibited unseemly interest in another woman. Naturally, Lizzie was not about to put up with that kind of monkey business.

So she burned his barn down. Sparks, on the other hand, did not take this barn burning business lightly. The next day he drove into Crowell, filed criminal charges against Lizzie, and had her arrested for arson. But neither Sparks nor the local constabulary could keep the infuriated Lizzie caged for long. She promptly posted bond, borrowed a car, loaded up her son Roy, and raced out to the Sparks farm to confront Tom.

It was a fatal mistake. Sparks ordered them not to get out of the car. Lizzie, of course, was not in any mood to take orders from anybody—and especially not from Tom Sparks. Lizzie and Roy leaped out of the car. Sparks opened fire. He shot Lizzie in the chest with a large-caliber revolver, killing her instantly. Then he opened fire on Roy with a shotgun. Roy was wounded, but not seriously. Sparks was quickly arrested but then released on a five-thousand-dollar bond.[6]

Lizzie was killed on January 6, 1916, less than nine months after her sister, Helen Sparks, died. Roy bought a plot in the Crowell, Texas, cemetery and erected a large and impressive tombstone over her grave. She was buried under the name Jessie Sparks, and the epitaph Roy had carved reads: "No love like a mother's love ever was known." While such an extravagant expression of emotion may not be all that unusual for a child upon the loss of a mother, it hints at another side—perhaps a gentler side—of Lizzie's character. Moving in with Sparks only a few months after her sister's death may well have been motivated, at least in part, by her love and concern for Helen's four small children.

Meanwhile, Tom Sparks was indicted for murder, and the trial was set to begin on April 4, 1916, three months after he killed Lizzie. On that day Lizzie's sons, twenty-year-old Roy and twenty-three-year-old Dick, both of whom were living in Oklahoma City, drove to Crowell to appear as witnesses for the prosecution. But they were not satisfied with playing that supporting role. Roy and Dick decided to personally administer a full measure of Old Testament justice and thus ensure that Tom Sparks paid the ultimate penalty for killing their mother. On April 4, 1916—the day the murder trial was to begin—they confronted Sparks in downtown Crowell in front of the Bank of Crowell, just across the street west of the Foard County courthouse. Both men opened fire on their stepfather, and he was fatally wounded in a hail of bullets.[7] (Family legend has it that Roy and Dick pumped as many as forty-eight slugs into Tom's body.) Although the Bank of Crowell went defunct many years ago, the building still stands, and two bullet indentations can be seen in the granite slab on the building's northeast corner—evidence that Roy or Dick aimed a bit too high and missed their target at least twice. Sparks was also armed, and before falling he once again managed to hit Roy in the arm, but once again the wound was not serious.

Dick and Roy Isaacs were indicted for the murder of Tom Sparks. On November 9, 1916, they were tried jointly in the district court in Crowell. There was a final note of irony in that. The town of Crowell is located only twenty miles south of Quanah, Texas., and it was in the town of Quanah that some twenty-one years earlier (almost to the day) their father, George Isaacs, was tried, convicted, and sentenced to life imprisonment for the murder

Lizzie Byrne Isaacs Sparks seated between her sons by George Isaacs: Richard Isaacs, age twenty-three *(left)*, and Roy Isaacs, age twenty. A few days later, on January 4, 1916, Lizzie was killed by her third husband, Tom Sparks. Courtesy Carol Morse.

of Canadian, Texas, sheriff Tom McGee. Roy and Dick were more fortunate, however. The Foard County jury that heard the murder cases took only eight minutes to declare both of them "not guilty."[8]

Some observers would later wonder why the Isaacs brothers chose to shoot Tom Sparks when he was literally on the steps of the courthouse about to go on trial for murdering their mother. Why kill Tom Sparks *before* the trial? Perhaps they doubted that a Crowell jury would find Sparks guilty and exact a satisfactory sentence. After all, the Sparks family was well respected in the community, while, to put the best face on it, Lizzie's past was checkered. Still, why risk a cell for life or a trip to the gallows by killing Tom Sparks—at least before the trial? Why not wait and see what the court would do to Sparks? Even if a jury acquitted him or imposed only a lenient sentence, the brothers could then bring their pistols into play and exact a full measure of revenge.

Most likely logic had little to do with it, and they gave the possible consequences of their acts little consideration. In that place and time—even after the turn of the century—subliminal echoes of the Old South's Code of Honor still resonated powerfully in the sons of the South and the West. As President Andrew Jackson's mother told him when he was still a boy, there are some crimes so personal and so outrageous that court justice is simply too tepid to yield full satisfaction. By that doctrine, a man—if he is to call himself a man—has to personally avenge the wrong and thus restore honor to himself and his family. Or, as a typical frontiersman might have put it: a man has to kill his own snakes.[9]

And that was the mind-set of the brothers Isaacs. Whatever a judge or a jury might have done to Tom Sparks, it simply would not have been enough. Even if the law hanged him, it would not have been enough. Not enough because the noose would not have been tied, or the trap sprung, by the sons of Lizzie Isaacs.

CHAPTER EIGHTEEN

FITTING THE PIECES TOGETHER

GEORGE ISAACS'S ACCOMPLICES: THE MAN BEHIND JIM STANLEY'S MASK

The tales of George Isaacs and his rambunctious wife, Lizzie, have been told. Yet there remain unanswered three questions: Who were the masterminds behind the ill-fated 1894 attempt to scam Wells Fargo out of twenty-five thousand dollars? Who rode behind the mask of Jim Stanley? And, whoever he was, was the fourth long rider just another Oklahoma Territory outlaw, or was he also a mastermind behind the plot?

It's not difficult to believe that a plan to relieve Wells Fargo of an enormous sum of money (amounting to more than half a million dollars in today's money), and do so in one fell swoop, would have had great appeal to Will and Sam Isaacs, two cowboys who had somehow already managed to become very wealthy very quickly.

Dewey County, Oklahoma, grassroots historian Robert E. "Bob" King spent years studying the Woodward Wells Fargo heist, the Canadian Wells Fargo botched heist, and the murder of Fred Hoffman. He arrived at some conclusions he considered obvious and beyond doubt. He wrote: "In my mind there is no doubt that Sam and William [Isaacs] were involved in the [Canadian, Texas, Wells Fargo] scheme just as much as [their brother George] but George was the fall guy. He was the black sheep of the family because he was the one that got caught."

Bob King noted that Sam and Will were present on both ends of the money packet shipment: Will Isaacs in Kansas City when it was consigned to Wells Fargo and Sam Isaacs in Canadian when it arrived there. He continues:

> Sam and Will supported Harbolt's defense and even went on his bond, which he jumped. Harbolt was tried after George Isaacs, so why were the Isaacs brothers so interested in trying to get him released? They said at the start they were not paying for his defense but time proved they lied about it. They also paid for Joe Blake's defense and succeeded in getting both men freed at a tremendous sum of money, and not because they were good Samaritans. If the three brothers were in the scheme at the start and George was the fall guy, he and his family were the ones to pay for the foiled robbery, something they have paid for many years. . . . The Isaacs [*sic*] living today would like to forget that poor George ever lived.[1]

King might also have pointed out that there was yet another incentive—and a very powerful one—for Sam and Will to ensure that both Harbolt and Blake kept their mouths shut. If either had revealed that Sam and Will were involved in the plot, then Sam and Will were as much of an accessory to the murder of Sheriff McGee as was brother George.

As historian King did note, however, it was just too much of a coincidence to be dismissed as a mere coincidence that Will Isaacs was in Kansas City when George shipped the money packets to Canadian and that Sam Isaacs was "Johnny-on-the-spot" in Canadian when the packets arrived there. Sam (who claimed he hadn't seen George in seven years) showed up the morning after the bungled robbery attempt at agent A. B. Harding's Wells Fargo office in Canadian, brother George in tow, introducing George to Harding and doing all he could to help shield the phony packets from discovery. First they tried to persuade Harding to ship the incriminating packets back to George in Kansas City. When that didn't work, then Sam took the packets to J. A. Chambers's store and had him lock them in his safe. That only succeeded in delaying the discovery until the next day, when the citizens' committee showed up.

Will, on the other hand, who claimed he hadn't seen George for eleven years, was forced to admit on cross-examination in the Joe Blake trial that he was, in fact, in Kansas City the day George shipped the packets. Although he denied it, he was almost certainly the man whom Wells Fargo Express agent A. A. Rinehart saw with George when George posted the packets. That became clear when Will Isaacs's role as a defense witness played out in the trials of George Isaacs, Jim Harbolt, and Joe Blake. George was tried first. Will did not appear as a defense witness for his brother even though his testimony would have been of critical importance to the defense, since it was designed to cast doubt on the veracity of two key prosecution witnesses: Cap Arrington and Dan McKenzie. (Brother Sam did testify to that effect in the George Isaacs trial.) However, during the subsequent trials of Jim Harbolt and Joe Blake, Will did appear and testify for both defendants. The question was, why didn't Will testify on his own brother's behalf?

There was a very good reason. A. A. Rinehart testified *in person* at the first trial, George Isaacs's trial, and therefore Will Isaacs could not afford to appear in court and risk Rinehart's recognizing him and identifying him as the man who accompanied George Isaacs to his office when George shipped the phony money packets. However, in that day when transportation facilities were slow and expensive, the opposing attorneys agreed after the George Isaacs trial that Rinehart's testimony could be transcribed and then read to the juries in the upcoming trials of Harbolt and Blake, thus avoiding the time, trouble, and expense of having Rinehart make two more trips from Kansas City to Texas. Therefore, since Rinehart was not present during the Harbolt and Blake trials, it was safe for Will Isaacs to appear in person as a defense witness without the risk of being recognized and identified by Rinehart and thus being incriminated as George's accomplice and companion at Rinehart's Kansas City office.

Other strands of circumstantial evidence yoked Sam and Will to the Wells Fargo fiasco in Canadian: Where did George get the cattle he sold in Kansas City to raise the relatively small amount of cash that he stuffed into the Wells Fargo packets? Neither George nor his unsavory associates Jim Harbolt, Joe Blake, or Tulsa Jack Blake owned any cattle. But Sam and Will Isaacs did. Or could the cattle have belonged to the man behind the Jim Stanley mask?

Since George was not a resident of Canadian—hadn't been there for years, if ever—then why did he have the money packets shipped to himself in Canadian? Why not choose a closer destination, one nearer his home in Chickasha? Perhaps Canadian was selected as the destination for a very good reason: because George's brothers lived there. If the scam had gone down as planned, then George's prominent and apparently law-abiding brothers, Sam and Will, would have been available to provide the appearance of legitimacy to the scam when George appeared in the Canadian express office to press his claim against Wells Fargo for his stolen twenty-five thousand dollars.

There were two other reasons to send the packets to Canadian. First, if George had to sue Wells Fargo to collect the twenty-five thousand dollars, it would have been much better—a much more favorable venue—to have filed the lawsuit in a state court in Texas rather than in a federal court in the Oklahoma Territory or the Indian Territory. Second, if George had to press his claim anywhere near Chickasha in the Indian Territory, he would have risked having Deputy US Marshal Luther J. Smith show up and reveal that George had previously tried to enlist his involvement in a similar plot to defraud Wells Fargo in that area.

From the beginning, Captain G. W. Arrington believed that George Isaacs had lied when he blamed the Wells Fargo plot on Bill Doolin and his compatriots. The attempted robbery just didn't have the "feel" of the Doolin gang.[2] As Arrington surmised, Tulsa Jack probably freelanced the Canadian robbery attempt because his brother Joe Blake was involved, and as it turned out, Tulsa Jack was the only member of the Doolin gang who participated. Arrington was equally convinced that Sam and Will Isaacs were somehow involved in the Wells Fargo scam, and he was determined to get to the bottom of the conspiracy and nail all the conspirators. It was also evident to Sam and Will Isaacs that Cap Arrington was on their trail. That's why Sam and Will mounted such a determined effort in the November 1895 election to unseat Cap Arrington as the sheriff of Hemphill County. They were successful in getting their candidate, W. R. Boyd, elected.

Meanwhile, Jim Harbolt had jumped his appearance bond posted by Sam and Will Isaacs and fled to the Indian Territory. He was later recaptured and subsequently returned to the Hemphill County jail in Canadian in December 1896 to await trial for the murder of Sheriff McGee. The trial was scheduled to begin on February 1, 1897—slightly more than a month later. That was the state of affairs when, on the night of January 19, 1897, Jim Harbolt broke out of the Canadian jail—with a little help from friends who slipped him the necessary tools. Will Isaacs's friend, W. R. Boyd, the new sheriff of Hemphill County, was conveniently out of town that night. He was over in Oklahoma supposedly looking after his farming interests.

The incident touched off a firestorm in the Canadian community. *Cana-*

dian Record editor W. S. Defibaugh ran a story on the jailbreak in his January 21, 1897, edition in which he stopped just short of naming Sheriff Boyd and Sam and Will Isaacs as accessories to the escape—an escape apparently engineered to allow Harbolt to avoid a near certain conviction for murder in his impending trial. But when the escape attempt failed, Jim Harbolt once more found the stark specter of the hangman's noose dangling ever closer. Would Harbolt's will power crumble? Would he be tempted to save his own neck by striking a deal with the prosecution to turn state's witness and finger all his criminal associates? That was a risk that Will and Sam Isaacs didn't want to take—couldn't afford to take.

District Judge Baker meanwhile fired off a telegram demanding that Texas adjutant general W. H. Mabry send the Texas Rangers to investigate, informing him that Cap Arrington was "defeated for Sheriff of this county by the influence of Will Isaacs the wealthy brother of George Isaacs." Will Isaacs, Sam Isaacs, and Sheriff W. R. Boyd responded by circulating a petition addressed to Texas governor Charles Culberson disputing Judge Baker's allegations.

After much ado, two Texas Ranger privates were dispatched to conduct an investigation. Meanwhile, Jim Harbolt, half frozen and suffering from pneumonia, showed up at the Canadian home of his friend and supporter, Will Isaacs, and surrendered. Harbolt was returned to jail, but he managed to derail the rangers' investigation by claiming that Dan McKenzie had furnished the escape tools. The rangers—two rookies who were unfamiliar with the background of the case—accepted Harbolt's unsupported testimony, dropped the investigation, and left town. Although McKenzie was charged as an accessory to the jailbreak, he steadfastly denied any part in it and was never tried for it, and it later became obvious that McKenzie had once again served as a handy scapegoat, this time shielding from blame the real culprit who slipped the escape tools to Harbolt. Sam and Will once again had managed to keep out of harm's way.

Jim Cloyd's roots reached deep in Hemphill County. His great-grandparents, E. E. Polly and wife, Kate, settled in a dugout along Monument Creek, a tributary of the Canadian River, in 1874—the first white family to settle in the Panhandle—and in 1887 Polly was elected the first county judge of Hemphill County. Jim Cloyd's father, E. R. Cloyd, served as sheriff of Hemphill County from 1945 to 1949, an office that Jim Cloyd later filled from 1965 to 1972. In

1976 Jim Cloyd was named field inspector for the Texas and Southwestern Cattle Raisers Association as well as being named as a Special Texas Ranger, positions he held until his retirement in 1997. After retirement he continued to live in Canadian.

When I interviewed him in 2003, Jim Cloyd retold the 1894 Wells Fargo story. Cloyd said that the original plan was for George Isaacs's outlaw cronies to hijack the train between Higgins and Canadian, but the outlaws later decided to wait until that night and rob the express office instead. He recounted Cap Arrington's heroic ride the next day following the outlaws' trail into D County, Oklahoma Territory, where he captured Joe Blake.

As to the role that Sam Isaacs and Will Isaacs played in the debacle, Sheriff Cloyd was less forthcoming about details, limiting his comment to this: "They [Will and Sam] were kinda tricky." After a pause, Cloyd amended that last observation: Will, he added, was more than "kinda tricky," he was just "crooked."[3]

In an interview with another local historian who wished to remain anonymous, the interviewee commented that nearly everybody in the Hemphill County, Texas, and D County, Oklahoma Territory, area believed that Sam and Will Isaacs were "in cahoots" with brother George Isaacs in that Wells Fargo plot. In the end—despite all the fingers of circumstantial evidence pointing in their direction—for more than a century the frontier's code of silence insulated Will and Sam Isaacs from any whispers of scandal audible to anyone living outside their tightly knit community.

In later years Will and Sam Isaacs did attempt to safeguard their reputations from exposure to the truth by passing along to family members one whopper of a tale: they claimed they had acquired for a pittance in 1893 a thirty-thousand-acre ranch and four thousand head of cattle at a forced sale on the steps of the Hemphill County courthouse in Canadian. According to Will and Sam, the ranch and cattle had been owned by an Oklahoma Territory cattle baron, William E. Malaley, who had gone bankrupt. That story was later accepted as factual and turned up in print more than half a century later in area histories (as heretofore recounted) and finally in the edition of the 1996 *New Handbook of Texas*. The problem was, as revealed by a search of the official records of Hemphill County, Texas, that family fable was a lie. Although there was indeed a forced sale on the steps of the Hemphill County courthouse in 1893, and Sam and Will did buy some cattle (apparently only seventy-nine head, not four thousand) that had belonged to the bankrupt W. E. Malaley (who had gone broke back in 1886), there was no forced sale of a thirty-thousand-acre ranch to Will and/or Sam Isaacs—not in 1893 or any other year. In fact, William E. Malaley never owned any land in Hemphill County, Texas.

Who was the real outlaw behind the Jim Stanley mask? The Wells Fargo heist at Woodward and the attempted Wells Fargo heist at Canadian, during which Sheriff McGee was murdered, were in fact conducted by separate gangs. Yet when all the bits and pieces of evidence relating to those two depot invasions are assembled with what was later uncovered in the Fred Hoffman murder investigation, it is apparent that there is a connection between the crimes. And when those bits and pieces are fit together, the face behind the Jim Stanley mask comes into focus, and the role he played in the skullduggery becomes clear.

Consider first what we know about the man everyone insisted was Jim Stanley. It is absolutely certain that Jim Stanley was not his real name. We do know that he was one of the four long riders who rode over from the Oklahoma Territory the fateful day that Sheriff McGee was killed; that his companions were Oklahoma Territory hoodlums Jim Harbolt, Joe Blake, and Tulsa Jack Blake. We know that they launched their mission that day from Dan McKenzie's cabin in D County some eighty miles east of Canadian, Texas, and about twenty-five miles west of Taloga and then returned there after the botched robbery attempt, where they met fellow outlaw Bitter Creek Newcomb. We know that Jim Stanley was a tall man--larger than his three long rider companions. All of the outlaws who referred to him always called him Jim Stanley, except once when Joe Blake in his supposedly confidential jailhouse letter to Dan McKenzie referred to him as Tom Brown—another fictitious name. Joe Blake in his letter made oblique reference to him as "the big fellow with sideburns." Dan McKenzie, after he turned state's evidence, described the mystery man as a tall, light-complected man with sideburns. McKenzie's wife, when she also testified for the state, gave the same description. However, we do not have to rely upon the outlaw contingent for that description. J. W. Conaster and Doc Walton, two of the locals who observed the four long riders approaching Canadian on November 22, 1894, agreed that three of the horsemen were small dark-complected men, but the fourth was a tall, light-complected man with sideburns and a light mustache. Doc Walton said the fellow was a large man—large for those times—weighing about 175 or 190 pounds. George Isaacs, who laid the blame on Jim Stanley for masterminding the Wells Fargo scam, told Detective F. J. Dodge that Jim Stanley was a tall, light-complected man, 180–85 pounds, with blue eyes. He denied that Jim Stanley was Bill Doolin. Moreover, Bill Doolin didn't fit the physical description of being a "tall, light-complected man with sideburns and a light mustache" weighing about 180 pounds.

It was more than a little curious that none of the outlaws or outlaw associates gave any further information about Jim Stanley. One wonders why Detective Dodge didn't press George Isaacs for more details when George was making his semiconfession. And why didn't law enforcement or prosecutor Cowan press Dan McKenzie for more information after McKenzie turned state's witness? Likewise, when Joe Blake testified in his case, although denying that he was one of the four outlaws who attempted to rob the Wells Fargo office in Canadian, he nevertheless testified that he had seen Jim Stanley at McKenzie's cabin the night after the botched attempt, adding that he had also seen Jim Stanley previously. Inexplicably, prosecutor Cowan let it go at that. Countless cross-examination questions come to mind: How did you know him? Where did you see him before? What was he doing then? Who was he with? And so on.

All of the above considered, one question begs an answer: Why were the outlaws and their sympathizers so determined to conceal Jim Stanley's actual identity? They exhibited no reluctance in speaking about their acquaintance and association with some of the worst outlaws in the territory and calling their names. George Isaacs, for instance, talked about his association with Bill Doolin. McKenzie also said he knew Bill Doolin, and he had no hesitation in naming Tulsa Jack Blake and Bitter Creek Newcomb and others as houseguests. Known outlaws lounged around McFadden's saloon in downtown Taloga with no fear of being observed or identified as outlaws by other D County residents. So why the secrecy? The answer that readily comes to mind is this: Jim Stanley was not a known outlaw, and he did not want to become known as an outlaw. And he certainly did not want to be identified as one of those responsible for the killing of Sheriff McGee. A further inference is that Jim Stanley was a man of some prominence, wealth, and standing in D County, and he could not afford, at any cost, to have his identity revealed and thus his status compromised. Conversely, Oklahoma outlaws in the area needed the ongoing support of the man behind the Jim Stanley mask—especially those who had been implicated, or who could become implicated, in the Wells Fargo scam or the murder of Sheriff McGee or the murder of undercover agent Fred Hoffman. It was also vital to Will and Sam Isaacs that they have somebody of means to help them shoulder the heavy burden of mounting legal costs in defending Jim Harbolt and Joe Blake. Especially Joe Blake—for reasons soon to come into clearer focus. Jim Harbolt and Joe Blake in particular undoubtedly realized that they would lose their ace in the hole if they identified the man behind the Jim Stanley mask. Then, too, the whole territory had by now heard what had happened to Fred Hoffman when he got the righteous urge to name Oklahoma Territory villains.

Where then does that leave us when it comes to naming suspects who fit the profile? Logic compels the conclusion that the mystery man was a prominent man—probably known as "outlaw friendly" but not somebody known as an active outlaw—and one who was a permanent resident of the Taloga-Seiling area, the home of Dan McKenzie; Jim Harbolt; the Blake brothers; Joe Blake's half-brother, the outlaw Charlie Pierce; and Pierce's running buddy, Bitter Creek Newcomb. (One piece of corroborating evidence: all four of the long riders gathered at Dan McKenzie's home the night before the murder of Sheriff McGee and returned there the next night and stayed there until word was received that McGee was dead.) But who? Who was the prominent resident of the area who might be tempted to step outside his usual role as being merely a friend and sympathizer of known outlaws and ride the owl hoot trail himself for a quick and very lucrative payoff? Two names come to mind. In that respect, let's recall historian Homer Croy's article "Where the Outlaws Hid." The two prominent ranchers in the area who "welcomed the saddle boys" and sometimes shared in the loot were Big Jim Riley and Amos Chapman.[4]

Then recall the recollections of an early-day county attorney of D County, George E. Black, writing about the assassination of Fred Hoffman. Black related that D County official Cicero Davis witnessed Fred Hoffman mailing a letter presumably addressed to his Wells Fargo superiors, a letter that must have contained some very incriminating information. Black stated that Cicero Davis intercepted the letter at the Taloga post office. Black continued: "[Davis] took [Hoffman's letter] to a man who lived near Lenora, and he and a man who lived near Seiling together paid Red Buck [Waightman] $500 to kill Hoffman. Lee Moore paid this money to Red Buck, and there was an eye-witness to the payoff."[5]

"The man who lived near Lenora" is obviously a thinly veiled reference to Big Jim Riley, a known outlaw colleague whose ranch headquarters was located about a mile east of Lenora. He owned a sizable ranch in the area, and at the north end of his ranch he had established an outlaw hideout, a post office, and a store. (See Map 2, D County.) "The man who lived near Seiling" is obviously a thinly veiled reference to Lee Moore's father-in-law, Amos Chapman. Lee Moore was also the foreman of Chapman's ranch as well as the brother of Alfred Son.

If Amos Chapman and Jim Riley each ponied up $250 to silence Fred Hoffman, what secrets were they trying to keep? Fred Hoffman had previously informed his Wells Fargo superiors that his investigation on both the Woodward and Canadian Wells Fargo heists was focusing on Alfred Son and his "near relatives." That intercepted and incriminating letter must have informed authorities that his investigation had implicated others, namely, Big Jim Riley and Amos Chapman. Chapman and Moore were undoubtedly interested in protecting Alfred Son as well as themselves and some other outlaw friends who might get caught up in Hoffman's investigation. Yet Amos Chapman may have had still another reason to silence Fred Hoffman. As Homer Croy noted, Chapman sometimes hosted known outlaws. He and foreman Lee Moore had even constructed a hideout cabin at a remote location on Chapman's ranch for just that purpose. Another interesting historical fact to feed into the mix is this: when, in March 1894, the Doolin gang successfully robbed the Wells Fargo Express office in Woodward of army payroll funds, a posse was organized to track and capture the gang. The posse, however, soon gave up the pursuit and returned, reporting that they had lost the trail in rough country—in D County.

The posse was led by Amos Chapman.

While no evidence was ever uncovered to implicate Amos Chapman in such a scheme to intentionally lose the Woodward bandits, still, to put Amos Chapman, an outlaw-friendly host, in charge of a pursuit of the bandits seems very much like putting the fox in charge of guarding the henhouse. And Woodward is not very far—less than fifty miles—from the outlaw hideout cabin Amos Chapman and Lee Moore had previously constructed on Chapman's ranch.

Was Big Jim Riley the fourth long rider, the one who went under the moniker of "Jim Stanley" to protect his true identity? His actions were consistent with that conclusion. He was the only man in the area who fit the physical description of the large fellow the Canadian-area locals witnessed riding toward Canadian that fateful day. Moreover, Big Jim Riley lived in D County; he was a prominent man, a friend of known outlaws who shielded them from the law; he testified for George Isaacs, Jim Harbolt, and Joe Blake in their murder trials; his ranch headquarters was but a short distance from Dan McKenzie's claim as well as the Blake brothers' claim and not too distant from Jim Harbolt's claim (see Map 3, Wells Fargo Robberies and Murders, 1894–95). By his own sworn admission in answer to written interrogatories in the Joe Blake murder trial, Big Jim was a drinking buddy and close friend of Joe Blake. In fact, during September and October of 1894—shortly before the failed Canadian robbery attempt in November 1894—Joe Blake not only worked for Big Jim Riley at his ranch but also lived with him in his home. Blake then moved to McKenzie's nearby claim in October; that was where he was living at the time of the Canadian depot shootout. Still more circumstantial evidence: during his first trial, Joe Blake testified that he and Big Jim Riley went on a two-day drinking spree in Taloga on the Wednesday and Thursday before Sheriff McGee was killed the following Friday evening.

It was initially thought that Will and Sam Isaacs had employed an expensive battery of attorneys to represent not only brother George and Jim Harbolt, but also Joe Blake during his trials and appeal. In retrospect, however, it seems more probable that it was really Joe Blake's friend, neighbor, and drinking buddy, Big Jim Riley, the wealthy D County rancher, who hired attorneys to defend Blake in his murder trials. That seems more probable yet when it is recalled that a different battery of lawyers represented Joe Blake than those who Sam and Will Isaacs had hired to represent George Isaacs and Jim Harbolt. The conclusion that Big Jim Riley hired Blake's attorneys seems even more compelling if, in fact, Big Jim Riley was that fourth long rider, the one who posed as Jim Stanley.

Although George E. Black, who was county attorney of D County from 1897 to 1898, reported that Big Jim Riley and Amos Chapman paid Red Buck Waightman five hundred dollars to assassinate Fred Hoffman, it is clear that Amos Chapman didn't fit the physical description of the fourth long rider, "Jim Stanley." In addition, by retaining the first name Jim for his fictional character, Riley would have ensured that if anybody slipped and called him Jim it wouldn't be a dead giveaway as to his true identity. Big Jim Riley couldn't afford to become exposed as an outlaw—much less risk getting himself indicted and tried, as had George Isaacs, as an accessory to the murder of Sheriff Tom McGee.

When Detective Fred Dodge interviewed George Isaacs shortly after his

Sam Isaacs, prominent Canadian, Texas, rancher and banker and brother of George Isaacs, about 1900–1910. 227/26-2, reprinted by permission of Panhandle-Plains Historical Museum, Canyon, Texas.

arrest, George inadvertently disclosed another important clue pointing to Big Jim Riley as the man behind the Jim Stanley mask. George said the original plan called for the four outlaws to hijack the train before it got to the Canadian depot. They were supposed to hijack it as it climbed a steep grade between Higgins and Canadian, and then not only rob the Wells Fargo express car, in order to recover his five money packets, but also disguise the real nature of the heist by robbing the passengers as well. But for a reason that George didn't understand at the time of his interview, apparently Jim Stanley had decided to change the plan. No doubt the change was due to the fact that had they gone with the original plan, it would have resulted in a daylight robbery. (Recall that the four long riders arrived in Canadian long before the sun went down. Joe Blake and Jim Harbolt were seen drinking in Paul Hoefle's saloon near the depot about five o'clock in the afternoon. Meanwhile, Tulsa Jack, a known outlaw, and "Jim Stanley" took care to keep well out of sight.) Big Jim Riley apparently had concluded that a daylight robbery of a passenger train that close to his home involved too much risk that some passenger would recognize him. Hence, he decided to lay low, keep out of sight, and wait until after dark to pull off the heist at the de-

Will Isaacs, prominent Canadian, Texas, rancher and banker and brother of George Isaacs, and his wife, Mary Brainard Isaacs, first president of the Pioneer Women of Culture and Charm Club, about 1900–1910. From F. Stanley, *Canadian, Texas: Rodeo Town*, 260, C.

pot. To play it even safer, he would let the other three outlaws execute the robbery while he stayed far away from the depot and held the horses at the stockyards.

To put any lingering doubts to rest, consider that George had not previously hesitated to enlist a nonoutlaw to participate in his Wells Fargo scam. In fact, he had done exactly that back in 1893. During George's murder trial Deputy US Marshal Luther J. Smith testified that George had approached him to participate in exactly the same scam in the Indian Territory.

All the circumstantial evidence points directly to Big Jim Riley as the man behind the Jim Stanley mask—to him and to nobody else.

If the above analysis is correct, then George Isaacs knew that Jim Stanley was a pseudonym for Big Jim Riley, and if he knew that, then so did brothers Sam and Will Isaacs. And they were all aware of it from the conception of the plot. Likewise, Big Jim Riley had to know that George's two brothers were players behind the scene and participants in the scheme to score big from Wells Fargo. Furthermore, at the time the Canadian Wells Fargo plot was hatched, it is also beyond doubt that Sam and Will Isaacs were acquaint-

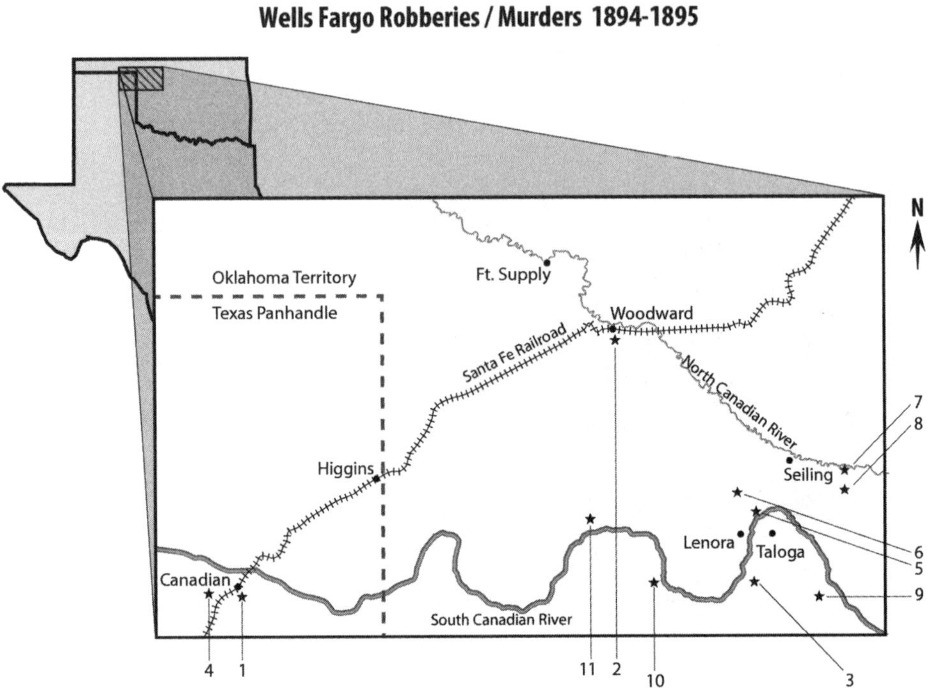

Wells Fargo Robberies / Murders 1894-1895

Map 3. Wells Fargo Robberies and Murders 1894–95

Key to Map Locations

1. Attempted robbery of Wells Fargo and murder of Hemphill County sheriff Tom T. McGee at Santa Fe depot in Canadian, Texas, on November 23, 1894.
2. Robbery of Wells Fargo office in Santa Fe depot in Woodward, Oklahoma Territory, on March 13, 1894.
3. Assassination of Wells Fargo undercover agent Fred Hoffman on January 22, 1895, south of Taloga, Oklahoma Territory.
4. Brothers Sam and Will Isaacs homes in Canadian, Texas, and ranches nearby in Hemphill County, Texas.
5. Headquarters of outlaw-friendly Big Jim Riley, wealthy D County, Oklahoma Territory, rancher.
6. Outlaw hideout on Big Jim Riley's ranch.
7. Amos Chapman/Lee Moore ranch.
8. Outlaw hideout on Amos Chapman ranch.
9. Settler's claim of Jim Harbolt in D County, Oklahoma Territory.
10. Settler's claim of Dan McKenzie in D County, Oklahoma Territory.
11. Settler's claim of Blake brothers (Joe, Sam, and Tulsa Jack) in D County, Oklahoma Territory.

ed with Big Jim Riley. By 1894 all three were wealthy ranchers, and their ranches were located in the same thinly populated area: Sam and Will Isaacs owned a ranch in Hemphill County, Texas, near Canadian, and Big Jim Riley, the second largest rancher in D County, Oklahoma Territory, owned a spread about seventy miles east of Canadian. Also, before Sam and Will Isaacs settled in Hemphill County they both had run cattle for other outfits in the Oklahoma Territory near Riley's place.

Will and Sam Isaacs and Big Jim Riley probably saw the Wells Fargo scheme as a low-risk venture that would yield a high rate of return. Big Jim Riley must have been tempted to briefly step outside his traditional role as merely an outlaw-friendly rancher and reap a bountiful harvest for a short one-day joyride to Canadian escorting three second-string outlaws to pick up a few packets. After all, Bill Doolin and company had made it look like a cakewalk at Woodward.

But the best-laid plans of mice and men sometimes backfire. Big Jim Riley's joyride turned into an expensive nightmare. Most likely Big Jim had to pitch in and help Sam and Will shoulder the heavy load of attorney's fees and other litigation expenses that it took to finance the murder trial defenses for Jim Harbolt and for Big Jim Riley's close friend and drinking buddy Joe Blake.

CHAPTER NINETEEN

STRIVING FOR RESPECTABILITY

SAM AND WILL ISAACS

> *As a result of economic change, Lincoln County [New Mexico] began to turn respectable. Churches, schools, newspapers, and other marks of settled respectability took root. Crime and violence while still common surrendered gradually to more effective sheriffs and judges and to the community's growing insistence on stability, order and security.*
>
> *Not surprisingly, therefore, respectability also overtook many of the Lincoln County warriors of the 1870s. Men who had pursued every crooked, deceitful, devious and lethal means to attain their ambitions or to gratify their whims now emerged as reputable citizens, even as pillars of the business or political community. They suppressed or rationalized the criminal and immoral behavior of their youth and turned to the task of transforming a wild frontier settlement into a model of staid, orderly community life.*
>
> *Robert M. Utley*[1]

After they had achieved prosperity, and after they had avoided an indictment in the McGee murder scandal, Will and Sam Isaacs refocused their attention on achieving respectability. In this endeavor the two brothers were treading down a path that numerous other outlaws on the western frontier had trod.

Although Will and Sam apparently did, during the late nineteenth century, engage in cattle rustling on a grand scale, still wholesale cattle rustling in the Texas Panhandle was not that uncommon, and neither brother served any time in the penitentiary. However, Will and Sam Isaacs took their outlaw careers a whole octave higher when they decided in 1894 to participate with brother George in swindling Wells Fargo out of the whopping sum of more than half a million dollars in today's money, and then compounded their involvement and risk by relying on a gang of second-string Oklahoma Territory armed outlaws to rob the company office at the Canadian depot. Even worse, the resulting murder of Sheriff McGee ratcheted their outlawry to the highest level of criminality: first-degree murder. Under Texas law, had their involvement as behind-the-scenes accomplices in the ill-fated Wells Fargo scheme been exposed, Sam and Will Isaacs would have found themselves facing the same murder indictment that netted brother George a life sentence in the Texas penitentiary. They succeeded in dodging that bullet due to their skillful and determined—and expensive—efforts to avoid exposure.

Even though Will and Sam managed to avoid being indicted, it is clear that Cap Arrington, Judge Baker, editor Defibaugh, and others didn't entertain any serious doubts about their culpability. And comments made by other longtime area residents confirm the belief that many—probably most—of the locals felt that Will and Sam were as much a part of the scheme to defraud Wells Fargo as was George. Witness, for example, the recent comments of others such as the lady who advised the author "not to get into that Isaacs mess," as well as the comments of former Hemphill county sheriff Jim Cloyd, of local historian Robert King, and of others who requested anonymity. That does, however, raise a puzzling question: Why would a substantial number of Hemphill County citizens at the turn of the twentieth century, some of whom were prominent, in effect grant Will and Sam Isaacs a pass even if they believed that the brothers were a part of the plot that ended up in the murder of their popular sheriff who died in the line of duty? At least a part of that answer has to be this: The mores of the western frontier were still potent and gunplay still common. No heritage of violence ingrained as deeply as it had been in the Old West could be overcome easily or quickly. Meanwhile, Will and Sam were by then prominent and wealthy neighbors—ranchers and bankers in the community. If the law couldn't or wouldn't administer justice, then why should a private citizen jeopardize his or her safety, livelihood, or standing in that pioneer community by pointing fingers and voicing accusations? A victim of gunplay could neither harm nor help anybody from the grave. On the other hand, the victor was alive and had to be dealt with. Better to mind one's own business: clamp a lid on the community scandal and get on with the task of trying to make a living in those difficult times. Likely also was the thought that technically, while Will and Sam might have been guilty of murder under the laws of Texas, nevertheless neither Sam nor Will pulled the trigger, neither was present at the scene of the killing, and neither foresaw the likelihood that Sheriff McGee, or anybody else, would be killed. Then, too, nothing could be done at that point to bring the sheriff back to life.

In the end, both Sam and Will Isaacs were able to outlive their outlaw pasts, reinvent themselves, and attain respectability.

For the Isaacs brothers, the first step in achieving their goal was to erase George Isaacs from mind, memory, and print. He just never existed. And neither did Lizzie. *The New Handbook of Texas*, a highly respected and authoritative source, devotes a substantial amount of print to the Isaacs Brothers. Biographical material and histories of the careers of William C., Sam, and John Childress Isaacs are discussed in detail. But nowhere is there to be found any mention of George.[2] More telling still is what is said, and what is not said, in the local county history: *Cowmen and Ladies: A History of Hemphill County*. Surely, one would think, a history of Hemphill County would not be complete without a lengthy article detailing the most sensational crime in the county's history: the murder of its first sheriff in a dramatic shootout with outlaws and the ensuing scandal and murder trials. Not so, however. The county history's account of this sensational event is limited to the following: "On November 30, 1894, Commissioners Court met and approved G. W. Arrington as sheriff to replace Tom T. McGee as sheriff and tax collector. Tom McGee died on the 24th of November 1894 by murder."[3]

At another page in the same local history, the author repeats the fiction that in 1893 Will and brother Sam Isaacs purchased from their employers (presumably Malaley and Forbes) "at a forced sale" thirty thousand acres of land in Hemphill County.[4] As previously noted and documented, the official Hemphill County deed records disprove that statement. There never was such a sale.

Also as previously noted, Jim Cloyd, former Hemphill County sheriff and son of a Canadian pioneer family, made this comment to the author during a September 25, 2003, telephone interview. He said that Sam Isaacs was "sneaky" but that Will Isaacs was "a crook." Then, without further conversation, elaboration, or explanation, he added this: "They stole that ranch."

The three remaining Isaacs brothers—Will, Sam, and John—lived out their lives in Hemphill County, all becoming wealthy ranchers and bankers. John married Viola Bloom of Medicine Lodge, Kansas, in 1898, and they had four children. He continued to operate his ranch on Needmore Creek east of Canadian until his death in 1937 at age seventy-one. John was a past president of the T Anchor Ranch Reunion Association and the Panhandle Old Settler's Association.

For their part, Sam and Will Isaacs struggled hard after the Wells Fargo debacle to become model citizens and, in the end, succeeded in achieving respectability. In 1906 the brothers helped establish the Canadian State Bank with Edward H. Brainard as president, Will as vice president, and Sam as cashier. Will subsequently was president for several years. Brothers Will, Sam, and John Isaacs also organized the Canadian Building and Loan Association.

In 1892 Will married Mary K. Brainard, sister of rancher and banker Ed Brainard. Mary was the first schoolteacher in Canadian. The Mary K. Isaacs school in Canadian is named for her. Will and Mary did not have any children. Will Isaacs died in 1934 at age eighty-one. Mary Isaacs remained active in the Women's Christian Temperance Union and social affairs of Canadian until her death in 1950.

Sam married May Louisa Stevens of Coats, Kansas, in 1907. They had no children. For a number of years Sam and May provided high school boys with room and board at their two-story brick home on Main Street in Canadian in exchange for doing chores around the house. Still later, Sam achieved even greater respectability. He helped establish the Masonic Lodge in Canadian and took an active part in the affairs of the organization. As a Mason he laid the cornerstone of the Panhandle-Plains Historical Museum in Canyon, Texas, in 1932. Sam was not only a founder of that museum, but also a charter member of the Panhandle-Plains Historical Society. Sam Isaacs died in 1943 at age seventy-nine.[5]

EPILOGUE: SUNSET ON THE TRAIL

THE FATE OF THE OTHER SURVIVORS

Nobody was ever convicted for the murder of Fred Hoffman, a crime that cried out for justice—cried out for a conviction and a hard sentence. Yet, in another sense, Fred Hoffman's sacrifice on the altar of law and order was not in vain. The cowardly assassination of Fred Hoffman shocked the community and emboldened law-abiding citizens to champion honest law enforcement and court-administered justice.

By the late 1890s the days of rampant outlawry in Oklahoma Territory were slowly drawing to a close.[1] Until 1892, when the Cheyenne-Arapaho Indian Reservation was opened for settlement, the western part of Oklahoma Territory had been the almost unchallenged domain of outlaws. Even for quite a spell thereafter, as honest settlers rushed in and staked their claims, the outlaws were seldom bothered or reported. The intimidating presence of these violent hard cases was one reason. But there was also another good reason: the hardscrabble settlers had their hands full simply trying to eke out a living and survive. Trouble with outlaws was the last thing they needed, and thus an uneasy truce between the settlers and the outlaws developed during the early settlement years. Dewey County historian Robert E. King calls it "an unwritten treaty," or a "leave-us-alone-and-we'll-leave-you-alone" understanding.

But as time passed, tensions increased. The outlaws became more arrogant, and the settlers became more numerous and more resentful—resentful because many of their county officials were not only unresponsive to their needs but also corrupt and tucked securely in the pockets of the outlaws. Once Fred Hoffman dared to speak out against the outlaw faction—and paid the ultimate price—the "unwritten treaty" was broken. His shocking murder alarmed the ever-increasing number of law-abiding settlers and galvanized them into action. As a result, according to King, within two or three months after Hoffman's murder, the D County settlers formed a vigilante chapter of the Anti–Horse Thief Association. The group never lynched any outlaws, but they did succeed in running a number of thieves out of the country as well as serving as a bridge between "no law" and the fledgling system of "justice under enacted law."[2] In addition to the citizens, deputy US marshals and bounty hunters began taking a toll on the outlaws' numbers.

Within two years of the Hoffman murder, Bill Doolin and the main members of his gang—Bitter Creek Newcomb, Tulsa Jack Blake, Charlie Pierce, Red Buck Waightman, Bill Dalton, Zip Wyatt, and others—were dead by violent means. Jim Harbolt, a killer himself, was killed on December 8, 1903. During one of his drunken holiday binges, Harbolt was shooting up the town in the small burg of Siboney near Lawton, in Tillman County, Oklahoma Territory, when he fired off a couple of celebratory rounds at Oscar Donahoe, a local farmer. Harbolt missed, but Donahoe took it personally. He drew his pistol and fired once. He didn't miss.[3] Grant Pettyjohn got his comeuppance on August 30, 1906, when O. J. Young, a disgruntled speculator in one of Pettyjohn's get-rich-quick schemes, gunned him down on the streets of McCracken, Kansas.[4]

Sam Blake, brother of Tulsa Jack Blake and Joe Blake, was indicted in Hemphill County as an accessory to the murder of Sheriff Tom T. McGee. Before he could be captured he fled the Oklahoma Territory and headed back to his native Missouri. A one-thousand-dollar reward was posted for his capture. He was also wanted for robbing the post office in Independence, Missouri. In May 1895 Sam Blake was sighted in Independence, but once again, before officers could raid his home, he decamped those parts in haste.[5] The only other reference to Sam was a one-liner in the Dewey County, Oklahoma, county history book: "Sam Blake was hanged."[6] Where, when, and by whom, he was hanged was not disclosed. Similarly, no record has been discovered regarding the fate of Sam's brother, Joe Blake, after he narrowly escaped the noose when a jury in Vernon, Texas, found him "not guilty" for the murder of Sheriff McGee in February 1898.

Dan McKenzie, although indicted three times—first for the murder of Wells Fargo undercover agent Fred Hoffman in D County, Oklahoma Territory, in 1895; second for being an accessory to the 1894 murder of Sheriff McGee in Hemphill County, Texas; and finally for assisting Jim Harbolt in his 1897 escape from the Canadian jail—was never tried for any of those offenses. No report of any subsequent adventures of Dan McKenzie has been found.

After three trials, Temple Houston finally succeeded in winning an acquittal for Alfred Son, who had been indicted for the 1895 murder of Wells Fargo undercover agent Fred Hoffman. After his acquittal in 1897, Son left the Oklahoma Territory and went straight. George E. Black, who was on the prosecution team during Son's first trial, served as D County's county attorney from 1897 to 1899. In later years Black wrote his "Dewey County Memories," which appeared in six consecutive weekly editions of the *Taloga Times-Advocate* in 1941. In the May 22, 1941, edition he related a surprise encounter with Alfred Son in 1909 in a saloon in Melrose, New Mexico. Black relates that they shook hands, shared a couple of drinks together, and enjoyed reminiscing about those early days in D County. Then they shook hands again and departed. Black added that he was glad Son was not convicted—that Son was really only an observer and not a participant in the murder of Hoffman. Red Buck Waightman was the hired killer.

The man behind the Jim Stanley mask—whether Big Jim Riley, as compelling circumstantial evidence indicates, or another—never paid the price for the murder of Sheriff McGee or undercover agent Fred Hoffman. Jim Riley died of natural causes at his ranch home near Lenora on December 10, 1903. After Dick and Roy Isaacs were acquitted in 1916 for the killing of Tom Sparks, they went back to Oklahoma and lived long and law-abiding lives. Captain George Washington Arrington, seventy-eight, suffered a heart attack and died in bed at his home in Canadian, Texas, on March 31, 1923. His wife, Sallie, died June 1, 1945. The Arrington family had three sons and six daughters.[7]

That left George Isaacs on the lam—somewhere in parts unknown and free at last, thanks to a forged pardon penned by that consummate con man, William J. Dent, and financed by brothers Sam and Will Isaacs. Ironically, the only man to serve any serious time (ten years as it turned out) on account of the killing of Sheriff McGee was William J. Dent, a man who had never even seen or heard of McGee until several years after the sheriff's death.

Other than that, by hook or by crook or by failure of both the Texas and Oklahoma judicial systems, the cowardly murders of Sheriff Tom T. McGee, a good man and a fine officer, and Fred Hoffman, a brave and honorable champion of law and order, went unavenged.

APPENDIX

DEPUTY TODAY, OUTLAW TOMORROW—AND VICE VERSA

*The [Texas] Pan-handle [*sic*] was full of bad men in the early nineties. Most of them had graduated from other schools of crime and found here a last resort. Some of them—a good many of them—had obtained official positions and were outlaws and deputies by turns. . . . Local authorities, even when conscientious, were poorly equipped to cope with such an element. . . . That was a wild epoch—chaotic and picturesque—a time of individual administration and untempered justice. . . . Next to cattle raising, cattle stealing was the chief industry.*

Captain Bill McDonald, Texas Ranger[1]

As Texas Ranger captain Bill McDonald pointed out in his autobiography, the Texas Panhandle in the last quarter of the nineteenth century was a wild, chaotic, and picturesque place, and some of the most picturesque of those who called it home were "outlaws and deputies by turns." Two of the characters appearing in our main story that snugly fit into that category are John N. Webb and Captain George Washington Arrington. A second look at their careers is informative, interesting, and illustrious of that time and place.

John N. Webb

Wind back the reel of our Wells Fargo scam story to November 23, 1894. John N. Webb was one of the four locals who witnessed the four strangers riding out of the Oklahoma Territory headed toward Canadian the afternoon before Sheriff Tom T. McGee was killed that evening.

While Webb made only a brief appearance along the main trail of our story, his was another side trail that proved not only captivating in and of itself, but also instructive. It tells us much about the life and times of the late nineteenth century and early twentieth century in West Texas, the Texas Panhandle, and the Oklahoma Territory. And that, in turn, reveals much about the motives and actions of our main characters in that time and place. It also illuminates the thin, shifting line between good and evil—between law and lawlessness, between lawmen and outlaws—a shifting line that often seemed to leave only a gray and blurred division between the two.

On the day Webb spied those four long riders headed for their date with infamy at Canadian, he was thirty-eight years old and a resident of Day County, Oklahoma Territory.[2] The county had been formed only two years earlier, in 1892, when it was carved out of the Cheyenne-Arapaho Indian Reservation. (Day County was wedged between Hemphill County, Texas, on its west and D County, Oklahoma Territory, on its east.) During the murder trials of George Isaacs, Jim Harbolt, and Joe Blake, Webb testified about observing the desperadoes approaching Canadian. In retrospect, however, a close examination of his testimony reveals something very peculiar.[3]

As it later turned out, of the four locals who witnessed the approach of the four outlaws, only John Webb testified that he didn't recognize any of them. That seems mighty strange given the fact that both D County and Day County (where Webb was a county commissioner) were not only adjoined but also very thinly populated in 1894. Even more remarkable was the fact that all of the other three locals who observed these strangers riding out of outlaw country with Winchester rifles clearly visible sticking out of their saddle scabbards suspected that they were outlaws up to some kind of mischief, and therefore focused their attention on the men. On the other hand, John Webb—if his testimony is to be believed—apparently paid scant attention to these men and so was not able to give a description of any of them. Instead, Webb seemed fixated on the horses they were riding. He described in detail all four horses: one was a sorrel, one was black, and two were bays. He even noticed that none of the horses were shod except the black horse and that the black horse was shod only on his hind feet. He also noticed that the black horse "turned his hind feet out as he walked." He testified that he could positively identify the horses even if he couldn't identify any of those well-armed strangers. Webb was not even able to identify Jim Harbolt or Joe Blake after they had been arrested and paraded before him. Moreover, if, as we have posited, Big Jim Riley was one of those four riders—the one posing as Jim Stanley—it is impossible to believe that Day County commissioner John N. Webb would not have recognized the most prominent rancher in next-door D County.

It's also worth noting that John Webb, shortly after observing those four long riders approaching, but prior to giving his testimony in the murder cases, packed up and left Day County, Oklahoma Territory, where he had been a county commissioner, and moved to Canadian, Texas. Could it have been that Webb's inability to identify or describe any of the four long riders—except for their horses—earned him some favors from friends in high places?

Webb next appeared in Dublin, Erath County, Texas. On December 29, 1896, he was convicted of having fraudulently signed a bank note and was sentenced to two and one-half years in the Texas penitentiary, but the conviction was overturned on appeal.[4] The next recorded sighting of John Webb was way up in the tip-top of the Texas Panhandle in Dalhart, the county seat of newly formed Dallam County. Apparently he had turned over a new leaf and come down squarely on the side of law and order. When the first term of the district court in Dallam County was convened on November 1903, J. N. Webb was in attendance and listed as the first sheriff of that county.[5] Webb was also the owner of a general store in downtown Dalhart. While sheriff of Dallam County, Webb led a large posse that pursued an outlaw gang that had robbed the No. 4 Rock Island passenger train at Logan, New Mexico. Apparently Sheriff Webb was popular with most, but not all, of his constituents—particularly not with one prominent citizen, Tom Black, "a high-collared gambler with diamonds all over him," the owner of eight saloons and a house of prostitution operated by his wife, Laura. Sheriff John Webb delivered an ultimatum to Tom Black—an Old West ultimatum worthy of John Wayne himself: "Get out of town, or else." Tom Black didn't get. Soon thereafter he was shot dead in front of Webb's store, and John Webb found himself under indictment for Black's murder. However, when the Dallam County jury returned its verdict in Webb's trial on May 25, 1904, the jury foreman announced its verdict: "not guilty." (Years later, when John Webb's son, Claude Webb, lay dying, he confessed that he was the one who had shot and killed Tom Black when he observed Black lying in wait to ambush his father.)[6]

While still the Dallam County sheriff, Webb became involved with "Deacon" Jim Miller. Miller had previous experience as a lawman in Pecos, Texas. In 1891 he had served as a deputy sheriff of Reeves County, Texas, under Sheriff George A. "Bud" Frazer until the sheriff fired him for misconduct and the suspected murder of a prisoner. Deacon Jim was soft-spoken, he dressed in a black suit like a frontier parson decked out for the mayor's funeral, he was well-mannered, and, at least when it suited the image he wished to portray, he attended church. But he fell somewhat shy of sainthood. He was a professional killer: a notorious, cold-blooded, remorseless hit man widely feared by folks all over West Texas as well as the New Mexico and Oklahoma Territories. Deacon Jim Miller was—and still is—a prime suspect in the unsolved 1908 assassination murder of Pat Garrett, the famed lawman who killed Billy the Kid.[7] Before the assassination of Pat Garrett, at least seven men died at Miller's hands between 1896 and 1907, and there were rumors of more.

How John N. Webb, the Dallam County sheriff, became involved with Deacon Jim Miller in 1904 remains a mystery. What we do know is that on March 10, 1904, in the men's room of the Delaware Hotel in Fort Worth, Deacon Jim shot and killed Frank Fore, a detective who was conducting an investigation into Miller's alleged participation in a land fraud scheme. Miller was released on bond the day of the shooting, whereupon he boarded the next train headed for Dalhart, Texas. Later the same day, the trial judge in Fort Worth determined that Miller's bond was insufficient and issued another warrant for his arrest. A Tarrant County deputy tracked Miller down in Dalhart and brought him back to Fort Worth. Later, at a pretrial hearing on Miller's plea for a continuance, he listed John N. Webb, sheriff of Dallam County, as a material witness who was needed when his murder trial was called. Miller claimed that Sheriff Webb had been in a public saloon in Fort Worth just before the killing and had heard Fore threaten to kill Miller. When the case was eventually tried, John Webb did appear as a defense witness for Deacon Jim Miller and testified as predicted. A Fort Worth jury found Deacon Jim not guilty on May 4, 1906.[8]

Meanwhile, back in Dalhart, Sheriff Webb had decided not to run for reelection as sheriff when his term was up in 1905. Instead, he moved his family to El Paso, where he found much more lucrative financial opportunities. He bought cattle for a butcher shop, and he was a partner in the firm of Brock, Webb, and Company, commission brokers. But, as it turned out, this was only his day job. Webb became active in a gigantic Chinese smuggling operation that was booming in El Paso at that time. Webb was a principal in the racket that he operated out of the Coney Island Saloon in El Paso, and his friend Deacon Jim Miller may have been involved. Hundreds of illegal Chinese immigrants were being smuggled into the United States each year by a smoothly operating organization. The organization charged fifty dollars per head for each illegal Chinese immigrant it placed with an American employer.

A man named Carl Adamson and a railroad employee named William Sullivan were associated with John Webb in the Chinese smuggling ring. In June 1908 John Webb, working out of his office in the Coney Island Saloon, rented horses and a covered wagon for Adamson and Sullivan. Shortly thereafter, on June 22, 1908, the pair were arrested near Tularosa, New Mexico, driving that covered wagon, and when immigration authorities removed the cover they discovered sixteen illegal Chinese immigrants.

In November 1908 John Webb, Carl Adamson, and William Sullivan were all indicted by a grand jury at Alamogordo, New Mexico, for conspiracy to smuggle Chinese laborers into the country. In 1909 Adamson and Sullivan were tried and convicted of the charge, but Webb was acquitted. A subsequent investigation revealed that only one juror had initially held out for acquittal of Webb, but finally the other jurors caved in. The investigation also uncovered the fact that the holdout juror was, at the time of the trial, under indictment in Lincoln County for yet another crime. Not only that, but the investigation further revealed that the juror had been bribed.[9]

John N. Webb was never in the news again after that close call. Apparently Webb closed down his shop at the Coney Island Saloon and drifted over the horizon, perhaps retreating into a reborn respectability. He died on February 19, 1935, in Brown County, Texas.

John N. Webb's close friend and associate, Deacon Jim Miller, didn't last near that long. In early 1909 Miller was hired to kill a former lawman and rancher named A. A. "Gus" Bobbit of Ada, Oklahoma. (It will be recalled that Gus Bobbit, while serving as a deputy US marshal in the Indian Territory back in 1896, arrested the fugitive Jim Harbolt, whom Bobbit discovered sleeping in the woods near Pauls Valley.) On February 7, 1909, Deacon Miller ambushed Bobbit on a country lane about six miles southwest of Ada, shooting him twice with a double-barreled shotgun loaded with buckshot. But he bungled the job. He left the dying man lying in agony and fled the scene. Bobbit lingered for about an hour before dying, but before he died he described the assassin to his wife. One of Bobbit's employees also described the killer. Authorities were able to track Miller's horse to a nearby farm. Deacon Miller and three of his cohorts, including Miller's employer, were soon arrested and lodged in the jail in Ada. This time, the enraged citizens of Ada were not about to let Deacon Jim Miller hire the famous Oklahoma defense attorney, Moman Pruiett, or any other defense lawyer, for that matter, and thus persuade fear-crazed jurors to find him not guilty once again. After midnight on April 13, 1909, an irate mob broke into the Ada jail and seized Deacon Jim Miller and his associates, Jesse West, Berry Burrell, and Joe Allen. They dragged the condemned men to a nearby barn, where there were ropes aplenty waiting, and there Deacon Jim Miller finally got his well-deserved comeuppance—quite literally.[10]

John N. Webb was only one of many in the Old West who slipped back and forth between law and lawlessness. As one wag later observed: to find out who was the good guy and who was the bad guy after a gunfight in the Old West, you had to turn the corpse over to see if he was wearing a badge that day.

Captain George Washington Arrington

When the Civil War erupted in 1861, George Washington Arrington was only sixteen years old. Nevertheless, the Alabama lad enlisted in the Confederate army and went through the bloodiest battles of the war, fighting for the Confederacy at both battles of Manassas, at Harpers Ferry, and at Antietam, where he was wounded. Later, he soldiered with Robert E. Lee at the Battle of Gettysburg, and during the retreat from that battle Union forces captured him. He was not imprisoned for long. Arrington escaped and made his way back to Confederate lines. During the last year of the war he was attached to a famous guerrilla band—Colonel John Singleton Mosby's Rangers—where he often did undercover work as a spy.[11]

After the Civil War, Arrington joined the Texas Rangers in 1875 and served for seven years. During those seven years he battled outlaws, Indian raiders, and fugitives from justice along the slowly advancing western frontier of Texas from the Rio Grande Valley all the way north to the Red River. Due to Arrington's fearlessness, audacity, and effectiveness in combat as well as his demonstrated leadership skills, he rose through the ranger ranks from enlisted man to captain of Company C of the Frontier Battalion, leaving him the handle "Cap" Arrington. He resigned from the Texas Rangers in August 1882 but was promptly elected as sheriff of Wheeler County and fourteen other adjoining but as yet unorganized Texas Panhandle counties, in which capacity he served for eight years ending December 31, 1890. In November 1894, Arrington was appointed as sheriff of Hemphill County after its first sheriff, Tom T. McGee, was murdered at the Santa Fe depot in Canadian.[12]

Yet for all of Cap Arrington's heroic deeds as a lawman, his record was not without blemish. To begin with, George Washington Arrington was not his real name. He was born December 23, 1844, bearing the name John C. Orrick Jr.[13] He returned to his hometown of Greensboro, Alabama, after the Civil War, but he was not hailed as a hero. Instead, he waded into a simmering caldron of Reconstruction-era strife and animosity. For reasons not entirely clear, Orrick got into a heated argument on a downtown street with Alex Webb on June 13, 1867. Webb, an African American, was a businessman and a family man, and he had recently been appointed one of the registers for the district of Hale and Greene Counties, Alabama. The dispute escalated. The words became louder and more inflammatory. Orrick abruptly terminated the argument by pulling his pistol and shooting the unarmed Webb three times. Alex Webb fell dead. Orrick walked down the street to his store, pistol in hand.

The violent incident quickly inflamed the black community, and Orrick barely escaped mob justice and a murder indictment by fleeing the state. That's when he changed his name to George Washington Arrington and took refuge in Honduras, a country that did not have an extradition treaty with the United States.[14] In 1870 Arrington surfaced in Galveston, Texas. In 1875 he began his Texas law enforcement career. He never returned to Alabama to face the pending murder indictment.

There would, however, be yet another murder indictment filed against Cap Arrington, and this time he would have to stand trial. In 1887 Arrington was serving as a Panhandle sheriff when he shot and killed John Leverton. Leverton and his brother, George, had previously worked as cowhands for several ranches in West Texas and the Texas Panhandle before starting a small cattle operation of their own in 1884 in the Evans Canyon some forty-five miles north of the Canadian River. Their small spread was located either near or adjacent to two large Panhandle Ranches—the LX and the Turkey Track. A railroad surveyor named B. C. Evans had surveyed the Evans Canyon in about 1882 and built a small rock house there. The house was located on land that the LX Ranch owned, or at least claimed, and in the summer of 1885 the Leverton brothers and their wives moved into that house with the permission of the LX Ranch, with the understanding that they would vacate the house in the fall of that year so the LX could locate its winter camp there. But when fall came the Levertons refused to move out, claiming that the house was actually located on state school land. The LX Ranch took the Levertons to court, claiming trespass, and also sued the brothers for five thousand dollars.

The Leverton incident came to a head in December 1886 when Cape Willingham, general manager of the Turkey Track Ranch, filed a criminal complaint against John Leverton and his brother George, charging them with stealing a calf from the Turkey Track. Earlier that month, a Turkey Track cowboy named Ellington reported to his boss, Willingham, that he had witnessed the Leverton brothers steal an unbranded Turkey Track calf. Ellington said that when the brothers spied him they threatened him, telling Ellington that if he mentioned what he had just seen, "his horse would come in without a rider." One of the Turkey Track cowhands later described John Leverton as being "hot headed, but not a fool"—an assessment that would soon prove to be truly prophetic. But Ellington was not intimidated. He described the encounter to Willingham, and Willingham filed a formal complaint charging the Leverton brothers with theft of a calf. In response to that complaint an arrest warrant was issued and delivered to Sheriff Arrington, who proceeded to form a posse and set out to arrest the Leverton brothers. The posse was led by Arrington and included Cape Willingham and four other men.

What happened next depends on the perspective of the storyteller. According to the ranchers, the Levertons were cattle thieves as well as trespassers. According to the Levertons and their friends, they were small nesters being victimized by those predatory tycoons who wanted to get rid of them—as well as any other nester who intruded on what they considered their territory.[15]

This is the version as told by Cap Arrington, Cape Willingham, and the four possemen: They arrived at the Levertons' cabin shortly before dawn on December 1, 1886. George Leverton had already departed, leaving only brother John, John's wife, and their infant son inside the cabin.

Arrington said that when he and his posse approached the Leverton cabin, a thin spiral of smoke rose from the rock chimney and light flickered through the curtained window. Arrington and his posse silently dismounted. Inside the cabin Leverton's wife was cooking breakfast; Leverton was grinding cinnamon bark at the kitchen table. The baby was in a crib nearby. Leverton was unarmed, although his loaded pistol was hanging on the baby's crib an arm's reach away.

Arrington was armed with a ten-gauge shotgun loaded with double-ought buckshot—a magnum load. The five other posse members were armed with pistols and Winchester rifles. Arrington didn't announce his presence—didn't knock on the cabin door. He cocked the ten-gauge shotgun and kicked open the door.

John Leverton was startled but not stunned. He quickly grabbed his pistol from a holster hanging on the end of his bed and fired point-blank at Arrington. The bullet scorched Arrington's scarf and set it afire. Leverton fired again. The bullet ricocheted off the rock wall behind Arrington, hitting Willingham in the calf of his leg and then burning a scar across the cheek of Leverton's baby. Then Arrington fired his shotgun. Three large shotgun pellets hit Leverton in the shoulder. Leverton fell, momentarily stunned but not mortally wounded. Arrington thought he had killed him. He raced quickly into the back room searching for George Leverton.

Meanwhile, John, bleeding profusely, staggered to his feet and raced outside, heading toward a log crib at the side of the house. Arrington came back into the smoke-filled front room and pursued. He hollered for Leverton to stop.

But Leverton, one arm dangling, turned, fired his pistol, and then kept running.

"Stop!" Arrington again commanded. But Leverton didn't stop. While still running away he kept firing back at the posse. Arrington fired another shotgun blast, and this time John Leverton fell, mortally wounded. Four hours later he died.[16]

His wife, Mollie, the only other eyewitness to the shootout, told John Leverton's story posthumously. She related her version of events to Charles Rudolph, editor of the weekly *Tascosa Pioneer*, an outspoken critic of all big ranchers and their supporters. Rudolph printed the story in three differing versions on December 8, 15, and 29, 1886. The first was an outraged version:

> All six of Arrington's posse burst into the house. Arrington asked if this was Leverton, and upon being answered that it was, fired a shot that took effect in the man's arm. Other shots were fired and Leverton fell to the floor and under the edge of the bed. He had no weapon and was in reach of none. But seeing that his murder was inevitable, his wife endeavored to get him out and arm him for something like a defense. He then fired five shots himself, whether any of them took effect or not is not known. . . . Thirteen shots were said by the brother and brother-in-law of Leverton to have struck him. . . . Arrington read the warrant for Leverton's arrest after the man to be arrested was in a dying condition, shot thirteen times!

Rudolph added the comment that Leverton's murder was "a cold-blooded murder" and "a bloody tragedy . . . which is . . . regarded in but one light by all our citizens and that is . . . horror." As a parting shot, he added that Arrington had "an unsavory reputation" as a lawman.

Before the next week's edition, Rudolph had had the opportunity to hear what Arrington's possemen had to say about the incident. His second take on the Leverton killing stated that the possemen's account was "very different from the story of the surviving Levertons." He continued: "It is made to appear that John Leverton was a cow thief and desperado, and that he invited the first shot by jumping for his weapon while two guns were leveled on him."

Rudolph's third version retreated further and said in effect that perhaps people shouldn't jump to conclusions, but rather should wait until the facts come out during the upcoming trial. The editor did report in his story that both Arrington and Willingham "insisted they would stand trial if indicted, and if not indicted, demand trial."

Arrington and Willingham, as well as the four possemen—Woods Coffee, Rube Hutton, Mack Sanford, and T. N. Adams—were indicted for murder on May 5, 1887, by a grand jury in Oldham County. At the trial the testimony of Arrington, Willingham, and the possemen supported the defense's contention of self-defense—that John Leverton fired the first two shots in the exchange. The only other eyewitness to the encounter was John Leverton's wife. During her uncorroborated testimony she claimed that Arrington intentionally shot an unarmed man "who had no weapon and was not within reach of one," a rather improbable version of the encounter from a biased witness—particularly improbable considering the fact that Willingham was wounded in the initial exchange of fire. Unsurprisingly, both Willingham and Arrington were acquitted by juries on the grounds of self-defense: Willingham was tried in Oldham County in Tascosa, Texas, and Cap Arrington was tried in Donley County in Clarendon, Texas. Arrington was acquitted on July 18, 1887. Charges against the four possemen were dismissed.

Despite the verdict of not guilty, despite the fact that Arrington was not the one who had accused John Leverton of cattle theft, and despite the fact that Arrington's role was that of a lawman who had been handed an arrest warrant that required him to capture Leverton, Arrington was nevertheless singled out by the nester faction as the prime villain. Their supporters also contended, with some merit, that Arrington's tactics in his "botched" attempt to arrest Leverton were questionable. On the other hand, it could be argued that his tactics were designed to avoid any gunplay. Knowing that John Leverton was hot-headed, Arrington might well have concluded that the safest way to capture him without igniting a deadly duel was to suddenly, without warning, kick in the door and immediately confront him with six armed men all pointing weapons at him and order "Hands up!" It was a tactic that would become a common law enforcement practice decades later when a specially-trained police SWAT team was dispatched to confront and arrest a subject believed to be armed and dangerous.

Did John and George Leverton really steal a Turkey Track Ranch calf? Did John Leverton resist a lawful arrest and fire the first shot in an attempt to kill Sheriff Arrington? Did Cap Arrington kill John Leverton in self-defense? In the end, these issues proved secondary to the basic drama underlying the Leverton incident. The killing of John Leverton by Cap Arrington brought to a boiling point a kettle of bitterness that had been simmering for several years between the big ranchers and the settlers. Cap Arrington was viewed by the nester faction as a pawn of the big cattle barons who, by intimidation, threats, and force, were denying them their right to claim a fair share of the Texas Panhandle and South Plains, while John Leverton was viewed as their sacrificial hero. Cap Arrington was viewed by the cattlemen as the protector of their rights against cattle thieves and those who were determined to intrude on their territory, while John Leverton was viewed as another intruder and cattle rustler—this one caught in the act.

However viewed, the killing of John Leverton touched off a storm of controversy between cattle barons and settlers.[17]

Resolution of the Controversy: The Long, Hard Road

When in 1875 Charles Goodnight drove the first herd of longhorns into the Texas Panhandle, it was a wild and lawless land—a land with no lawmen or courts for more than two hundred miles in every direction and no roads or railroads connecting it to the rest of the nation. It was a great cow country. It was also a ready-made haven for hardcases of every stripe, including killers, hardened criminals, hustlers, gamblers, drunks, prostitutes, and fugitives on the run from the law back East who rode in under assumed names. But particularly threatening to the ranchers who followed Goodnight into the Panhandle was the army of major cattle rustlers. Though badly outnumbered, Goodnight and the big ranchers played a heroic role in battling the outlaws. In 1880, to protect themselves from rampant cattle thievery, most of the big ranches joined in organizing the Panhandle Stockman's Association with Goodnight as president. Longtime Amarillo newsman, publisher, and Panhandle historian John C. McCarty later wrote that Goodnight "was the most powerful influence for order and law in the Panhandle."[18]

By 1883, however, times had changed significantly, and Goodnight and the other big ranchers found themselves playing a less than heroic role on another front: opposing cash-strapped settlers who, although poor in the world's goods, were rich in energy and boundless hope, demanding their fair share of the open ranges of the Llano Estacado. In particular, the settlers focused on attempting to settle on small tracts of state-owned land, known as school sections, scattered across the range. (A section of Texas land contains 640 acres.) Many of these school sections were located within the barbed wire–enclosed boundaries of the big ranches. As time passed, the animosity between the big and the small escalated.[19] It was brought to a boiling point when, in December 1886, Cap Arrington shot and killed John Leverton.

The bitter controversy between cattle barons and settlers would subside, but that would take years. Two events proved to be significant milestones in the long, hard road to resolution. First was the coming of the railroads. In 1887 the Fort Worth and Denver City Railroad finally reached the Panhandle. Soon other railroads followed, thus connecting the Texas Panhandle with the rest of the nation. Ready markets for cattle and crops were opened up. Commerce developed, and towns located along the railroad began growing. More immigrants arrived.

The second important milestone was the enactment by the Texas legislature in 1895 of the Four-Sections Act, as amended in 1897.[20] The law enabled small settlers to purchase from the state up to four sections of school land in the western part of the state for one dollar per acre, and that could be paid out over forty years at 3 percent interest. There was, however, one final requirement a settler had to satisfy in order to obtain full legal title to the tract: the settler had to live on the tract of land for at least three years and make improvements on it.

Judge James D. Hamlin, a Panhandle pioneer, in his colorful biography noted that this act "set off an influx of settlers fanning out through the large ranches in decrepit wagons, often containing their families, all their earthly goods, and pulled by tired plow horses."[21]

The Four-Section Act, more than any other factor, brought about settlement of the entire area.[22]

NOTES

Preface

1. Sallie B. Harris, *Cowmen and Ladies: A History of Hemphill County*, 25.

Chapter One

1. *Oklahoma State Capital*, March 14, 1894; Glenn Shirley, *West of Hell's Fringe: Crime, Criminals, and the Federal Peace Officer in Oklahoma Territory, 1889-1907*, 188; Colonel Bailey C. Hanes, *Bill Doolin: Outlaw O.T.*, 139.
2. *Oklahoma Daily Press-Gazette*, March 14, 1894; *Guthrie Daily Leader*, March 14, 1894.
3. *Oklahoma State Capital*, March 13 and 14, 1894.
4. Amos Chapman was not the only casualty of the Buffalo Wallow fight. One of the enlisted men, Private George W. Smith, was killed and Sergeant A. T. Woodhall and Private John Harrington were wounded, although they recovered and resumed their duties. All six men were awarded the Medal of Honor, including Private Smith, posthumously. For a summary of the battle, see H. Allen Anderson, "Buffalo Wallow Fight," Handbook of Texas Online, Texas State Historical Association, http://www.tshaonline.org/handbook/online/articles/btb03. Also see Millie Jones Porter, *Memory Cups of Panhandle Pioneers*, 80–81, wherein the author quotes from J. Evetts Haley's interview of J. E. McAllister, a teamster who had warned Amos Chapman about the Indian threat two days before the attack (July 1, 1926, Panhandle-Plains Historical Museum, Canyon, Texas). See also a biographical sketch of Amos Chapman

in Dewey County Historical Society (DCHS), *Spanning the River: Dewey County Family Histories*, 1:3. For an account of army scout Billy Dixon and his role in the Battle of Adobe Walls, see T. C. Richardson, "Dixon, William," Handbook of Texas Online, Texas State Historical Association, http://www.tshaonline.org/handbook/online/articles/fdi22.

5. Homer Croy, "Where the Outlaws Hid," *True West*, October 1962. See also Robert E. King, "Till the Drums Beat Again: The Fred Hoffman Story," unpublished treatise in the Oklahoma State Archives, Oklahoma City, Oklahoma, 40, 44, 57n87; Robert E. King, interview with the author, Seiling, Oklahoma, March 21, 2003.
6. *Guthrie Daily Leader*, March 15, 1894; MeasuringWorth.com, http://www.measuringworth.com/uscompare.

   One of the staunchest defenders of law and order on the western frontier, Wells Fargo was organized in 1852 initially to speed up shipments from the California gold fields to banking and minting offices back East. By 1870 Wells Fargo had expanded into a network of 396 bank offices, stagecoach routes, and railway express franchises that reached into virtually every cow town and mining camp in the West. Noel M. Loomis, *Wells Fargo: An Illustrated History*.

Chapter Two

1. MeasuringWorth.com, http://www.measuringworth.com/uscompare.
2. Robert J. Chandler, Senior Research Historian, Historical Services, Wells Fargo Bank, email to the author, May 30, 2002. Chandler cites the 1888 Wells Fargo instructions, which were then in effect. Paragraph 221 states, in part: "In delivering money sealed with the 'Public' seal . . . in no case shall [the packet] be opened and contents counted . . . nor will the Company be responsible for any discrepancy in the amount or character of the money."
3. *Cheyenne Sunbeam* (Robert Mills County, Oklahoma Territory), December 1, 1894.
4. Colonel Bailey C. Hanes, *Bill Doolin: Outlaw O.T.*

Chapter Three

1. Testimony of C. W. Jones taken on September 6, 1895, during a habeas corpus hearing on George Isaacs's application for bond in Cause No. 110, *State of Texas v. George Isaacs*, in the 31st Judicial District Court of Hemphill County, Texas.
2. The testimony of J. W. Conaster, John N. Webb, Doc Walton, and Mrs. John Miller, the four local citizens who witnessed the approach of the four Oklahoma Territory outlaws on November 23, 1894, is taken from transcripts of trial testi-

mony in the murder trials of George Isaacs (Cause No. 334 in the 46th Judicial District Court of Hardeman County, Texas); Jim Harbolt (Cause No. 647 in the 46th Judicial District Court of Donley County, Texas); and Joe Blake (Cause No. 939 in the 46th Judicial District Court of Wilbarger County, Texas). The testimony of Mrs. John Miller is taken from page 16 of the Jim Harbolt trial transcript and from pages 17 and 18 of the Joe Blake trial testimony.

3. Sallie B. Harris, *Cowmen and Ladies: A History of Hemphill County*, 7–8. Quote from *Cheyenne Sunbeam*, December 1, 1894. Thomas T. McGee was born on September 13, 1849, in West Virginia. In 1884, after working as a cowboy for a time in Colorado, he accompanied Henry Creswell's CC Bar herd to its new location in Ochiltree County in the northern Texas Panhandle. Later, he worked on the Moody-Andrews PO Ranch in Hemphill County, Texas, and also helped drive herds to Dodge City for several ranchers. In December 1883 he registered his own Quarter Circle brand at Mobeetie. Then, in about 1886, McGee bought William Young's interest in the PO Ranch and became the ranch foreman. When Hemphill County was organized in 1887, with the town of Canadian as its county seat, McGee was elected as its first sheriff. On June 5, 1889, he married Mary Blandy Taylor in Kansas City. With his deputy sheriff, Vastine "Vas" Stickley, as a partner, McGee operated the wagon yard and livery stable in Canadian until 1893. H. Allen Anderson, "McGee, Thomas T.," Handbook of Texas Online, Texas State Historical Association, http://www.tshaonline.org/handbook/online/articles/fmcbz.
4. Walter Prescott Webb, *The Texas Rangers*, 422; John Miller Morris, *A Private in the Texas Rangers: A. T. Miller of Company B, Frontier Battalion*, 90.
5. Walter Prescott Webb, "George W. Arrington: The Iron-Handed Man of the Panhandle," *Panhandle-Plains Historical Review* 8 (1935): 7–20. See also Jerry Sinise, *George Washington Arrington: Civil War Spy, Texas Ranger, Sheriff and Rancher*; Frederick Nolan, *Tascosa: Its Life and Gaudy Times*, 311–12n26; Allen G. Hatley, "Cap Arrington: Adventurer, Ranger and Sheriff," *Wild West*, June 2001, 8; and L. F. Sheffy, "The Arrington Papers," *Panhandle-Plains Historical Review*, no. 1 (1928): 30–66.
6. Sinise, *George Washington Arrington*, 47–51; H. Allen Anderson, "Arrington, George Washington," Handbook of Texas Online, Texas State Historical Association, http://www.tshaonline.org/handbook/online/articles/far20; Mike Cox, *Texas Ranger Tales II*, 105.

As soon as Arrington was sworn in as sheriff, the iron-handed former ranger wasted no time in cleaning up Mobeetie. He made a tour of the saloon and red-light district and announced that the tolerant, easy-going ways of his predecessor were over. No one doubted him, and soon a raft of gamblers, con men, shills, bums, deadbeats, and outlaws decided it in their best interest to vacate Mobeetie. Most of them headed west to Tascosa on the west side of the Panhandle—a community that was not located in Sheriff Arrington's district. The red-light district closed down, and all the prostitutes—ladies of the evening with such colorful frontier titles as Frog Lip Sadie, Rowdy Kate, Gizzard Lip, Homely Ann, Canadian Lilly, Slippery Sue, Midnight Rose, and Box Car Jane—headed for Tascosa, where they joined the sisterhood of ladies in the same profession with equally colorful names, such as Bronco Bride, Mustang May, Pissin' Jenny, and the most famous of them all, Frenchy McCormick, who was destined to become a Tascosa legend. Nolan, *Tascosa*, 140; John L. McCarty, *Maverick Town: The Story of Old Tascosa*, 100.

7. The testimony of G. W. Arrington is summarized here and is taken from the transcript of his testimony in the murder trials of George Isaacs, Jim Harbolt, and Joe Blake as cited above, note 2, this chapter.
8. Testimony of A. B. Harding in *State v. Jim Harbolt*, Cause No. 647 in the 46th Judicial District Court of Donley County, Texas.

Chapter Four

1. George Isaacs, Jim Harbolt, and Joe Blake were all indicted for the murder of Sheriff Tom T. McGee by the 31st Judicial District Court of Hemphill County, Texas, at Canadian, but the murder cases were all transferred on change of venue motions to three separate counties in the 46th Judicial District of Texas: *State v. George Isaacs*, Cause No. 334, Hardeman County; *State v. Jim Harbolt*, No. 647, Donley County; and *State v. Joe Blake*, No. 939, Wilbarger County. All quotations and incidents referred to in this chapter are taken from transcriptions of trial testimony in the Jim Harbolt and Joe Blake murder trials and from summaries of trial testimony contained in the Texas Court of Criminal Appeals opinion in George Isaacs's appeal: *George Isaacs v. State*, 36 Tex.Crim. 505; 38 S.W. 40 (Tex. Ct.Crim.App., 1896).
2. All quotations attributed to Sheriff Tom T. McGee are quoted from testimony of his attending physician, Dr. A. M. Newman: pp. 1–4 in the Joe Blake transcript, pp. 1–3 in the Jim Harbolt transcript, and in *George Isaacs v. State*, 36 Tex.Crim. 505 (1896), 510–11.
3. Jerry Sinise, *George Washington Arrington: Civil War Spy, Texas Ranger, Sheriff and Rancher*, 77.

4. Testimony of Captain George Washington Arrington in the Jim Harbolt transcript, 23–25; in the Joe Blake transcript, 27–31 and 45–46; and in *George Isaacs v. State*, 36 Tex.Crim. 505 (1896), 514–17.

Chapter Five

1. Testimony of A. B. Harding in the Jim Harbolt transcript, 10–11; in the Joe Blake transcript, 10–13; and in *George Isaacs v. State*, 36 Tex.Crim. 505 (1896), 507–9. Testimony of J. A. Chambers in the Jim Harbolt transcript, 11–12; in the Joe Blake transcript, 13–14; and in *George Isaacs v. State*, 36 Tex.Crim. 505 (1896), 513–14.
2. Testimony of D. J. Young in the Jim Harbolt transcript, 12–13; in the Joe Blake transcript, 14–16; and in *George Isaacs v. State*, 36 Tex.Crim. 505 (1896), 514–15.

Chapter Six

1. William (Will or Bill) Conn Isaacs was born in Alabama on December 4, 1853; George W. Isaacs was born in Bosque County, Texas, on November 30, 1858; Samuel Allen Isaacs was born in Bosque County on January 26, 1864; and John Childress Isaacs was born in Bosque County on January 31, 1866. All were sons of Joseph C. and Mary Jack Isaacs. See also H. Allen Anderson "Isaacs Brothers," Handbook of Texas Online, Texas State Historical Association, http://www.tshaonline.org/handbook/online/articles/fis08. Note that by the time this article for the Handbook of Texas Online was written, the Isaacs family had succeeded in publicly disclaiming any kinship with "black sheep" brother George Isaacs.
2. Minnie Timms Harper and George Dewey Harper, *Old Ranches*, 54–56.
3. *Quanah Tribune-Chief*, February 17, 1931.
4. Carol Byrne Morse, interview with the author, August 10, 2004, Ardmore, Oklahoma. The background of the William Rufus and Mary Horton Ellis family as well as the history of Lizzie Ellis Byrne Isaacs up to and through the 1910 federal census was obtained from Carol Morse.

Chapter Seven

1. Testimony of Wells Fargo detective Fred J. Dodge is summarized in the opinion of the Texas Court of Criminal Appeals in *George Isaacs v. State*, 36 Tex.Crim. 505 (1896), 516–19.
2. Ibid., 517–18.
3. Walter Emerson "Jake" Hocker was an intelligent and multitalented man who had a remarkable career. The son of Dr. Phillip S. Hocker, a Missouri druggist, and his second wife, Jake was born March 21, 1869, in Middle Grove, Missouri.

The family migrated to the Indian Territory when Jake was seventeen. His law enforcement career began in June 1891, when he received an appointment as a deputy US marshal for the US Eastern District Court of Texas and for the Indian Territory federal court. In January 1895, US Marshal Sheb Williams deployed Hocker to keep a close watch on George Isaacs, who, it was hoped, would lead lawmen to identify the outlaws, including Jim Stanley, responsible for murdering Sheriff Tom T. McGee. Shortly thereafter, on August 23, 1895, Hocker became involved in a gun battle with outlaws, during which "Black Jack" Bill Christian shot Hocker in the back. The rifle ball passed through his body, barely missing his heart but puncturing a lung. The wound was severe, but Hocker survived. Afterward, he was instrumental in several successful frontier enterprises. In 1906 he married Martha Malone.

In 1907 Hocker was employed by the Anderson Clayton Cotton Company of Memphis, Tennessee, and was sent to Elk City, Oklahoma, where he oversaw the construction and management of a cotton oil mill for the company. He resigned in 1910 to join Wichita Falls, Texas, founding fathers Joseph A. Kemp and Frank Kell in obtaining the right-of-way for and the construction of a railroad from Wichita Falls to Abilene, Texas. In 1911 Hocker began a career in banking. He was instrumental in establishing banks in a number of small towns in Oklahoma. In 1917 he purchased controlling interest in the Farmers State Bank in Elk City and remained its president throughout the remainder of his life. When he died on September 21, 1939, the mayor of Elk City issued a proclamation requesting all business houses to close in honor of Jake Hocker.

Sources on Hocker's biography include Glenn Shirley, *West of Hell's Fringe*, 297; Mike Tower, "Black Jack Shot Lawman Hocker," *Wild West* 20, no. 5 (February, 2008): 20; *Purcell Register*, June 12 and 19, 1891, and August 23 and 30, 1895. Jake Hocker's obituary appeared in the *Elk City Journal*, September 21, 1939, and the obituary of his wife, Martha Malone Hocker, appeared in the *Elk City Journal*, September 15, 1953.

4. *Canadian Record*, March 21 and May 28, 1895.
5. From testimony of George Washington Arrington taken on September 6, 1895, at a hearing on a habeas corpus motion filed by George Isaacs seeking a bail bond, in *State of Texas v. George Isaacs*, Cause No. 110 in the 31st Judicial District Court of Hemphill County, Texas.
6. Jerry Sinise, *George Washington Arrington: Civil War Spy, Texas Ranger, Sheriff and Rancher*, 78.
7. *Wichita Eagle*, November 24, 1894, reporting the current cattle market prices at the Kansas City stockyards.

8. Indictments returned by the grand jury in the 31st Judicial District Court of Hemphill County, Texas: a murder indictment against Joe Blake in Cause No. 108, a murder indictment against Jim Harbolt in Cause No. 109, a joint murder indictment against Jim Harbolt and George Isaacs in Cause No. 110, and a joint indictment for conspiracy to rob Wells Fargo in Cause No. 111 against "Tulsa Jack" Blake, Joe Blake, Sam Blake, Jim Harbolt, George Isaacs, George "Bitter Creek" Newcomb, and Dan McKenzie.

Chapter Eight

1. Robert E. King, "Till the Drums Beat Again: The Fred Hoffman Story," 1–4, unpublished treatise, 2002, Oklahoma State Archives, Oklahoma City.
2. Glenn Shirley, *West of Hell's Fringe: Crime, Criminals, and the Federal Peace Officer in Oklahoma Territory, 1889-1907*, 54; Colonel Bailey C. Hanes, *Bill Doolin, Outlaw O.T.*, 10; King, "Till the Drums Beat Again," 5; *Taloga Advocate*, December 10, 1903; http://www.okgenweb.org/~okdewey/rileycem.html.
3. Interview of Efies Jackson, Roll 7, p. 510, Oklahoma Historical Society at Oklahoma City and Calera, Oklahoma.
4. Dewey County Historical Society (DCHS), *Spanning the River: Dewey County Family Histories*, 1:484. Dewey County was named for the American naval hero Commander George Dewey (1837–1917), famed for completely destroying the Spanish fleet during the Spanish-American War at the Battle of Manila Bay.
5. Homer Croy, "Where the Outlaws Hid," *True West*, October 1962; DCHS, *Spanning the River*, 1:500.
6. Croy, "Where the Outlaws Hid."
7. DCHS, *Spanning the River*, 1:500.
8. Ibid., 484.
9. "Sheriff's Report of US Prisoners in County Jail, Sedgwick County, Kansas, 1886–1894," 69–71, cited in Shirley, *West of Hell's Fringe*, 61–62 and 436n43.
10. Other D County outlaws staking claims in D County during the 1890s include Nannie Wray, who extended hospitality to her son-in-law, Joe Beckham, a renegade Texas sheriff who was wanted for the murder of another sheriff back in Texas; Levi Moors Smith, who harbored his daughter's boyfriend, the notorious Doolin rider George "Red Buck" Waightman; E. C. Kinney, who was married to Bill Doolin's sister; Doolin rider Roy Daughtery (aka Arkansas Tom Jones), who sometimes harbored and horsed other Doolin gang members; and Alfred Son's older brother, who went under the alias of Lee Moore and was foreman of the Amos Chapman ranch, which also often harbored Doolin members. According to later memoirs of the county attorney of D County, George E. Black, other

known outlaw sympathizers living in D County at the time included Dutch Anderson, John Brooks, and the Edwards brothers, Bill, John, and Charles. Bill Neal, *From Guns to Gavels: How Justice Grew Up in the Outlaw West* (Lubbock: Texas Tech University Press, 2008), 10–44

The map included in the text of chapter 8 showing outlaw locations in D County, Oklahoma Territory, in the 1890s is adapted from the map printed in DCHS, *Spanning the River*, Vol. 1, inside cover, and a Taloga-area map in King, "Till the Drums Beat Again," 43. Information about, as well as the locations of, known outlaws and outlaw sympathizers was obtained from DCHS, *Spanning the River*, 1:499–502; King, "Till the Drums Beat Again," 5–25, 30–49; personal interviews by the author with Robert E. King and Patsy Smart, local Dewey County historians, on March 21, 2003, in Seiling, Oklahoma; and a six-part series, "Dewey County Memories," written by former County Attorney George E. Black, that appeared in six weekly installments of the *Taloga Times-Advocate*, April 17 and 24 and May 1, 8, 15, and 22, 1941.

11. DCHS, *Spanning the River*, 1:499, 500–502. See also Black, "Dewey County Memories," *Taloga Times-Advocate*, April 17, 1941, et. seq.

12. Colonel Bailey C. Hanes in his history of Bill Doolin made this pertinent observation: "There were those in the community who knowingly sheltered the outlaws and gave them sympathy, but there were many more that did not take them in and were not in sympathy with lawlessness."

Hanes went on to note that the outlaws—at least those who filed homestead claims—were usually careful to keep a low profile in the community where they lived. "They refrained from taking part in any stealing or robbing in this particular community, where they wanted peace and quiet"—and anonymity. And the honest settlers, who were engrossed in a daylight-to-dark struggle to eke out a meager existence on the frontier, were not inclined to borrow trouble by becoming involved in any righteous crusades or, for that matter, becoming unduly inquisitive about their neighbors' affairs. Hanes went on to observe: "In territorial days, it was not wise to take sides, and a man was seldom asked where he came from or just what his business was. 'The boys,' as the outlaws were referred to, were seldom molested, and many of them were not suspected of being outside the law because many worked on ranches in the area between forays." Colonel Bailey C. Hanes, *Bill Doolin: Outlaw O.T.*, 31.

13. Charles K. Cary, *Kaffir Woolies*, 26.

14. *Oklahoma State Capital*, May 17, 1894; Shirley, *West of Hell's Fringe*, 241–42, 315–16; Bob Blackburn, "The Anti–Horse Thief Association," *Oklahombres: The*

Journal of Lawmen and Outlaw History of Oklahoma 2, no. 2 (Winter, 1991); *El Reno Democrat*, May 31, 1894. As the outlaws' arrogance and blatant banditry increased, so did the outrage of the law-abiding Oklahoma Territory settlers. In May 1894 a group of stockmen living near Watonga, thirty-five miles southeast of Taloga, became so incensed that they organized to challenge a gang that had been systematically stealing their livestock and driving them into the Texas Panhandle. The strident demands of the stockmen reached the sympathetic attention of Thomas J. Lowe, the Oklahoma Territory's secretary of state, who issued a charter for the organization of the Mutual Protection Association of the Oklahoma Territory, which permitted the base organization to charter local, subordinate lodges throughout the territory to be known in each area as the Grand Lodge of the Anti–Horse Thief Association of the Oklahoma Territory. Each lodge joined in a pledge to make horse and cattle thieves scarce, "even if we have to plant more trees to hang them all." Soon these citizen law enforcers began arresting and obtaining indictments against numerous offenders, including some prominent residents of their communities. At Taloga, D County settlers followed suit and formed their own Anti–Horse Thief Association.

15. King, "Till the Drums Beat Again," 40, 44; Bill Neal, *Getting Away with Murder on the Texas Frontier: Notorious Killings and Celebrated Trials*, 113–14; Robert E. King, interview with the author, March 21, 2003, Seiling, Oklahoma; King, "Till the Drums Beat Again," 40, 44; Glenn Shirley, *Temple Houston: Lawyer with a Gun*, 256; Hanes, *Bill Doolin: Outlaw O.T.*, 60, 65.

For years Lee Moore was thought to be the half-brother of Alfred Son. However, when he married Amos Chapman's daughter, Minnie Chapman, at Watonga, Blaine County, Oklahoma Territory, on February 23, 1896, he listed his name as "J. Lee Moore alias Son" on the affidavit on application for the marriage license, giving his father's name as J. W. Son and his mother's maiden name as Sarah Logan. The Son family had originally settled in Brown County, Texas, and the federal census for 1880 lists five-year-old Alfred Son as being the child of John W. and Sarah Son.

Glenn Shirley states that "Alfred Son was not an outlaw," although he states that he was a friend of McKenzie, "Harbold [*sic*]," and Red Buck Waightman. Hanes states that "Alf Sohn [*sic*] was a lesser member of Doolin's gang: Of Alf Sohn, little is known except that he was another cowboy of unknown origin who rode with Doolin on a few occasions but was not a regular in the real sense."

16. Refer to Map 3, D County (later Dewey County), Oklahoma Territory about 1895, for the location of Fred Hoffman's home, the path he rode on that fateful

morning of January 22, 1895, en route to his office, and the site where he was ambushed and assassinated.

17. *The Territory of Oklahoma v. Dick Yeager (alias Zip Wyatt), Bailey Son, Alford Son, Dan McKinzie and Grant Pettyjohn*, Cause No. 15, 2nd Judicial District Court of D County.

Chapter Nine

1. *Purcell (Indian Territory) Register*, February 24, 1898, quoting from article in previous week's edition of the *Chickasha (Indian Territory) Express*.

Chapter Ten

1. Bill Neal, *From Guns to Gavels: How Justice Grew Up in the Outlaw West*, 10–11.
2. An ironic sidebar note here: On October 22, 1895, two days after George Isaacs went on trial for his life in Quanah, his wife, Lizzie, back in the Indian Territory, gave birth to their second child, Roy Isaacs. It will be recalled that the previous January, after his arrest in Canadian, George had been released on bond on the strength of his promise to "assist" law enforcement in determining the identities and locations of all the Oklahoma outlaws who were involved in the Sheriff McGee murder. With the birth of his son, Roy, the following October, it thus became apparent that George had not devoted all of his time during his January reprieve to that noble task of sleuthing villains.]
3. *Quanah Tribune-Chief*, February 17, 1931.
4. *Quanah Tribune*, October 24, 1895.
5. *Quanah Tribune-Chief*, February 17, 1931; Billy Mitchell, "Judge A. J. Fires, Childress Pioneer," *Panhandle-Plains Historical Review* 19 (1946): 27; Thomas F. Turner, "Prairie Dog Lawyers," *Panhandle-Plains Historical Review* 2 (1929): 116; H. C. Randolph, *Panhandle Lawyers*, 22–25.
6. *State of Texas v. George Isaacs*, Cause No. 334, 46th Judicial District Court of Hardeman County, Texas; *Quanah Tribune*, October 24, 1895.
7. The account of the George Isaacs trial that follows is taken from the opinion of the Texas Court of Criminal Appeals as reported in *George Isaacs v. State*, 36 Tex. Crim. 505 (1896). A condensed version of that opinion is reported in *George Isaacs v. State*, 38 S.W. 40 (Tex.Ct.Crim. App., 1896).
8. Luther Jarrett Smith was born December 5, 1867, the son of Sarah Jarrett Smith. He married Retta Cecil, a widow and mother of one son. Smith apparently arrived in the Indian Territory during the first land run in 1889. His law enforcement experience began as a posse member for Bob Nestor, deputy US marshal for the Eastern District Court of Paris, Texas, but by 1890 he was a fully accred-

ited deputy marshal for the Paris court. In 1903 he was appointed as a jailer for the federal jail in Chickasha, Indian Territory. By mid-1904 he had moved to Gainesville, Texas. The 1910 federal census reports that Luther Jarrett Smith and wife and one daughter of their own were living in Amber Township, Grady Oklahoma. His occupation was listed as farming. Smith died on September 17, 1936. Mike Tower, interview with the author, December 3, 2012, Elmore City, Oklahoma. Tower cites his sources of information as being correspondence with Luther J. Smith's grandniece, Thelma Nolan; historian and author Norm Brown of Ransom Canyon, Texas; and various newspaper articles.

9. *Quanah Tribune-Chief*, February 17, 1931.
10. *Canadian Record*, November 2, 1895; *Quanah Tribune-Chief*, April 16, 1916.
11. *George Isaacs v. State*, 36 Tex.Crim. 505, 532 (1896); 38 S.W. 40, 42 (Tex. Ct.Crim.App., 1896).
12. *State v. Grant Pettyjohn* for suborning perjury, Cause Nos. 399, 406, 407, and 436; *State v. Bert Sexton* for perjury, Cause Nos. 405 and 437; and *State v. John Shumate* for perjury, Cause No. 404; all in the District Court of Hardeman County, Texas.

Chapter Eleven

1. L. F. Sheffy, "Sam Isaacs," *Panhandle-Plains Historical Review*, 1946, 40–44.
2. Sam P. Ridings, *The Chisholm Trail*, 108–13.
3. Laban S. Records, *Cherokee Outlet Cowboy*, 346.
4. *Quanah (Texas) Tribune-Chief*, February 17, 1931.
5. James L. Haley, *The Buffalo War: The History of the Red River Indian Uprising of 1874*; Rupert Norval Richardson, *The Comanche Barrier to South Plains Settlement*; J. Evetts Haley, *Charles Goodnight: Cowman and Plainsman*, 276–78; Frederick Nolan, *Tascosa: Its Life and Gaudy Times*, 21; James L. Haley, *Texas: From the Frontier to Spindletop*, 218.
6. Laura V. Hamner, *Light 'n Hitch: A Collection of Historical Writing Depicting Life on the High Plains*, 115–16.
7. Charles Goodnight, undated material no. 11, J. Evetts Haley Collection, Haley Museum and History Center, Midland, Texas; Nolan, *Tascosa*, 101–2.
8. Haley, *Charles Goodnight*, 376; Also see John Arnot, "Tascosa Trails: John Arnot's Memories of an Old Cowtown," Earl Vandale Collection, 1813–1946, Center for American History, University of Texas, Austin.
9. Hamner, *Light 'n Hitch*, 115.
10. Nolan, *Tascosa*, 251. Late in his career Harry Koch, pioneer country newspa-

per editor and longtime owner of the weekly *Quanah Tribune-Chief* who had migrated from East Texas and settled in Quanah, Texas, in 1891, published in that newspaper (August 26, 1938) these insightful memoirs on West Texas in the late nineteenth century:

> Guns were very much in evidence in those days. Captain Bill McDonald and Co. B of the Texas Rangers made their headquarters in Quanah, and I became acquainted with several killers. While running a newspaper, I discovered that notoriety was something many Rangers aspired to, and I had no trouble to stand well with them by giving ample space to their exploits. There was plenty of work for the rangers, and other representatives of the law. Cattle thieves operated all over the West, and had established regular routes all the way from Old Mexico to the Kansas line. Driving a stolen herd at night, they managed to throw the cattle into a pasture belonging to one of their gang, and after a few nights others stood ready to drive the stock farther North.
>
> There were a number of fellows in the country under suspicion of whom it was known that they slept in daytime and rode all night, but mere suspicion did not go far with the juries of those days when even peace officers might stand in with the thieves. It had not been long since when "mavericking" was still considered more or less of a joke that even big cow outfits would indulge in. Several of them employed "bad men" who terrorized their smaller neighbors, and it was not uncommon for a herd starting for Dodge City from South Texas to pick up several hundred head en route.
>
> At cow camps one could hear some great tales about cattle stealing, always told in the light of a joke, and as cattle were of little value, a man operating on not too large a scale could get by for years. In fact, many a man handy with a branding iron got started in business that way. English syndicates owned big ranches in West Texas, and frequently were lax in their business methods of which their neighbors were not slow to take advantage.

11. John L. McCarty, *Maverick Town: The Story of Old Tascosa*, 82–83; Hamner, *Light 'n Hitch*, 94; Nolan, *Tascosa*, 78; Orville H. Nelson, "The Story of the First Panhandle Stockmen's Association," unpublished manuscript, February 12, 1926, J. Evetts Haley Collection, Panhandle-Plains Historical Museum, Canyon, Texas.
12. Hamner, *Light 'n Hitch*, 93–95; Peter R. Rose, *The Reckoning: The Triumph of Order on the Texas Outlaw Frontier*, xxii. In a foreword of *The Reckoning*, p. xv,

Rose added these words: "Order must come before law, and civilization cannot exist without the will and power to defend it. This, after all, was what the Old West was all about."

13. Boone McClure, "The Laws and Customs of the Open Range," *Panhandle-Plains Historical Review* 10 (1938): 71–72.
14. Nolan, *Tascosa*, 121.
15. Estelle D. Tinkler, "Nobility's Ranche: A History of the Rocking Chair Ranche," *Panhandle-Plains Historical Review*, 1942, 57.
16. Nolan, *Tascosa*, 261–62.
17. Jerry Sinise, *George Washington Arrington: Civil War Spy, Texas Ranger, Sheriff and Rancher*, 61–65.
18. *Oklahoma State Capital*, May 17, 1894; *El Reno Democrat*, May 31, 1894; ; Bob Blackburn, "The Anti-Horse Thief Association," *Oklahombres: The Journal of Lawmen and Outlaw History of Oklahoma* 2, no. 2 (1991).
19. L. F. Sheffy, "Sam Isaacs,"40–44; F. Stanley [Stanley F. L. Crocchiola], *Rodeo Town: Canadian, Texas*, 318, 320; Sallie B. Harris, *Cowmen and Ladies: A History of Hemphill County*, 56; H. Allen Anderson, "Isaacs Brothers," Handbook of Texas Online, Texas State Historical Association, http://www.tshaonline.org/handbook/online/articles/fis08.

F. Stanley was an ordained Catholic priest who became fixated on regional histories of towns and communities in West Texas and New Mexico. A grassroots historian, Father Stanley wrote and self-published 177 books and pamphlets on the subject beginning in 1940. He was born in New York's Greenwich Village and eventually, after his ordination in 1938, became a southwesterner for good. Mary Jo Walker, *The F. Stanley Story* (Santa Fe: The New Mexico Book League and the Lightning Tree, 1985).

20. The Hemphill County deed records do reflect that Will Isaacs made a purchase of land in 1893, but it was not made at a public auction sale, and it was not for 30,000 acres. Volume 5, p. 64 of the deed record books reflect that on April 11, 1893, Will Isaacs purchased 2,302.5 acres of land at a private sale from Rhodes Fisher for $1.00 per acre, and then on May 8, 1893, he deeded one-half interest in that tract to his brother Sam Isaacs (Vol. 5, p. 69). The deed records also reflect that over a period of years from 1889 to 1901, Sam and Will Isaacs did make a number of land purchases in Hemphill County, none of which, however, were at a public auction sale. All were private transactions, including the purchase of 19,974.5 acres of land on November 2, 1900, from J. M. McCook, the Texas Land & Cattle Co., et al. (Vol. 6, p. 429), paying the sellers $1.25 per acre. Altogether the brothers eventually managed to acquire a total of 30,221 acres of

land in Hemphill County. On June 29, 1912, Sam and Will executed a partition deed whereby they divided those 30,221 acres between themselves as per their agreement (Vol. 21, p. 587).

21. *Willliam C. Isaacs v. Kate Malaley, W. E. Malaley, John D. Miles, Lucy D. Miles and John D. Miles administrator of the Estate of Lucy D. Miles*, in Cause No. 35 in the District Court of Hemphill County, Texas.
22. Records, *Cherokee Outlet Cowboy*, 346.

Chapter Twelve

1. *Fort Worth Daily Gazette*, January 2, 1889, and May 3, 1890; *Territorial Topic*, May 3, 1890; *Fort Smith Elevator*, May 9, 1890; *Dallas Morning News*, June 28, 1896; *Galveston Daily News*, December 10, 1903.
2. *Galveston Daily News*, January 29, 1889; *Fort Worth Gazette*, January 29, 1889; *Graham [Texas] Leader*, January 31, March 28, and October 29, 1889.

   Some sources claim George Harbolt was killed in an altercation before being brought to trial. Glenn Shirley, *The Fighting Marlows: Men Who Wouldn't Be Lynched*, 84–86; William Rathmen and Robert K. DeArment, *Life of the Marlows: A True Story of Frontier Life of Early Days*, 104–5. But other records, including the 1900 and 1910 federal censuses and the Oklahoma City directory, refute that claim. He died in Oklahoma City on February 22, 1953, and was buried in the Marlow, Oklahoma, cemetery. Mike Tower, interviewed with the author, October 16, 2012, Elmore City, Oklahoma.

   Also see Charles Marlow and George Marlow, *Life of the Marlows, A True Story of Frontier Life in the Early Days, as Related by Themselves* (1893), revised by William Rathmen (1928); Shirley, *Fighting Marlows*; Rathmen and DeArment, *Life of the Marlows*; and various other books and articles. The tale was glamorized still later in a movie entitled *The Sons of Katie Elder*, starring John Wayne and Dean Martin.
3. *Canadian Record*, September 12, 1895; *Harbolt et al. v. State*, 44 S.W. 1110 (Tex. Ct.Crim.App., 1898). The March 13, 1896, edition of the *Canadian Record* incorrectly informed its readers that Jim Harbolt and his renegade sidekick George "Hookey" Miller had ambushed and killed a farmer named W. W. Glover about three weeks earlier some five miles west of Arapaho in Day County, Oklahoma Territory. The news account then said that the two killers had fled the scene and escaped. But as it turned out, the *Canadian Record* had it all wrong. Jim Harbolt was not the killer of W. W. Glover; he was not even near the scene of the crime. The killer of W. W. Glover was correctly identified as Red Buck Waightman

in the March 5, 1896, edition of the *Arapaho Argus*. A more complete version of the incident was later printed in Charles Power Rainbolt, *In Pursuit of the Outlaw "Red Buck,"* 60–62. Contemporary news accounts incorrectly identifying Harbolt as the killer include the *Cheyenne Sunbeam*, February 21, 1896; *Canadian Record*, March 13, 1896; *San Antonio Light*, March 8, 1896; and the *New York Times*, March 10, 1896. The *Fort Wayne Gazette*, March 10, 1906, also carried the story about the killing of W. W. Glover, telling its readers that the killers were George Miller and Jim Harbolt, and then it went on to give quite a different version of the event, including mistakenly identifying W. W. Glover as sheriff of Day County, Oklahoma Territory.

4. *Dallas Morning News*, June 28, 1896.
5. Ibid.
6. G. W. Arrington to Adjutant General, December 10, 1896, General Correspondence Files, Texas Adjutant General, Texas State Archives, Austin.
7. Ibid.
8. *Canadian Record*, January 21, 1897; F. Stanley, *Rodeo Town: Canadian, Texas*, 195.
9. *Canadian Record*, January 28, 1897; Stanley, *Rodeo Town*, 193–96.
10. Ibid.
11. *Canadian Record*, January 28, 1897; Stanley, *Rodeo Town*, 196–97.
12. Petition, January 23, 1897, in General Correspondence Files, Texas Adjutant General, Texas State Archives, Austin.
13. Ibid.
14. Telegram, January 24, 1897, in General Correspondence Files, Texas Adjutant General, Texas State Archives, Austin.
15. January 1897 Monthly Report for Company B, Frontier Battalion, Texas Rangers, Texas State Archives, Austin.
16. *George Isaacs v. State*, 36 Tex.Crim. 505; 38 S.W.40 (Tex.Ct.Crim.App., 1896).

Chapter Thirteen

1. *State v. Jim Harbolt*, Cause No. 647 in the 46th Judicial District Court of Donley County, Texas; *State v. Joe Blake*, Cause No. 939 in the 46th Judicial District Court of Wilbarger County, Texas.
2. The following account of the trial of Jim Harbolt on February 1, 1897, in the Donley County District Court is taken from the opinion of the Texas Court of Criminal Appeals, styled *Jim Harbolt v. State*, 40 S.W. 983 (Tex.Ct.Crim.App., 1897).

3. *Canadian Record*, February 19, 1897.
4. *Jim Harbolt v. State*, 40 S.W. 983 (Tex.Ct.Crim.App, 1897).

Chapter Fourteen

1. Joe Blake to Dan McKenzie, August 11, 1895, attached to the trial transcript in the case of *State v. Joe Blake*, Cause No. 939 in the 46th Judicial District Court of Wilbarger County, Texas. The letter was written while both were incarcerated in separate cells in the Hemphill County, Texas, jail awaiting trial for the murder of Sheriff Tom T. McGee.
2. Thomas F. Turner, "Prairie Dog Lawyers," *Panhandle-Plains Historical Review* 2 (1929): 117.
3. Charles E. Coombes, *The Prairie Dog Lawyer*, ix, x.
4. The following account of the trial of Joe Blake for the murder of Hemphill County sheriff Tom T. McGee, held on March 1, 1897, is taken from the transcript of trial testimony in that case: *State v. Joe Blake*, Cause No. 939 in the 46th Judicial District Court of Wilbarger County, Texas.
5. *Joe Blake v. State*, 43 S.W. 107 (Tex.Ct.Crim.App., 1897).
6. Charles K. Cary, *Kaffir Woolies*, 26.
7. *Territory of Oklahoma v. Lew Herring and William Kopp*, Vol. 1, p. 13, D County, Oklahoma Territory Criminal Docket Book.
8. Nancy B. Samuelson, *Shoot from the Lip: The Lives, Legends and Lies of the Three Guardsmen of Oklahoma and US Marshal Nix*, 69–70.

Chapter Fifteen

1. Glenn Shirley, *Temple Houston: Lawyer with a Gun*, 266–71. Background and early career adventures of Temple Houston were obtained from Shirley, *Temple Houston*; Hank Bass, "Temple Lea Houston—Gun-Toting, Bible-Quoting Lawyer of the Old West," *Texas Bar Journal* 64, no. 1 (January 2001): 69; and Bill Neal, *Getting Away with Murder on the Texas Frontier: Notorious Killings and Celebrated Trials*, 116–18.
2. Shirley, *Temple Houston*, 3–7.
3. Ibid., 5.
4. Temple Houston marched to the beat of a different drummer, and he often took cases for reasons other than financial. In a eulogy for Temple upon his untimely passing at age forty-five in 1905, fellow lawyer H. E. Hoover made these remarks: "He was a friend to and an admirer of children, horses, dogs, the outcast, the unfortunate, the underdog, the one in trouble who had need of his sympathy and support. . . . His rough, sympathetic nature naturally inclined him to the defense

rather than the prosecution. . . . He often had to reject a good fee to devote his time and his efforts in defense of some unfortunate outcast from whom he expected and received no compensation." Sallie B. Harris, *Cowmen and Ladies: A History of Hemphill County*, 41. See also H. C. Randolph, *Panhandle Lawyers*, 17–21.

5. George E. Black, "Dewey County Memories," *Taloga Times-Advocate*, May 1, 1941.
6. Shirley, *Temple Houston*, 256–61.
7. Ibid., 257; Black, "Dewey County Memories," *Taloga Times-Advocate*, May 29, 1941. Ironically, Red Buck Waightman, the cold, steel-nerved killer, had a sensitive side. He was an untutored but accomplished musician. He played the violin at country dances, his tender, romantic ballads enchanting the dancers. A biography of Waightman noted that the "man who could make a fiddle whisper love after his guns had spoken death" was killed in a battle with lawmen on March 4, 1896. *Hennessey (Oklahoma Territory) Clipper*, March 12, 1896; and "George Waightman," Vertical Files, Library Resources Division, Oklahoma Historical Society, Oklahoma City.
8. *Alfred Son v. Territory of Oklahoma*, 5 Okla. Rep. 526, 49 P. 923 (Okla.Sup.Ct., 1897).
9. Shirley, *Temple Houston*, 260–61.
10. Black, "Dewey County Memories," *Taloga Times-Advocate*, May 22, 1941.
11. DCHS, *Spanning the River*, 1:501.
12. Robert E. King, "Till the Drums Beat Again: The Fred Hoffman Story," 5, 7, 17; Robert E. King, interview with the author, Seiling, Oklahoma, March 21, 2003; *Territory v. Amos Chapman*, Vol. 1, p. 70, and *Territory v. Lee Moore*, Vol. 1, p. 72, D County Criminal Docket Book.
13. Black, "Dewey County Memories," *Taloga Times-Advocate*, May 29, 1941; Dewey County Historical Society (DCHS), *Spanning the River: Dewey County Family Histories*, 1:500.

Chapter Sixteen

1. Convict Record Ledger for George Isaacs, prisoner no. 15531, in the Department of Criminal Justice Records, Texas State Archives, Austin.
2. "Dent's Criminal Career," article with pictures and illustrations in the *Syracuse (NY) Sunday Herald*, June 30, 1901.
3. Ibid.
4. *Brown v. State*, 43 S.W. 986 (Tex.Ct.Crim.App., 1898).

5. *Brown v. State*, 38 S.W. 1008 (Tex.Ct.Crim.App., 1897).
6. *Brown v. State*, 43 S.W. 986 (Tex.Ct.Crim.App., 1898).
7. W. J. Dent to Texas Governor Joseph D. Sayers, July 13, 1899, attached to Dent's Application for Pardon in Cause No. 19573, *The State of Texas v. W. J. Dent alias J. W. Brown*, in the District Court of Tarrant County, Texas, and in No. 5392, Department of State, Executive Clemency, Reasons For, Box No. 470, Texas State Archives, Austin, Texas.
8. Ibid.
9. William G. Hill to Governor Joseph D. Sayers, July 8, 1899, forged by W. J. Dent, in Pardon No. 19573, August 28, 1899, of J. W. Brown alias W. J. Dent, State of Texas Executive Office, Texas State Archives, Austin. The letter purported to have been written by William G. Hill, financial agent of the Texas State Penitentiaries, to Governor Sayers attesting to the good conduct and character of prisoner J. W. Brown, alias W. J. Dent.
10. Hon. J. J. Jackson, Judge of US District Court of West Virginia, to Governor Joseph D. Sayers, June 1, 1899, and July 26, 1899, in W. J. Dent, Pardon No. 19573, Texas State Archives, Austin.
11. J. W. Atkinson, Governor of West Virginia, to Governor Joseph D. Sayers, June 1 and August 25, 1899, in ibid.
12. *Raleigh (West Virginia) Herald*, August 26, 1906.
13. The original of the forged pardon is missing from the Texas State Archives, but a complete copy of the forged pardon was printed by the *Galveston Daily News*, January 23, 1900.
14. Chuck Parsons, *Captain John R. Hughes: Lone Star Ranger*, 178–79.
15. The letter dated December 9, 1899, written by Mrs. J. W. St. Clair, was reprinted in its entirety in the *Galveston Daily News*, May 17, 1911.
16. Ibid.
17. *Dent v. State*, 65 S.W. 627 (Tex.Ct.Crim.App., 1901).
18. Pardon of W. J. Dent, Pardon No. 10654, May 16, 1911, signed by Governor O. B. Colquitt, Texas State Archives, Austin.

Chapter Seventeen

1. *Purcell (Indian Territory) Register*, February 24, 1898.
2. Carol Byrne Morse, interview with the author, August 10, 2004, Ardmore, Oklahoma.
3. Mrs. Warren (Jo) Haynie, director of the Crowell, Texas, Firehouse Museum, interview with the author, January 15, 2006, Crowell, Texas.
4. Foard County, Texas, Death Certificate of Helen Gertrude Sparks, No. 145, Foard

County Courthouse, Crowell, Texas, and Crowell Cemetery records, Crowell, Texas.

5. *Foard County News*, January 7, 1916.
6. *Quanah Tribune-Chief*, January 6, 1916. See also Foard County, Texas, Death Certificate of Mrs. Jessie Sparks, No. 172, Foard County Courthouse, Crowell, Texas, and Crowell Cemetery records, Crowell, Texas.
7. *Quanah Tribune-Chief*, April 6, 1916. See also Foard County, Texas, Death Certificate of Thomas Niri Sparks, No. 185, Foard County Courthouse, Crowell, Texas, and Crowell Cemetery records, Crowell, Texas.
8. *Quanah Tribune-Chief*, November 16, 1916.
9. Michael P. Rogin, *Fathers and Children: Andrew Jackson and the Subjugation of the American Indian*, 58; Frederick Nolan, *Bad Blood: The Life and Times of the Horrell Brothers*, 160–61.

Chapter Eighteen

1. Robert E. King, Dewey County historian, Seiling, Oklahoma, to Patsy Smart, fellow Dewey County historian, Seiling, Oklahoma, September 2003; copy in author's possession.
2. Testimony of Captain George Washington Arrington taken on September 6, 1895, at a hearing on a habeas corpus motion filed by George Isaacs seeking a bail bond in *State v. George Isaacs*, Cause No. 110 in the 31st Judicial District Court of Hemphill County, Texas.
3. Jim Cloyd, telephone interview with the author, September 25, 2003.
4. Homer Croy, "Where the Outlaws Hid," *True West*, October, 1962.
5. Dewey County Historical Society, *Spanning the River: Dewey County Family Histories*, 1:501.

Chapter Nineteen

1. Robert M. Utley, *High Noon in Lincoln: Violence on the Western Frontier*, 160–61.
2. H. Allen Anderson, "Isaacs Brothers," Handbook of Texas Online, Texas State Historical Association, http://www.tshaonline.org/handbook/online/articles/fis08.
3. Sallie B. Harris, *Cowmen and Ladies: A History of Hemphill County*, 25.
4. Ibid., 56.
5. All personal and family history stated above was derived from "Isaacs Brothers," in Ron Tyler, Douglas E. Barnett, and Roy R. Barkley, eds., *The New Handbook of Texas*.

Epilogue

1. This chapter is based on my book *Getting Away with Murder on the Texas Frontier: Notorious Killings and Celebrated Trials*, 129–30.
2. Robert E. King, interview with the author, Seiling, Oklahoma, March 17, 2003.
3. *Lawton News-Reporter*, December 10, 1903; *Taloga Tomahawk*, December 17, 1903; *Hutchison Daily News*, December 10, 1903; *Galveston Daily News*, December 10, 1903; *Daily Ardmorite*, December 11, 1903; *Dallas Morning News*, January 12, 1904.
4. *McCracken (Kansas) Enterprise*, August 31, 1906; *Taloga Times*, September 13, 1906.
5. *Oklahoma State Capital* (Guthrie, Oklahoma Territory), May 23, 1895, quoting the *Kansas City Journal.*
6. Dewey County Historical Society (DCHS), *Spanning the River: Dewey County Family Histories*, 1:500.
7. H. Allen Anderson, "Arrington, George Washington," Handbook of Texas Online, Texas State Historical Association, https://www.tshaonline.org/handbook/online/articles/far20.

Appendix

1. Albert Bigelow Paine, *Captain Bill McDonald, Texas Ranger*, 154–58.
2. *Day County (Oklahoma Territory) Tribune*, December 7, 1893.
3. *State v. George Isaacs*, Cause No. 334, Hardeman County, Texas, District Court (1895); *State v. Jim Harbolt*, Cause No. 647, Donley County, Texas, District Court (1896); *State v. Joe Blake*, Cause No. 939, Wilbarger County, Texas, District Court (1896).
4. *State v. John N. Webb*, 39 Tex. Crim. 534, 47 S.W. 856 (Tex.Ct.Crim.App., 1898).
5. Lillie Mae Hunter, *The Book of Years: A History of Dallam and Hartley Counties*, 57.
6. Ibid., 57–58.
7. Mark Lee Gardner, *To Hell on a Fast Horse: Billy the Kid, Pat Garrett, and the Epic Chase to Justice in the Old* West, 231–42; Leon C. Metz, *Pat Garrett, the Story of a Western Lawman*; Jerry J. Lobdill, "Rethinking the Murder of Pat Garrett," *Journal of the Wild West History Association* 4, no. 4 (August 2011): 26–40.
8. *State v. James B. Miller*, Cause No. 16869, Tarrant County District Court, Fort Worth, Texas.
9. Lobdill, "Rethinking the Murder of Pat Garrett," 34–38. See also the *Galveston Daily News*, November 5, 1907, and the *Albuquerque Journal*, August 23, 1911.

10. Glenn Shirley, *Shotgun for Hire: The Story of "Deacon" Jim Miller, Killer of Pat Garrett*; Ellis Lindsey, "The Lynching of Jim Miller," *Wild West*, October 2012, 40–47.

11. Jerry Sinise, *George Washington Arrington: Civil War Spy, Texas Ranger, Sheriff and Rancher*, 1–11; Millie Jones Porter, *Memory Cups of Panhandle Pioneers*, 269–71; Frederick Nolan, *Tascosa: Its Life and Gaudy Times*, 311n26; H. Allen Anderson, "Arrington, George Washington," Handbook of Texas Online, Texas State Historical Association,http://www.tshaonline.org/handbook/online/articles/far20.

12. Sinise, *George Washington Arrington*, 17–48; Walter Prescott Webb, *The Texas Rangers: A Century of Frontier Defense*, 2nd ed., 411–22; John L. McCarty, *Maverick Town: The Story of Old Tascosa*, 100, 175.

13. Arrington was his mother's maiden name. His father, John C. Orrick Sr., born August 17, 1816, married Mariah Arrington on November 11, 1841, and he died February 7, 1848, when his son was four years old. Sinise, *George Washington Arrington*, 14–15; L. F. Sheffy, "The Arrington Papers," *Panhandle-Plains Historical Review* 1 (1928): 48–49.

14. Sinise, *George Washington Arrington*, 11–15; *Alabama Beacon*, June 15 and 22, 1867.

15. Nolan, *Tascosa*, 213–15; John Miller Morris, *A Private in the Texas Rangers, A. T. Miller of Company B, Frontier Battalion*, 92-97; Porter, *Memory Cups of Panhandle Pioneers*, 520–25; Sinise, *George Washington Arrington*, 50–59; John Arnot, "Leverton Brothers," Earl Vandale Collection, 1813–1946, Center for American History, University of Texas at Austin.

16. Sinise, *George Washington Arrington*, 50–59.

17. Porter, *Memory Cups of Panhandle Pioneers*, 520–25, and McCarty, *Maverick Town*, 238–39. Both authors record how the existing bitterness between ranchers and nesters was inflamed by the Leverton tragedy.

18. McCarty, *Maverick Town*, 12.

19. H. Allen Anderson, "Grass-Lease Fight," Handbook of Texas Online, Texas State Historical Association, http://www.tshaonline.org/handbook/online/articles/azg01.

20. H. P. N. Gammel, *The Laws of Texas, 1822–1897*, 10:63–77.

21. J. Evetts Haley and William Curry Holden, *The Flamboyant Judge, James D. Hamlin: A Biography*, 11–12; Paul H. Carlson, *Empire Builder in the Texas Panhandle: William Henry Bush*, 95–97; Paul H. Carlson, *Amarillo: The Story of a Western Town*, 60–62. Most of the cattle barons strongly opposed the enact-

ment of the Four-Section Act, but not all. Several of the big ranchers, including the managers of the XIT Ranch and the most prominent cowman of them all, Charles Goodnight, supported it. In fact, it was Charles Goodnight who originally proposed this concept of legislation to W. B. Plemons. Charles Goodnight had mellowed in his attitude toward "progress," declaring, "Nothing will ruin us that settles this country." J. Evetts Haley, *Charles Goodnight: Cowman and Plainsman*, 401; H. Allen Anderson, "Goodnight, Charles," Handbook of Texas Online, Texas State Historical Association, http://www.tshaonline.org/handbook/online/articles/fgo11.

22. Haley and Holden, *Flamboyant Judge*, 12.

BIBLIOGRAPHY

Unpublished Sources

Manuscripts and Records

Arnot, John. "Leverton Brothers." Earl Vandale Collection, 1813–1946, Center for American History, University of Texas at Austin.

———. "Tascosa Trails: John Arnot's Memories of an Old Cowtown." Earl Vandale Collection, 1813–1946, Center for American History, University of Texas at Austin.

Dent, W. J. Pardon File, No. 10654. State of Texas Executive Office Files, Texas State Archives, Austin.

Haley, J. Evetts. "Charles Goodnight." Undated Material No. 11. J. Evetts Haley Collection, Haley History Center, Midland, Texas.

Hamner, Laura V., and John L. McCarty. "Jess Jenkins, King of Hogtown." John L. McCarty Collection, Amarillo Public Library.

Hemphill County, Texas. Deed Records, 5:64, April 11, 1893; 5:69, May 8, 1893; 6:429, November 2, 1900; and 21:587, June 29, 1912. Hemphill County courthouse, Canadian, Texas.

Isaacs, George. Convict Record Ledger No. 15531. Department of Criminal Justice Records, Texas State Archives, Austin.

———. Pardon File No. 19573. State Texas Executive Office Files, Texas State Archives, Austin. (Also see copy of George Isaacs's forged pardon printed in *Galveston Daily News*, January 23, 1900.)

King, Robert E., "Till the Drums Beat Again: The Fred Hoffman Story," 2002. Oklahoma State Archives, Oklahoma City.

——— to Patsy Smart, Seiling, Oklahoma, September 2003; copy in possession of Bill Neal.

Nelson, Orville H. "The Story of the First Panhandle Stockman's

Association," February 12, 1912. J. Evetts Haley Collection, Panhandle-Plains Historical Museum, Canyon, Texas.

Sparks, Helen Gertrude. Death Certificate No. 145. Foard County, Texas, and Crowell Cemetery records, Foard County courthouse, Crowell, Texas.

Sparks, Mrs. Jessie. Death Certificate No. 172. Foard County, Texas, and Crowell Cemetery records, Foard County courthouse, Crowell, Texas.

Sparks, Thomas Niri. Death Certificate No. 185. Foard County, Texas, and Crowell Cemetery Records, Foard County courthouse, Crowell, Texas.

Texas Adjutant General. General Correspondence Files, December 10, 1896, and January 23, 24, 1897. Texas State Archives, Austin.

Texas Rangers. Monthly Report for January 1897, Company B, Frontier Battalion, Texas Rangers. Texas State Archives, Austin.

Waightman, George. "George Waightman." Vertical Files, Library Resources Division, Oklahoma Historical Society, Oklahoma City.

Interviews

Chandler, Robert J., email interview with Bill Neal, May 30, 2007.

Cloyd, Jim, interview with Bill Neal, Canadian, Texas, September 25, 2003.

Haynie, Warren (Jo), interview with Bill Neal, Crowell, Texas, January 15, 2004.

King, Robert E., interview with Bill Neal, Seiling, Oklahoma, March 17 and 21, 2003.

McAllister, J. E., interview with J. Evetts Haley, Canyon, Texas, July 1, 1926.

Morse, Carol Byrne, interview with Bill Neal, Ardmore, Oklahoma, August 10, 2004.

Smart, Patsy, interview with Bill Neal, Seiling, Oklahoma, March 21, 2003.

Tower, Mike, interview with Bill Neal, Elmore City, Oklahoma, October 16 and December 3, 2012.

Legal Records

Alfred Son v. Territory of Oklahoma, 5 Okla.Rep. 526, 49 P. 923 (Okla.Sup.Ct., 1897).

George Isaacs v. State of Texas, 36 Tex.Crim. 505; 38 S.W. 40 (Tex.Ct.Crim.App, 1896).

Jim Harbolt et al v. State, 44 S.W. 1110 (Tex.Ct.Crim.App., 1898).

Jim Harbolt v. State of Texas, 40 S.W. 983 (Tex.Ct.Crim.App, 1897).

Joe Blake v. State of Texas, 43 S.W. 107 (Tex.Ct.Crim.App., 1897).

J. W. Brown v. State, 38 S.W. 1008 (Tex.Ct.Crim.App, 1897).

J. W. Brown v. State of Texas, 43 S.W. 986 (Tex.Ct.Crim.App, 1898).

State of Texas v. Bert Sexton, Cause Nos. 405 and 437 in the 46th Judicial District Court of Hardeman County, Texas (1895).

State of Texas v. George Isaacs, Cause No. 110 in the 31st Judicial District Court, Hemphill County, Texas (1895).

State of Texas v. George Isaacs, Cause No. 334 in the 46th Judicial District Court of Hardeman County, Texas (1895).

State of Texas v. Grant Pettyjohn, Cause Nos. 399, 406, 407, and 436 in the 46th Judicial District Court, Hardeman County, Texas (1895).

State of Texas v. Jim Harbolt, Cause No. 647 in the 46th Judicial District Court, Donley County, Texas (1897), and Cause No. 109 in the 31st Judicial District Court, Hemphill County, Texas (1895).

State of Texas v. Joe Blake, Cause No. 939 in the 46th Judcial District Court, Wilbarger County, Texas (1897), and Cause No. 108 in the 31st Judicial District Court, Hemphill County, Texas (1895).

State of Texas v. John N. Webb, 39 Tex.Crim. 534, 47 S.W. 856 (1898).

State of Texas v. John Shumate, Cause No. 404 in the 46th Judicial District Court of Hardeman County, Texas (1895).

State of Texas v. "Tulsa Jack" Blake, Sam Blake, Joe Blake, Jim Harbolt, George Isaacs, "Bitter Creek" Newcomb, and Dan McKenzie, Cause No. 111 in the 31st Judicial District Court, Hemphill County, Texas (1895).

State of Texas v. W. J. Dent, alias J. W. Brown, Cause No. 19573 in the Tarrant County District Court (1897).

State v. James B. Miller, Cause No. 16869 in the District Court of Tarrant County, Texas (1904).

Territory v. Amos Chapman, Vol. 1, p. 70, in the Criminal Docket Book, D County, Oklahoma Territory (1895).

Territory v. Dick Yeager (alias Zip Wyatt), Bailey Son, Alford [sic] *Son, Dan McKinzie* [sic], *and Grant Pettyjohn*, Cause No. 15 in the 2nd Judicial District Court of D County, Oklahoma Territory (1895).

Territory v. Lee Moore, Vol. 1, p. 72, in the Criminal Docket Book, D County, Oklahoma Territory (1895)

Territory v. Lew Herring and William Kopp, Vol. 1, p. 13, in the Criminal Docket Book, D County, Oklahoma Territory (1894).

W. J. Dent v. State of Texas, 65 S.W. 627 (Tex.Ct.Crim.App., 1901).

William C. Isaacs v. Kate Malaley et al., Cause No. 35 in the 31st Judicial District Court of Hemphill County, Texas (1892).

Books and Articles

Adams, Ramon F., et al. *The Book of the American West*. New York: Julian Messner, 1963.

Bass, Hank. "Temple Lea Houston: Gun-Toting, Bible-Quoting Lawyer of the Old West." *Texas Bar Journal* 64, No. 1 (January 2001).

Blackburn, Bob. "The Anti-Horse Thief Association." *Oklahombres: The Journal of Lawmen and Outlaw History of Oklahoma*, Winter 1991.

Carlson, Paul H. *Amarillo: The Story of a Western Town*. Lubbock: Texas Tech University Press, 2006.

———. *Empire Builder in the Texas Panhandle: William Henry Bush*. College Station: Texas A&M University Press, 1996.

Cary, Charles K. *Kaffir Woolies*. Canadian, TX: Southern Canadian River Cattle Company, and Dewey County, Oklahoma, Jailhouse Museum, 1999.

Coombes, Charles E. *The Prairie Dog Lawyer*. Dallas: Texas Folklore Society and University Press, 1945.

Cox, Mike. *Texas Ranger Tales II*. Plano, TX: Republic of Texas Press, 1999.

Croy, Homer. "Where the Outlaws Hid." *True West*, October 1962.

Dewey County Historical Society (DCHS). *Spanning the River:Dewey County Family Histories*, Vol. 1. San Angelo, TX: Newsfoto Yearbook Co., 1976.

Gammel, H. P. N. *The Laws of Texas, 1822–1897*, vols. 9 (1883) and 10 (1883). Austin: Gammel Book Company, 1898.

Gardner, Mark Lee. *To Hell on a Fast Horse: Billy the Kid, Pat Garrett, and the Epic Chase to Justice in the Old West*. New York: HarperCollins, 2010.

Gober, Jim. *Cowboy Justice: Tale of a Texas Lawman*. Edited by James R. Gober and B. Byron Price. Lubbock: Texas Tech University Press, 1997.

Haley, J. Evetts. *Charles Goodnight: Cowman and Plainsman*. Norman: University of Oklahoma Press, 1949.

———. *The Flamboyant Judge, James D. Hamlin: A Biography*. Canyon, TX: Palo Duro Press, 1972.

———. *The XIT Ranch of Texas, and the Early Days of the Llano Estacado*. Norman: University of Oklahoma Press, 1953.

Haley, James L. *The Buffalo War: The History of the Red River Indian Uprising of 1874*. Garden City, NY: Doubleday, 1976.

———. *Texas: From the Frontier to Spindletop*. New York: St. Martin's Press, 1985.

Hamner, Laura V. *Light 'n Hitch: A Collection of Historical Writing Depicting Life on the High Plains*. Dallas, TX: American Guild Press, 1958.

———. *Short Grass and Longhorns*. Norman: University of Oklahoma Press, 1943.

Hanes, Colonel Bailey C. *Bill Doolin: Outlaw O.T.* Norman: University of Oklahoma Press, 1968.

Harper, Minnie Timms, and George Dewey Harper. *Old Ranches*. Dallas, TX: Dealy and Lowe, 1936.

Harris, Sallie B. *Cowmen and Ladies: A History of Hemphill County*. Canyon, TX: Staked Plains Press, 1977.

Hatley, Allen G. *Bringing the Law to Texas: Crime and Violence in Nineteenth Century Texas*. LaGrange, TX: Centex Press, 2002.

———. "Cap Arrington: Adventurer, Ranger, and Sheriff," *Wild West*, June 2001.

Hemphill County Preservation Committee. *Hemphill County History*. Dallas, TX: Taylor Publishing Company, 1985.

Holden, William Curry, and J. Evetts Haley. *The Flamboyant Judge, James D. Hamlin: A Biography*. Canyon, TX: Palo Duro Press, 1972.

Hunter, Lillie Mae. *The Book of Years: A History of Dallam and Hartley Counties*. Hereford, TX: Pioneer Book Publishers, 1969.

Lindsey, Ellis. "The Lynching of Jim Miller." *Wild West*, October 2012.

Lobdil, Jerry. "Rethinking the Murder of Pat Garrett." *Journal of the Wild West History Association* 4, no. 4 (August 2011).

Loomis, Noel M. *Wells Fargo: An Illustrated History*. New York: Clarkson N. Potter, 1968.

Marlow, Charles, and George Marlow. *Life of the Marlows: A True Story of Frontier Life in the Early Days, as Related by Themselves*. Ouray, CO: Plaindealer Printing, Kelly & Hulanski, Publisher, 1893; revised ed., William Rathmell, Ouray Herald Print, W. S. Olexa, Publisher, 1928.

McCarty, John L. *Maverick Town: The Story of Old Tascosa*. Norman: University of Oklahoma Press, 1968.

McClure, Boone. "The Laws and Customs of the Open Range." *Panhandle-Plains Historical Review* 10 (1938).

McLoughlin, Denis. *Wild and Woolly: An Encyclopedia of the Old West*. Garden City, NY: Doubleday & Company, 1975.

Metz, Leon C. *Pat Garrett, the Story of a Western Lawman*. Norman: University of Oklahoma Press, 1974.

Mitchell, Billy. "Judge A. J. Fires, Childress Pioneer." *Panhandle-Plains Historical Review* 19 (1946).

Morris, John Miller. *A Private in the Texas Rangers: A. T. Miller of Company B, Frontier Battalion*. College Station: Texas A&M University Press, 2001.

Neal, Bill. *From Guns to Gavels: How Justice Grew Up in the Outlaw West*. Lubbock: Texas Tech University Press, 2008.

———. *Getting Away With Murder on the Texas Frontier: Notorious Killings and Celebrated Trials*. Lubbock: Texas Tech University Press, 2006.

———. *Sex, Murder, and the Unwritten Law*. Lubbock: Texas Tech University Press, 2009.

Nolan, Frederick. *Bad Blood: The Life and Times of the Horrell Brothers*. Stillwater, OK: Barbed Wire Press, 1994.

———. *Tascosa: Its Life and Gaudy Times*. Lubbock: Texas Tech University Press, 2007.

Nordyke, Lewis. *Cattle Empire: The Fabulous Story of the 3,000,000 Acre XIT*. New York: William Morrow, 1949.

Paine, Albert Bigelow. *Captain Bill McDonald, Texas Ranger*. Austin, TX: State House Press, 1986.

Parsons, Chuck. *Captain John R. Hughes: Lone Star Ranger*. Denton: University of North Texas Press, 2011.

Porter, Millie Jones. *Memory Cups of Panhandle Pioneers*. Clarendon, TX: Clarendon Press, 1945.

Rainbolt, Charles Power. *In Pursuit of the Outlaw "Red Buck."* Inola, OK: Evans Publications, 1990.

Randolph, H. C. *Panhandle Lawyers*. Amarillo, TX: Russell Stationery, 1931.

Rathmell, William, and Robert K. DeArment. *Life of the Marlows: A True Story of Frontier Life of Early Days*. Denton: University of North Texas Press, 2004; reprint of the original version of same book by Charles and George Marlow (Ouray, CO: Plaindealer Printing, Kelly and Hulanski Publisher, 1893), as revised by William Rathmell (Ouray Herald Print, W. S. Olexa, Publisher, 1928).

Records, Laban S. *Cherokee Outlet Cowboy*. Norman: University of Oklahoma Press, 1995.

Richardson, Rupert Norval. *The Comanche Barrier to South Plains Settlement*. Glendale, CA: Arthur H. Clark Company, 1933.

Ridings, Sam P. *The Chisholm Trail: A History of the World's Greatest Cattle Trail*. Medford, OK: Grant County Historical Society, 1975.

Rogin, Michael P. *Fathers and Children: Andrew Jackson and the Subjugation of the American Indian*. New York: Vintage Books, 1976.

Rose, Peter R. *The Reckoning: The Triumph of Order on the Texas Frontier*. Lubbock: Texas Tech University Press, 2012.

Roth, Randolph. *American Homicide*. Cambridge, MA: Harvard University Press, 2009.

Samuelson, Nancy B. *Shoot from the Lip: The Lives, Legends, and Lies of the Three Guardsmen of Oklahoma and US Marshal Nix*. Eastford, CN.: Shooting Star Press, 1998.

Sheffy, L. F. "The Arrington Papers." *Panhandle-Plains Historical Review* 1 (1928).

———. "Sam Isaacs." *Panhandle-Plains Historical Review* 19 (1946).

Shirley, Glenn. *Shotgun for Hire: The Story of "Deacon" Jim Miller, Killer of Pat Garrett*. Norman: University of Oklahoma Press, 1970.

———. *Temple Houston: Lawyer with a Gun*. Norman: University of Oklahoma Press, 1980.

———. *The Fighting Marlows: Men Who Wouldn't Be Lynched*. Fort Worth: Texas Christian University Press, 1994.

———. *West of Hell's Fringe: Crime, Criminals, and the Federal Peace Officer in Oklahoma Territory, 1889-1907*. Norman: University of Oklahoma Press, 1978.

Sinise, Jerry. *George Washington Arrington: Civil War Spy, Texas Ranger, Sheriff and Rancher*. Burnet, TX: Eakin Press, 1979.

Stanley, F. *Rodeo Town: Canadian, Texas*. Denver, CO: The World Press, 1953.

Tinkler, Estelle D. "Nobility's Ranche: A History of the Rocking Chair Ranche." *Panhandle-Plains Historical Review* 15 (1942).

Tower, Mike. "Black Jack Shot Lawman Hocker." *Wild West*, February, 2008.

Turner, Thomas F. "Prairie Dog Lawyers." *Panhandle-Plains Historical Review* 2 (1929).

Tyler, Ron; Douglas E. Barnett; and Roy R. Barkley, eds. *The New Handbook of Texas*. Austin: Texas State Historical Association, 1996.

Utley, Robert M. *High Noon in Lincoln: Violence on the Western Frontier*. Albuquerque: University of New Mexico Press, 1987.

Webb, Walter Prescott. "George W. Arrington: The Iron-Handed Man of the Panhandle." *Panhandle-Plains Historical Review* 8 (1935).

———. *The Texas Rangers: A Century of Frontier Defense*, 2nd ed. Austin: University of Texas Press, 1965.

Internet Articles

Anderson, H. Allen. "Arrington, George Washington," Handbook of Texas Online. www.tshaonline.org/handbook/online/articles/far20.

———. "Buffalo Wallow Fight," Handbook of Texas Online. www.tshaonline.org/handbook/online/articles/btb03.

———. "Goodnight, Charles," Handbook of Texas Online. www.tshaonline.org/handbook/online/articles/fgo11.

———. "Grass-Lease Fight," Handbook of Texas Online. www.tshaonline.org/handbook/online/articles/azg01.

———. "Isaac Brothers," Handbook of Texas Online. www.tshaonline.org/handbook/online/articles/fis08.

———. "McGee, Thomas T.," Handbook of Texas Online. www.tshaonline.org/handbook/online/articles/fmcbz.

———. "Rocking Chair Ranch," Handbook of Texas Online. www.tshaonline.org/handbook/online/articles/apr01.

Richardson, T. C. "Dixon, William," Handbook of Texas Online. www.tshaonline.org/handbook/online/articles/fdi22.

Newspapers

Alabama Beacon.

Albuquerque Journal.

Arapaho Argus.

Canadian Record.

Cheyenne Sunbeam.

Dallas Morning News.

Day County (Oklahoma Territory) Tribune.

Elk City Journal.

El Reno Democrat.

Foard County News.

Fort Smith Elevator.

Fort Wayne Gazette.

Fort Worth Daily Gazette.

Galveston Daily News.

Graham (TX) Leader.

Guthrie Daily Leader.

Hennessey (Oklahoma Territory) Clipper.

Hutchison Daily News.

Lawton News-Reporter.

McCracken (KS) Enterprise.

New York Times.

Oklahoma Daily Press-Gazette.

Oklahoma State Capital.

Purcell (Indian Territory) Register.

Quanah Tribune.

Quanah Tribune-Chief.

Raleigh (West Virginia) Herald.

San Antonio Light.

Syracuse (NY) Sunday Herald.

Taloga Advocate.

Taloga Times.

Taloga Times-Advocate.

Territorial Topic.

INDEX

Page numbers in *italic* refer to illustrations.

ABOUT THE AUTHOR

As a practicing criminal lawyer, **Bill Neal** spent more than four decades frequenting county courthouses in West Texas and hearing tales of sensational crimes and celebrated trials of bygone years. Shortly before his retirement from active law practice, Neal decided to resurrect these old tales of frontier justice—and injustice—through research in the basements and backshops of courthouses and country weeklies, family histories, and interviews with oldtimers. His multiple award-winning books are the results of his efforts. He lives in Abilene, Texas, with his wife, Gayla.